GOOD GOVERNANCE AND COALITION POLITICS

GOOD GOVERNANCE AND COALITION POLITICS

(PDP-Congress in Jammu & Kashmir)

M.M. Khajooria

KALPAZ

ISBN: 978-93-5128-118-4

Price: ₹ 750

First Published, 2016

Published by

Kalpaz Publications
C-30, Satyawati Nagar,
Delhi-110052
Ph. : 9212142040
E-mail: kalpaz@hotmail.com

Printed at : G. Print Process, Delhi

Cataloging in Publication Data—DK
Courtesy: D.K. Agencies (P) Ltd. <docinfo@dkagencies.com>

Khajooria, M. M., author.
Good governance and coalition politics : PDP-Congress in Jammu & Kashmir / M.M. Khajooria.
pages cm
Includes bibliographical references.
ISBN 9789351281184

1. Coalition governments—India—Jammu and Kashmir.
2. Jammu and Kashmir (India)—Politics and government—21st century. I. Title.

DDC 320.9546 23

Dedicated

To the respectful and everlasting memory of my parents
Shrimati Tara Devi, and Shri Hari Chand

Contents

Preface

In a parliamentary democracy people elect their representatives through secret ballot inspired by the programmes and policies enumerated in manifestoes of the contesting political parties. 'The party gaining the majority in the Legislative Assembly/Parliament was mandated to govern the state/country on their behalf for a predetermined period, six years in case of Jammu and Kashmir legislative assembly against a five years tenure constitutionally prescribed for the parliament and assemblies of other states of the union. After the lapse of this period in a fresh mandate the electorate either affirmed their faith in the party in power or returned an adverse verdict overthrowing the government. This determined who would run the affairs of the state for the next term. As the parliamentary system, which we have opted admitted of multi-party participation, coalition governments sometimes become unavoidable. In fact, election to Jammu and Kashmir Legislative Assembly-2015 have again returned fractured verdict. After protracted and somewhat tortured negotiations and about 49 days long Governor's Rule, PDP and BJP stitched a coalition. A PDP-BJP coalition government was accordingly in on 1st, March, 2015.

This is a tale of two coalitions PDP-Congress (2002–2008) and NC-Congress (2008–2014), and three chief ministers, their performance, monitoring and evaluation prefaced by "the concept and contours of Good Governance" detailing the criteria according to which the conduct of affairs of Jammu and Kashmir State by these chief ministers and their governments may be judged.

The Legislative Assembly elections 2002 dislodged the long time ruling party, Jammu and Kashmir National Conference from power but returned a fractured verdict. Even though National Conference emerged as the single largest party, it wisely decided to sit in the opposition. The Congress–PDP coalition brokered by the UPA chairperson Sonia Gandhi and Prime Minister, Man Mohan Singh earned the distinction of being the first real coalition government in Jammu and Kashmir state. Panthers Party and assorted independents also became coalition partners endowing the combine with the required numbers. A Common Minimum Programme was agreed upon, signed and sealed. The Congress–PDP coalition had two other unique features. First, the main coalition partners agreed to share the leadership of the government by rotation, three years term for each. Second, PDP, the minor partner managed the first term. Mufti Mohd. Syeed was the first to ascend the throne.

This arrangement should have worked, but it did not. The arrangement under which coalition partners shared the crown of Chief Ministership after three years turned to be the root cause of the trouble. A reluctant Mufti was replaced by aggressive Congress leader, Ghulam Nabi Azad. Persistent feuds within the cabinet, conflicts of interest between PDP ministers and the Chief Minister that spilled into the public domain made a mockery of the cabinet system designed to work on the principle of Joint responsibility. The tottering PDP-Congress coalition finally demissed on 28th of June, 2008 when the PDP pulled out of the cabinet on the contentious issue of Amar Nath Yatra land use. Elections-2008 returned a fractured verdict. The coalition put together this time around comprised of Congress and National Conference. It, however, sprung two surprises. Dr Farooq Abdullah under whose leadership the National Conference contested election and who was its declared Chief Ministerial candidate found himself sidelined and his son, Young Omar Abdullah crowned as the Chief Minister of Jammu and Kashmir. Dr Farooq was accommodated in the Union cabinet. Deviating from Congress-PDP coalition arrangement, it was decided that Omar Abdullah would head the coalition government for the full tenure of six years.

The book was divided into four parts excluding the conclusion. The first related to Concept and Contours of Good Governance in historical and philosophical contexts. The focus was on dynamic changes in the philosophy, structure, functions and goals of governance and the triangular relationship among state, society, and citizen that evolved during the last two centuries or so. Responsibility, responsiveness and accountability, the three main ingredients of good governance under democratic dispensations that settle the criteria for evaluating the performance of coalition governments come for comprehensive treatment and critical scrutiny. It may be mentioned here that in view of the crucial importance of was 'Accountability' and its centrality to the very idea of Good Governance a separate chapter was devoted to the subject.

The second part of the Book "dealt with the two coalition governments scanning, analysing and evaluation their conduct and performance. Also included the chronicling of developments and analysis thereof *published* in newspapers/journals on "As it happened basis". These reflect my perception of Issues, posturing and positioning by parties and individuals meriting public concerns and politico-administrative dissection and analysis. The purpose of publishing this collection of articles, was to provoke a meaningful, informed and objective debate on the crucial subject of functioning of the coalition governments under a somewhat modified cabinet system where under the ministers were nominated by the parties and allocated portfolios that came to the share of their parties but were required to function on the principle of "joint responsibility" as prescribed in its classical model. The PDP-Congress coalition manifestly violated the letter and spirit the cabinet system.

The chief minister was answerable to the Governor and accountable to the legislature and through them to the people of the state. He was vested with the authority to choose his cabinet colleagues and allocate to them portfolios. They actually held office at his pleasure even though technically the discretion was exercised by the Governor on advice of the chief minister, whose advice was binding. The rotation of chief minister after three years also effectively cut down the term of a chief minister to half of the stipulated life of the legislative assembly thereby interrupting the continuity and tenor of governance. This adversely impacted the designing of policies and programmes and even performance level of the bureaucracy charged with the responsibility of implementation.

Part three detailed the conduct of affairs under the Governors' Rule. Which had to be imposed after the collapse of the PDP-Congress Coalition government following the abject surrender of Gulam Nabi Azad led government before secessionist street action dictated from across the LOC and desertion the PDP. The cancellation of government order diverting two pieces of land to Shri Amarnath Ji Yatra Shrine Board for the duration of the Yatra gave rise to protests in Jammu region which snow balled into an unprecedented massive popular upsurge, without parallel in the post-independence India.

The fourth part surveyed analysed and evaluated the conduct of state affairs by Congress-National Conference government led by Chief Minister Omar Abdullah. It specifically and comprehensively mapped and clinically dissected number of contentious issues that impacted not only the political environment of Jammu and Kashmir but also triggered somewhat avoidable forays into national and international arena.

I hope readers find the subject provocative enough to generate an informed and meaningful debate on this subject of vital public interest and promote further research in this crucial field. The outcome of the debate might be helpful in concretising ideas, suggestions and systemic changes to help the future coalition governments to avoid pitfalls, drawbacks and functional disorders to which the PDP-Congress and National Conference-Congress Coalitions fell victim. There could be no doubt about the importance and urgency of such an exercise.

This book highlighted the flaws in the policy frame, processes and motivation that informed the decision-making on issues of great public importance and grave political and administrative import in the conduct of affairs of the state by multi-party governments. The objective was to arouse the conscience of the legislatures, intellectuals, scholars voters and other concerned segments of the civil society who had the power ability and above all the duty to ensure that the people's right to good governance was not sacrificed at the altar of petty personal or party interests. If interests of the people of this country can only be served through drastic constitutional changes or even total revamping of the system, so be it.

M. M. Khajooria

"Sahil" 20C-D/C, Gandhi Nagar
Jammu

PART: 1
GOOD GOVERNANCE

1

The Concept and Contours of Governance?

Governance is a complex and multi-dimensional concept. Historically it evolved and developed alongside the human civilisation. In its simplest form, it encompassed the process of decision-making and the mechanism through which such decisions were implemented. Any analysis of governance must, therefore, focus on the formal and informal actors involved in decision-making and implementing the decisions made and structures put in place for the purpose.

There was no unanimity about the meaning of governance amongst conservatives and liberals on the one side and socialists and the communists on the other. World Bank book, however defined governance, as "the manner in which power is exercised in the management of a country's economic and social resources for development" (World Bank, 1992).[1] In concrete terms, it dealt with scrutiny of processes through which governments were constituted and policies concerning the state, citizens, and institutions that govern economic and social communications among them formulated and implemented. This perspective was shared by International Institute On Governance (IOG) founded in Ottawa in 1990 to explore, share and promote good governance in Canada and overseas according to which "governance comprises the traditions, institutions and processes that determine how power is exercised, how citizens are given a voice, and how decisions are made on issues of public concern."[2]

The working definition adopted by the British Council, however stressed that "Governance involves interaction between the formal institutions and those in civil society. Governance refers to a process whereby elements in society wield power, authority and influence and enact policies and decisions concerning public life and social uplift." Governance is a dynamic connotation which according to the Oxford Advanced Learner's Dictionary means, the way in which a country is governed."[3] Simply put, governance means the activities or process of managing public affairs. It is different from government which is a physical entity encompassing various institutions (i.e., legislature, executive and judiciary) and their actors who are authorised to exercise sovereign power of the state. Governance is thus a qualitative expression and a normative concept. It essentially dealt with safeguarding the territorial integrity of the State and securing citizen security, rule of law and the delivery of services ranging from education, health to livelihood and food security.

The collapse of the neo-liberal oriented Structural Adjustment Policies (SAP) late 1980s and early 1990s as the tool for speedy development in developing countries pushed the concept on to the centre stage. The World Bank report on Sub-Sahara Africa in, 1989 argued that much of the failure was due to 'the crisis of governance' without addressing which no worthwhile progress was possible.

It should be remembered that in a democratic polity, the political executive and its civil and military appendages are not the only components of governance. The Civil Society in its widest connotation which included intelligentsia, Opinion makers, media, lobbyists, NGOs, research institutes, and finance institutions, was an equally vital stake holder. "Governance", therefore, not only encompassed but transcended the collective meaning of related concepts like the state, government, regime and good government. Some value-assumptions obviously add to governance when prefaced with word "good" placing public good at the core of its concerns. Good governance was therefore expressed in the quality of decisions and actions of public servants that enhanced citizens trust in the polity and its leadership.

Though the emphasis on good governance was of somewhat recent origin, its roots could be traced to more than two thousand years old treatises of Kautilya and Confucius wherein were elaborated the traits of the ruler dispensing good governance. Kautilya, wrote "The king who is well educated and disciplined in sciences, devoted to good government of his subjects, and bent on doing good to all people will enjoy the earth unopposed."[4]

Confucius believed that a well-ordered society required a government based on superior morality rather than on superior power. In order to achieve good governance, "the ruling class should represent the highest type of morally integrated individuals upon whom both political and social responsibilities were to fall."[5]

Many of the elements and principles underlying "good government" have by now become an integral part of the concept of "governance" itself. In the words of John Healey and Mark Robinson "good government" implies a high level of organisational effectiveness in relation to policy formulation and the policies actually pursued, especially in the conduct of economic policy and its contribution to growth, stability and popular welfare.

Under a democratic dispensation "Good governance is epitomised by predictable, open and enlightened policy-making, a bureaucracy imbued with a professional ethos acting in furtherance of the public good, the rule of law, transparent processes, and a strong civil society participating in public affairs." (definition provided by the World Bank).

According to a United Nations Economic and Social Commission for Asia and the Pacific publication. "Good governance has eight major characteristics. It is participatory, based on consensus, accountable, transparent, responsive, effective and efficient, equitable and inclusive and follows the rule of law. It ensures that corruption is minimised, the views of minorities are taken into account and that the voices of the most vulnerable in the society are heard in decision-making. It must be responsive to the present and future needs of the society."

1. Participation

Participation by all citizen irrespective of caste. Creed religious beliefs or gender was a key cornerstone of good governance. Participation could be either direct or through legitimate intermediate institutions or representatives. Participation should be informed and organised implying freedom of association and expression on the one hand and an organised civil society on the other hand.

"Public participation is a political principle or practice, and may also be recognised as a right (Public participation). The terms public participation may be used interchangeably with the concept or practice of stakeholder engagement and/or popular participation. Generally public participation seeks and facilitates the involvement of those potentially affected by or, interested in a decision. The principle of public participation holds that those who are affected by a decision have a right to be involved in the decision-making process. Public participation implies that the public's contribution will influence the decision."[6]

In democracies public participation "has become a central principle of public policy making. In the UK it has been observed that all levels of government have started to build citizen and stakeholder engagement into their policy-making processes. This may involve large scale consultations, focus group research, online discussion forums, or deliberative citizens' juries. There are many different public participation mechanisms, although these often share common features."[7]

Public participation may also be used to measure attainable objectives, evaluate impact and identify lessons for future practice. In the USA public participation in administrative rule-making refers to the process by which proposed rules are subject to public comment for a specified period of time. Public participation is typically mandatory for rules promulgated by executive agencies of the US government. Statutes or agency policies may mandate public hearings during this period. In our own country important bills introduced in the parliament were circulated for eliciting public opinion before finalisation and introduction for consideration by the legislature.

2. Rule of law

In any democratic dispensation it was imperative that legal frameworks were fair and equitable and enforced impartially ensuring full protection of human rights, particularly those of disadvantaged sections of society and minorities. Impartial enforcement of laws, an independent judiciary and an impartial and incorruptible police force were integral to Good governance. Legal and judicial systems where under laws were not enforced and noncompliance and corruption became the norm undermined respect for the rule of law, engendered social degradation, insecurity of life and property of citizens and undermined progress towards sustainable development.

"Practitioners in the development field have increasingly turned their attention to reforms to improve legal and judicial institutions and promote the rule of law and good governance. For example, various United Nations agencies such as the United Nations Environment Programme (UNEP) and the United Nations Development Programme (UNDP), as well as the

World Bank and other regional development banks, are directing increasing resources to reform legal and judicial institutions."

But what use were good laws if either not enforced at all or enforced in a crooked and discriminatory manner? The issue was addressed comprehensively in the Convention on Access to Information, Public Participation in Decision-making and Access to Justice in Environmental. "To date, however" it recorded "most of these efforts have concentrated on developing new laws and creating new institutions, rather than building capacity for ensuring compliance with existing rules. Yet without compliance, laws and regulations are meaningless–or worse, they undermine respect for the rule of law–and cannot promote sustainable development. As a result, many developing countries and countries with economies in transition still suffer from weak legal and judicial systems, lack investment, and have poor development prospects, sustainable or otherwise. Thus, donor-driven reform efforts need to ensure that their rule of law efforts include sufficient training and capacity building to establish the institutional foundation for compliance and enforcement, through both instrumental and normative efforts."[8]

3. Transparency

Transparency was widely perceived as a critical prerequisite for macro-economic sustainability, good governance and overall fiscal rectitude in the conduct of affairs of the government "A basic requirement for transparency in the overall structure and functions of government is a clear demarcation of the boundaries between the public and private sectors. Apart from some activities (e.g., education, healthcare, and public utilities) where both sectors may operate concurrently. In many countries, the government is solely responsible for public administration, internal safety, defence, foreign relations, and macroeconomic policy" wrote. George Kopits and Jon Craig in their paper "Transparency in Government Operations" (International Monetary Fund Washington DC, January 1998).[9]

According to them "Freedom-of-information legislation helps ensure government transparency and accountability by giving citizens access to public documents and assigning to government the burden of justifying non-disclosure." The Right to Information Act (RTI) took care of this concern. They recommended independent performance audits and studies on selected issues by a review agency to ensure transparency in government operations. "To be effective, such an agency must be accountable to the legislature and the public at large and must be endowed with wide investigative and reporting authority over government operations" they concluded.

Free availability and direct access to clear, accurate and up-to-date information to those who will be affected by decisions and their enforcement were the basic attributes of transparency in governance. Information should be provided by concerned agencies in commonly understandable language and format through easily accessible medium. Obviously, mere access to any quantum and quality of information would be meaningless and hypocritical if not followed by concrete, speedy and satisfactory response to complaints or demands made by citizens.

A historical perspective to the issue was lent by United Nations Department of Economic and Social Affairs which pertinently drew attention to changing world scenario and recorded "The end of the cold war; spreading democratisation; a shift in balance among the state, the market and civil society; globalisation; and changing social mores—among other factors–are altering the environment in which governments are operating. The explosion of new information and communication technologies is also allowing for a rapid, global diffusion of ideas and practices, enabling the public to demand higher standards of ethics, transparency and accountability in the public sector. These prerequisite values of good governance and sustainable development not only buttress responsive public policy and high levels of public sector performance but also play a crucial role in preventing the onset of systemic corruption." It emphasised that "There is now international recognition that corruption impedes economic development, undermines stability and erodes trust in public institutions. The pernicious effects of corruption—the lack or poor quality of essential public infrastructure and services—are borne by those the least able to do so: the poor."[10]

Declaring his commitment to Transparency and Open Government, President Barak Obama in his Memorandum for the Heads of Executive Departments and Agencies wrote, "My Administration is committed to creating an unprecedented level of openness in Government. We will work together to ensure the public trust and establish a system of transparency, public participation, and collaboration. Openness will strengthen our democracy and promote efficiency and effectiveness in Government. Transparency promotes accountability and provides information for citizens about what their Government is doing. Information maintained by the Federal Government is a national asset." He assured that, "My

Administration will take appropriate action, consistent with law and policy, to disclose information rapidly in forms that the public can readily find and use. Executive departments and agencies should harness new technologies to put information about their operations and decisions online and readily available to the public. Executive departments and agencies should also solicit public feedback to identify information of greatest use to the public."[11]

Obviously, it wasn't just at the state level but at all levels that government agencies must recognise the importance of making information available to desiring citizens online or otherwise. Driven by the mandate to foster good governance and sound public administration, the goal of transparency was brought within the reach of Indian citizens by the landmark enactment of Right to Information Act (RTI). A combination of principled determined action by public spirited citizens and positive and activist response from the Judiciary was already making waves. The Protection of Whistle Blowers legislation further strengthened the activism in public domain.

4. Responsiveness

Good governance required that institutions and processes were truly and transparently responsive and served all stakeholders within a reasonable timeframe. Even though responsiveness of officials at the grass root level was critical for the good governance most of them remained unresponsive towards to needs and demands of the common citizen. The prevailing situation and their attitude had to change. They must be made to realise and recognise their duty to respond to the calls and needs of all citizens and willingly and play a proactive role in protecting their rights irrespective of caste, creed, religion and social status.

The civil society which wielded influence amongst all sections of society also had a significant role in inculcating the spirit of responsiveness amongst government officials with a view to work towards well being of the common people. Working in tandem, the community leaders and citizens it had the undeniable potential to foster good governance through ensuring services for the common people and protect their rights.

"The evolution of the New Public Management movement has increased pressure on state bureaucracies to become more responsive to citizens as clients" wrote. Eran Vigoda in the article titled "From Responsiveness to Collaboration: Governance, Citizens, and the Next

Generation of Public Administration. He asserted that, "Without a doubt, this is an important advance in contemporary public administration, which finds itself struggling in an ultra dynamic marketplace. However, together with such a welcome change in theory building and in practical culture reconstruction, modern societies still confront a growth in citizens' passivism; they tend to favour the easy chair of the customer over the sweat and turmoil of participatory involvement." The author pointed towards two primary goals: "First to establish a theoretically and empirically grounded criticism of the current state of new managerialism, which obscures the significance of citizen action and participation through overstressing the (important) idea of responsiveness. Second, the article proposes some guidelines for the future development of the discipline. This progress is toward enhanced collaboration and partnership among governance and public administration agencies, citizens, and other social players such as the media, academia, and the private and third sectors." The article concluded that, "despite the fact that citizens are formal "owners" of the state, ownership will remain a symbolic banner for the governance and public administration–citizen relationship in a representative democracy. The alternative interaction of movement between responsiveness and collaboration is more realistic for the years ahead."[12]

5. Consensus Oriented

A broad consensus on what was in the best interest of the society and the manner in which this should be achieved formed the bed rock of good governance in a democracy. As societies were not omnibus entities, mediation between several actors holding diverse view points and cherishing different interests needed to be engaged in a sustained and meaningful consultation process.

Such periodic consultation through round table, community meetings, social networking and the like could be of substantial help in comprehending the people's needs, aspirations; and, obtain their views and recommendations on major public issues. The administration must therefore develop and nurture effective mechanisms to encourage such partnerships that facilitated the feel of the pulse of the constituency on a regular basis. The aim should be to work out a broad and long-term perspective on sustainable human development in the historical, cultural and social contexts.

Many local self-government organs had institutionalised such mechanisms as part of the governance process. Ideally those partnering consultative status or observer status within the municipalities, and Panchayat hierarchies should have no voting rights. It must be a two-way communication mechanism: not only to communicate to residents, but also to be communicated by them.

Under our constitutional arrangement, parliamentarians and legislators in two houses of the parliament/state legislative assemblies representing different political streams were expected to build consensus on issues of national/state level concerns. Consultative committees comprising members of parliament/state legislatives assemblies drawn from different political parties were appointed by the respective Speakers to monitor the functioning of concerned ministries/departments. Yet our esteemed public representatives managed to avoid or evade consensus mostly motivated by party and sectarian/regional considerations. Apparently the fault lay not with the institutions but with the mindset of the political class.

6. Equity and Inclusiveness

Fair play, impartiality and involvement of all sections of the society in governance and right to its fruits were the cardinal attributes of good governance. It should have a wide framework of law which was implemented impartially. The government should create structures where under all the members of the community and society were enabled to realise that all of them without any exception had responsibility towards the society and the people constituting the society. In this context, it was necessary that all the groups of the community particularly the most marginalised and vulnerable were empowered to contribute, improve and/or maintain their own well being and betterment. No one was excluded from the mainstream.

"A society's well being" pointed out T. Ayco "depends on ensuring that all its members feel that they have a stake in it and do not feel excluded from the mainstream of society. This requires all groups, and especially the most vulnerable to have opportunities to maintain or improve their well being. (*Local Good Governance* by Ramon T. Ayco, September 2007)."[13]

7. Effectiveness and Efficiency

Good governance implied that its processes and institutions produced results that squared with the aspirations of the society through the optimum, economical and most efficient utilisation of resources at their disposal. Assurance of the standard of security of life, honour and property and speed and quality of development-related activities free from taint of corruption were the primary touch stones on which its performance in this respect was tested. The concept of efficiency in the good governance had also come to cover the sustainable use of natural resources and the protection of the environment.[14]

8. Accountability

Accountability was a key requirement of good governance. The governmental institutions as also the private sector and civil society organisations must be accountable to the citizen and to their institutional stakeholders. Who was accountable to whom would be judged by whether decisions or actions taken were internal or external to an organisation or institution. In general, an organisation or an institution was accountable to those affected by its decisions or actions. Transparency and the rule of law were prerequisite for accountability. These were the yardsticks according to which the achievement of the goal of good governance shall be measured.

Institute of Governance, Ottawa in Policy Brief 15 took the position that "The concept of Governance opens new intellectual space. It allows us to discuss the role of government in coping with public issues and the contribution that other players may make. It opens one's mind to the possibility that groups in society other than government (e.g. 'communities' or the 'voluntary sector') may have to play a stronger role in addressing problems." Moreover "a universal set of principles for defining good governance can be fashioned and that the strength of their universality rests to a large extent on the body of international human rights and laws." It concluded that, "these principles can be usefully applied to help deal with current governance challenges. When they are applied it becomes apparent that there are no absolutes; that principles often conflict; that the 'devil is in the detail'; that context matters. Finally, the nature of governance–both the means and the ends–needs to be understood. Only then does it make sense to elaborate the principles in order to create a meaningful analytical tool."[15]

Good governance is now an acceptable goal for members of public services especially in developing countries who were required, besides acquiring professional excellence, to be more transparent and fair in all of their transactions. Moreover, highest standard of integrity must be integral to their responses to the demands of the citizens. Good governance, therefore was not an end in itself, but a means of achieving wider goal of public service. All this required experts and professionals in public services to be not only achievement-conscious but also pro-people and value caring. In short, governance must be productive of greater efficiency and effectiveness in delivering public goods and services and reducing corruption.

In the post-Independence India, the leadership of the nascent democracy was understandably in a hurry to build the basic infrastructure for development and economic self-sufficiency. In the extraordinary circumstances, it was not always possible to construct, operationalise and stabilise matching, viable, competent and credible institutions and structures. The gaps were, more often than not occupied and exploited by the corrupt and morally deficient amongst the state actors and informal actors like crime, mafia, kitchen cabinets, corporate giants, foreign investors/donors who had come to exercise significant influence in the formulation of governmental policy and designing of development strategies.

Good Governance as an ideal is universally acknowledged as difficult to achieve. Governments the world over have endeavoured to attain this goal with varying degrees of success. Very few have managed even to come close to the ideal, which was not only desirable but essential for well being of the people. It was, therefore, necessary that persistent public pressure demanding ceaseless and concerted efforts should be mounted to make Good Governance a reality–a precondition for peace, harmony, progress and overall accelerated sustainable human development of a nation.

References

1. Wehmeier, S. (ed). 2000. *Oxford Advanced Learner's Dictionary*, Sixth Edition. Oxford.
2. World Bank. 1992. Governance and Development.
3. Graham, J., Bruce A. and Plumptre, T. 2003. "Principles for Good Governance in the 21st Century," Institute on Governance, *Policy Brief No.15*.
4. Shamsastry, R. 1967. *Kautilya's Arthas Principles of Public Participation*. Co-intelligence.org. 2008-05-23.
5. Linebarger, P.M.A., Chu, D. and Burks, A.W. 1956. *Far Eastern Governments and Principles of Public Participation*. Co-intelligence.org. 2008-05-23.

6.
7. Rowe and Frewer, 2005.
8. Principles for Good Governance in the 21st Century, Policy Brief No.
9. Morita, Sachiko and Zaelke, Durwoo. (Rule of Law, Good Governance, and Sustainable Development).
10. Convention on Access to Information, Public Participation in Decision-making and Access to Justice in Environmental Matters, June 25, 1998.
11. George Kopits and Jon Craig. "Transparency in Government Operations" (International Monetary Fund Washington DC, January 1998).
12. United Nations Department of Economic and Social Affairs 2013, Report to Congress.
13. Eran Vigoda in "From Responsiveness to Collaboration: Governance, Citizens, and the Next Generation of Public Administration."
14. *Local Good Governance* by Ramon T. Ayco, September, 2007.
15. Institute of Governance, Ottawa Institute of Governance, Ottawa in Policy Brief.

2

Public Administration

Public administration is an ancient activity. The task of an administrator began with the very inception of the state irrespective of the form of governent. All Rulers, be they despots, elected Prime Ministers, Presidents or dictators took political decisions and set the goals for the system to achieve desired objectives. An organised body of government officials called 'administration' was designed to implement the policies and realise the goals to the satisfaction of the masters. Administrators were therefore in existence ever since kings and emperors required pages, treasurers, and architects to carry out the business of court, the army and the police to maintain order and keep crowns on their heads secure.

Even though word *'administration'* derived from Latin word *ad+ministrara, meant "to care for, or look after people, to manage affairs"*, the advent of feudal era and rise of dynasties and despotic regimes, distorted and corrupted its very meaning and purpose. These dispensations used administration as instrument of oppression for the preservation and strengthening of their exploitative and oppressive regimes and furtherance of their vested interests. Since then the very mention of word 'administration' conjured in the public mind images of power, arrogance and privileges.

With the passage of time, the concept of administration came to permeate all organised activity. In essence, it possessed three distinct features—purpose, functions and methodology. According to, *A Handbook of Public Administration* published by the United Nations, 'Its purpose has been completely re-oriented, its functions have enormously increased and its methodology has grown from trial and error stage into an orderly discipline with an organised ever increasing body of knowledge and experience.' In recent time credibility, transparency and public accountability have come to occupy the center-stage in the working and evaluation of an administration. In the word of John A Veig administration denoted "a determined action taken in pursuit of a conscious purpose. It is the systematic ordering of affairs and the calculated use of resources. Administrative decisions and actions must aim at making those things happen which we want to happen and simultaneously preventing developments that fail to square with our collective intent. It is the marshalling of resources in order to gain that what is desired at the lowest cost in energy, time and money."

The concept of 'Permanent and neutral' Civil Services was bequeathed by British to Independent India. The framers of our constitution adopted and integrated it into our constitutional framework. As a result the government apparatus had come to comprise of the political executive, the Public services and local self-government institutions. The latest addition was that of the Non-government organisations.

The dynamic changes in the structure and functions of government and the triangular relationship among state, society, and citizen during the last century or so have had the effect of giving a new direction to the discourse and brought divergent and competing views on the content and scope of public administration into the realm of serious and comprehensive debate. The advancement of civilisation and the great strides in science and technology also significantly impacted its nature, scope, and periphery necessitating the study and systematic exploration of the status of public administration right from its ancient somewhat disoriented state to the modern hi-tech-driven administrative system. This exercise should help to arrive at a broad view of basic patterns of public administration systems, as well as to trace clues for reforms in future.

Present day public administration was recognised as an extension of the concept of democratic governance propounded by classic and liberal philosophers like Aristotle, John Locke, John Stuart Mill, Thomas Hobbes, Rousseau, Montesquieu, Thomas Paine, Samuel Adams and Thomas Jefferson. During those times, the emphasis remained mainly on the organisation of the public administration till the birth of the nation state. Machiavelli's classic '*The Prince*', not only prescribed the guidelines for European rulers but also dwelt on in the philosophy and management techniques of administration.

In fact, the nation state became the reigning model of in Western Europe from the sixteenth century. With the passage of time and extension of the area of its scope and control, the task of governance became enlarged and complex. Organisational structures for defence, enforcement of law and order, managing relations with other states and routine court and public administration etc., had to be created and professional civil servants, with adequate knowledge and expertise found to man the crucial positions.

In the eighteenth century the need for administrative expertise grew further and became more pressing, as state intruded into fresh areas of concern. King Frederick William I of Prussia responded by setting up "professorates in Cameralism," at the Universities of Frankfurt, and Halle. These institutions laid emphasis on economic and social disciplines, with the goal of societal reform. Thus, from a Western European perspective, classic, medieval, and enlightened scholars formed the foundation of the discipline that was to be called public administration.

Lorenz von Stein, an 1855 German professor from Vienna, was credited by many to be the founder of the science of public administration. He found the then prevailing belief that the public administration was a form of administrative science as 'too restrictive'. He was of the opinion that the public administration was an integrating science which relied on many other disciplines like sociology, political science, administrative law and public finance. According to him, the science of public administration provided an interaction between theory and practice. He conceded that the public administration led practically, but affirmed that the theory had to form the base.

In the United States of America, Woodrow Wilson was considered the father of public administration. His formal recognition of public administration came in an 1887 article entitled, "The Study of Administration." He wrote that, "it is the object of administrative study to discover, first, what government can properly and successfully do, and, secondly, how it can do these proper things with the utmost possible efficiency and at the least possible cost either of money or of energy."[1] Wilson advocated four concepts:

1. Separation between politics and the public administration.
2. Consideration of the government from a commercial perspective.
3. Comparative analysis between political and private organisations and political schemes.

4. Crafting effective management by training civil servants and assessing their quality.

The separation between politics and the public administration had since been, perhaps the most fiercely debated issue.

Till the first quarter of the last century, public administration was generally accepted as a value free science dedicated to the enforcement of laws with efficiency and economy, and implement politically determined policies. But soon it was realised that in practice public officials not only implemented policies, but also significantly contributed in policy formulation and setting goals. The United Nations acknowledged that public administration played a significant but discrete role in policy formulation. This brought into focus three goals for the achievement of which public administration in a modern society must strive :

(1) to serve public interest;
(2) to establish rule of law; and
(3) to reflect people's expectations in governmental works (United Nations, 1961).[2] In effect the main purpose of public service was public welfare. That is why Government officials were called civil servants.

Public administration was in essence the "translation of politics into the reality that citizens see every day."[3] It's twenty first century version had, however acquired a new connotation requiring greater transparency, more participation by civil society and higher standards of efficiency. It must not only be sensitive to human rights but must respect them. The change in the public administration concept forced a radical restructuring of the local administrations in many countries. The citizen's concerns emerged as the main focus of legislations and debates. In the final analysis all acts of omission and commission by administration were to be explained to the citizens - the real masters of their destiny in a democracy.

Ethics

The word "'Ethics' derived from the Greek word *ethos*, meant good and bad, right and wrong and should and should not be related to concept or philosophical idea. This branch of philosophy dealt with values relating to human conduct with respect to the rightness or wrongness of certain actions."[4] Universal Dictionary (Readers Digest) described it as "A principle of right or good conduct or a body of such principles." In the context of public administration, adherence to a set of values held sacred and sanctioned by the society may be taken to denote the 'rules or the standards governing the conduct of the administrators in the performance of public service.

The concept was essentially interactive in nature and involved the people, peoples representatives and the public administrators. It may be emphasised that "Ethics is Not just doing the right thing—the reason or intention as well as the consequences of the act meant to be ethical or moral are equally important as the act itself, just as doing the right thing for wrong reasons is equally unethical or immoral…"[5]

Thus, ethics determined an expected mode of behaviour in society and organisations. "It was a guidance system to be used in making decisions. In administrative context, ethics involved the application of moral principles to the conduct of officials in organisations."[6] The Public servants were accordingly required to:

(1) serve citizens and be fair and friendly in that service;

(2) be accountable for what they do to management (government), to clients and to the public in general; and

(3) remain vigilant against corruption, and not allow a conflict of interest in their work?

These were undoubtedly ethical or moral questions which must be addressed by the civil servants in ensuring public interest.

It would, to say the least be erroneous to treat public administration as a value free process responsible only for implementation of public policy with efficiency and economy. As the public administration was closely linked with policy formulation and administrators were involved and do in certain circumstances make political decision, sufficient and effective moral guidelines (as opposed to mere mechanisms for arresting bad decisions) for making or participating in making of those decisions in the interest of the public therefore needed to be laid down. This would deny, public administrators the escape hatch for keeping themselves in safe distance from being directly accountable to people under the shadow of Ministerial responsibility and bureaucratic anonymity.[7]

Herbert A. Simon in his book entitled, *Administrative Behaviour*, argued that public administration was basically a decision-making process.[7] It could, therefore, be said that the soul of good governance resided in ethics and morality, and it demised with the erosion of values, moral deviation, aberration and corrupt behaviour and unjust dispensation.

Experience showed that public officials, while taking decisions, were specially influenced by psychological and social environment besides traditional values of rule conformity, efficiency and economy. According to experts, public bureaucracy while making decisions always faced two conflicting situations such as between serving the personal or group interest and serving public or national interest. "Since it was expected that government officials should always be guided by public interest and subjugate individual interest, the question of ethics or the feeling of right or wrong and just or unjust become important in day to day conduct of administration. It was therefore imperative for the civil servants to ensure that in the conduct of affairs of the state public interest always remained paramount."[8]

A sociological understanding of ethics would embrace norms of behaviour which emerged from self-discovery by people who had several subtle ways to integrate social cohesion with self-realisation. The two indicators to show that the social system is in happy equilibrium, required that:

"The system does not induce people to do to others what they would not like to be done to themselves."[9] "The system would yield the greatest happiness to the greatest number, happiness being defined the way the individuals want it."[10]

In specific terms, canons of ethics in administration dictated that substantive issues relating to Integrity, Corruptibility, Responsibility, Response, Reprisal and Accountability were seriously and persistently addressed in a systematic manner.

Lasswell and Bernard opined that in taking various decisions in the policy implementation process, the administrators, besides the considerations of efficiency and economy, were also influenced by social and psychological environment.[11] This meant that decision-makers at the time of making decisions, were influenced by both personal (or group) emotion and rationality. Thus, the administrators sometimes might take unethical or anti-democratic decisions. "For this reason, along with institutional accountability, the question of administrators' prudence or sense of responsibility and ethics become pertinent. According to '*The Standards and Techniques of Public Administration*' published by the UN in the 50s "the quality of public administration of a country largely depends on the honesty and integrity of its administrators."[12]

To be able to effectively and efficiently discharge its onerous duties under a democratic dispensation, it was necessary to inject a new preparedness within the administrative set-up that had hardly any precedence. It must aim at enhancing implementation capability, effective policy implementation and promote shared understanding of social reality. The capacity to cope with social and administrative complexity could be enhanced by a deliberate and caliberated policy of transparency. To be operative, innovative, risk-taking, and often adventurous entrepreneurial zeal could be expected to transform 'bureaucracy' into a viable and efficient tool of change. Obviously, the discipline of Public Administration cannot exist in isolation. It had to develop in close association with the dynamic social changes. "As a body of knowledge, it must develop explanatory strength to analyse socio-economic complexity and assist in the ushering in of a new-society free of exploitation and human misery, poverty and deprivation of the past era."

References

1. Wilson, Woodrow. June, 1887. The Study of Administration, Political Science Quarterly.
2. Pendleton Act, 1883.
3. Holmquist, 1993). Ethics-How Important it is in Today Office-Public Personnel Management 22(4).
4. Dr. Rene E. Mendoza, University of Philippines.
5. Thompson, D.F. 1985. The Possibility of Administrative Ethics, Public Administration Review 45(5).
6. Simon, H.B. 1947. Administrative Behaviour–Decision Making Process in Administrative Organisation. New York Free Press.
7. Noor, A. (2008). Ethics, Religion and Good Governance, JOAAG, Vol. 3. No. 2.
8. Bernard 1958. The Function of the Executive, Cambridge –Harvard University.
9. Kant–Foundation of Metaphysics and Morality, London, Long-man, 1985.
10. J.S. Mill, Utilitarianism, London, Longman, 1897.
11. Lasswell -1930. Psychopathalogy and Politics. New York. Viking 11.
12. United Nations Technical Assistance Programme-1951. Standards and Technique of Public Administration Special Reference to Under developed Countries.

3

Public Accountability

Accountability was often described as a relationship between an actor and a forum which obliged the actor to explain and justify his / her conduct to the later. The forum, on its part was entitled to demand explanation, require justification and pass judgment for acts done by the actor who bears the consequences of the judgement. Thus, in a democratic polity, the elected government exercising delegated authority for a limited specified period was accountable to the elected representatives, political parties, voters, media and the civil society. In a sense, public accountability boiled down to the obligations of persons/entities entrusted with public resources to be accountable for the fiscal, managerial and programme responsibilities conferred upon them and to report to those that have conferred these.

Accountability was recognised as one of three essential components of good governance, the other two being transparency and responsiveness. "Accountability is a key requirement of good governance. Not only governmental institutions but also the private sector and civil society organisations must be accountable to the public and to their institutional stakeholders. Obviously, who is accountable to whom varied depending on whether decisions or actions taken are internal or external to an organisation or an institution. In general, an organisation or an institution was accountable to those effected by its decisions or actions." But "Accountability cannot be enforced without transparency and the rule of law."[1]

Since the late twentieth century the Anglo-Saxon world was witness to the transformation of the traditional book keeping format to an exhaustive and much broader form of accountability. The transformation of finance accountability to public accountability broadly accompanied the introduction of the New Public Management by the Margret Thatcher's Conservative government in United Kingdom and the Reinventing Government Reforms initiated by the Clinton administration in the United States of America. The transformation provoked search for mechanism capable of dealing with the day to day problems citizen interface with Public Service generate. This quest finally ended with the formulation of the concept of Citizen's Charter. The Conservative Government of John Major was the first to articulate and implement this concept in the United Kingdom in 1991. It was designed as a national programme focussed at continuous improvement in the quality of public services for the people obliging these services to respond to the needs and wishes of the users.

The programme was re-launched in 1998 by the Labour Government of Tony Blair designated as "Services First. Accountability embodied the right of the citizens to speedy, non-discriminatory and quality service. This initiative aroused considerable interest around the world. Several countries followed suit. Others hitched on to service quality paradigm of the 'Total Quality Management' (TQM) movement or pitched somewhere in between the two." Even UK moved on to the Next Steps / Modernising Government Initiatives and injected Citizen's Charters with quality content in delivery of public services. The improved quality tools included the Business Excellence Model, Investors in People, Charter Mark, ISO 9000 and Best Value (Government of UK, 1999).[2]

The six principles of the Citizen's Charter movement as originally framed in UK were:

(i) *Quality:* Improving the quality of services.

(ii) *Choice:* Wherever possible.

(iii) *Standards:* Specifying what to expect and how to act if standards are not met.

(iv) *Value:* For the taxpayers' money.

(v) *Accountability:* Individuals and Organisations; and

(vi) *Transparency:* Rules/Procedures! Schemes! Grievances.

These were later elaborated by the Labour Government as the following nine principles of Service Delivery (1998) :

(i) Set standards of service.

(ii) Be open and provide full information.

(iii) Consult and involve.

(iv) Encourage access and the promotion of choice.

(v) Treat all fairly.

(vi) Put things right when they go wrong.

(vii) Use resources effectively.

(viii) Innovate and improve.

(ix) Work with other providers.[3]

The end of the cold war, the demise of colonialism and spread of democratisation spawned an unprecedented revolutionary alteration of the balance among the states, the market and civil society. The changing social mores and globalisation of economy drastically impacted the operating environment of governments the world over. The rapid global diffusion of ideas and practices promoted by the explosion on the information and communication technological fronts gave birth to the public demand for higher standards of transparency and accountability in the governance. Public accountability thus came to permeate the public discourse and policy documentation as it conveyed the sense of transparency and trustworthiness. By 1996, a consensus on effective, responsible and responsive administration emerged on Indian politico - administrative scene. Chief Ministers conference held on 24 May, 1997 in New Delhi presided over by the Prime Minister concretised the compelling public sentiment and adopted an "Action Plan for Effective and Responsive Government." It was decided in the conference that the Central and State Governments would formulate Citizen's Charters, starting with sectors with a large public interface (e.g., Railways, Telecom, Posts, Public Distribution Systems and the like).

These Charters were to include first, standards of service as well as the time limits that the public can reasonably expect for service delivery, avenues of grievance redress and a provision for independent scrutiny through the involvement of citizen and consumer groups. However, mere listing the rights of the citizen in Citizen's Charter would be meaningless without devising and putting in place a structured system to monitor and evaluate the quality of services provided based on feedback from actual users of services. An India-based NGO, the Public Affairs Centre, Bangalore, came up with the answer by crafting the instrument of Citizen Report Card (CRC) in year 1994. It took the cue from the private sector practice of collecting consumer feedback to undertake system correction measures being taken for improving the quality of the product/services aimed at enhancing consumer satisfaction and pushing up sales.

Application of this technique to the public goods and services did the trick. Interestingly, the CRC duplicated student's performance on different subjects as assessed by the teacher translated into scores recorded in a School Report Card. The CRC data similarly aggregated scores given by users for the quality and satisfaction with different services like health, education, police, etc...or scores on different performance criteria of a given service, such as availability, access, quality and reliability. The Citizen's Report Card thus contained the evaluation and assessment by citizens of the performance of the government, its administrative, economic, security and social service agencies. The Report Cards represented "Blending of the "sciences" of Surveys with the "Art" of Advocacy/reforms."[4] Citizen Report Cards, were also described as participatory surveys, providing quantitative measure of user perceptions on the quality, adequacy and efficiency of public services. In fact, they went beyond mere data collection exercises and effectively operated as instruments of exacting public accountability with the backing of a proactive and vibrant media and awakened civil society. The outcome and evaluation of surveys provided impetus for administrators and progressive politicians' intervention to take corrective action against bureaucratic inertia. CRCs were also being increasingly used as tools for civic engagement to demand better governance.

The use of Citizen's Charter and Citizen's Report Card was still more or less in experimental stage confined to a tiny part of this vast country. Then, there were strategic and structural limitations. For one, there was critical dependence on strong media support and external financing. The effort and time required to stimulate backing both from public officials and from citizens was quite daunting given the unpredictability and commitment quotient of different actors. In term of methodologically, also there existed the problem of comparing different services or regions based on user perceptions on account of varying expectations. This was not to underplay the utility and importance of the concept as well as the instrumentality. With enhanced public awareness and realisation of the critical role of the CRs and CRCs as engines for securing accountability and reform and combined efforts of a combination of citizen, political action groups and bureaucratic action, these would prove the ideal catalyst for moving ordinary people, including the poor, from 'coping to voice' and from 'shouting to counting'.

In the post-modern era, commitment to the ideals of democracy, rule of law and a culture of accountability, rooted in constitutionalism, and defined in terms of good and responsible, has become a core value in measuring the performance of governments and regimes' argued 'Dejo Olowu in his paper, "Public Accountability, Good Governance and Constitutional Validation in Commonwealth Africa."[5]

"The prevention of corruption in the public sphere, and the effective monitoring of the fiscal responsibility of one arm of government to another have thus became critical values from which no regime will officially or even consciously shirk" he concluded. It was therefore appropriate and necessary to locate and link the civil society to the pursuit of public accountability and good governance across the world, institutions of governance were witnessing a paradigm shift towards effective partnership between governments and civil society groups with the objective of creating conducive atmosphere for good and responsible governance through strong and active civil society initiatives. It may be pertinent to mention here that the concept of public accountability operated in the United Kingdom as convention (UK has no written constitution). The structure and function of the Public Accounts Committee (PAC) was part of the reforms initiated by William Ewart Gladstone as British Chancellor of the Exchequer in the 1860s. The first Public Accounts Committee was established in 1861 by a resolution of the British House of Commons proposing a standing committee designated as "The Committee of Public Accounts for the examination of the Accounts showing the appropriation of sums granted by Parliament to meet the Public Expenditure, to consist members, who shall be nominated at the commencement of every Session, and of whom five shall be a quorum."

We the people of India solemnly resolved to constitute India into a Sovereign Socialist republic on twenty sixth day of November, 1949 and gave ourselves a comprehensive Constitution. Under the constitution the governments at the centre and states were accountable to the parliament/ state legislatures and through them to the people. The founding fathers of our constitution took serious note of the challenge of curbing corruption through building in formal processes of accountability in the public realm. A provision was accordingly made for the constitution of the Public Accounts Committee (PAC) comprising members from both houses of the parliament to address the menace of corruption and abuse of fiscal responsibility. The Public Accounts Committee consisted of fifteen members elected by Lok Sabha every year from amongst its members according to the principle of proportional representation by means of single transferable vote. Seven members of Rajya Sabha were elected by that House in like manner. This system of election ensured that each Party/Group found representation on the Committee in proportion to its respective strength in the two Houses. The Chairman of the Committee was appointed by the Speaker from amongst the members of Lok Sabha elected to the Committee. As a convention, starting from the Public Accounts Committee of 1967-68, a member of the Committee belonging to the main opposition party/group in the House is appointed as the Chairman of the Committee. No member of the council of ministers was eligible to become a member of the PAC. The term of office of members of the Committee does not exceed one year at a time. Same provisions exist for the states.

The Public Accounts Committee performed wide ranging functions. It examined the accounts showing the appropriation of the sums granted by Parliament to meet the expenditure of the Government of India, the Annual Finance Accounts of the Government of India and such other accounts laid before the House as the Committee might think fit. In addition to the Reports of the Comptroller and Auditor General of India on Appropriation Accounts of the Union Government, the Committee examined the various Audit Reports of the Comptroller and Auditor General on revenue receipts, expenditure by various Ministries/Departments of Government.

Accounts of autonomous bodies Undertakings allotted to the Committee on Public Undertakings, however were outside the purview of the PAC. An important function of the Committee was to ascertain that money granted by Parliament was spent by Government "within the scope of the demand." More importantly, the functions of the Committee extended "beyond the formality of expenditure to its wisdom, faithfulness and economy." The Committee thus examined cases involving losses, nugatory expenditure and financial irregularities.

In India, Media, especially the electronic Media had taken over the highly proactive role of holding to account the governments, individual ministers, parliamentarians, public servants, corporate tycoon. In fact, all players in the field of law making, governance, trade, commerce, contractors who were involved in any activity relating to public affairs and requiring injection of public funds were under the scanner. The conduct of public servants big or small where it impinged on the rights and well being of the citizens and violated the rule of law was meticulously scrutinised and failures, faults and corrupt practices exposed mercilessly. In the process the Media had earned the odium of indulging in Media trials and sullying reputations pre-empting the task of courts of justice. The fact, however remained that but for the sustained pressure from and exposure by the Indian Media many a scam would have gone unexposed to the detriment of national interest. The issues were now in the realm of public debate and the options of self-regulation and state intervention were being hotly debated.

Decades of practicing a vibrant democracy, significant strides in the fields of economy, commerce and technology, spread of education and the information explosion made the citizens of India aware of their rights. "Citizens have become more articulate and expect the administration not merely to respond to their demands but also to anticipate them. It was in this climate that a consensus began to evolve since 1996 in the Government on effective and responsive administration. At a conference of the Chief Ministers of States and Union Territories held on 24th of May, 1997 in New Delhi presided over by the Prime Minister of India an "Action Plan for Effective and Responsive Government at the Centre and State levels was adopted."[6]

Unfortunately, the Central and State governments mostly paid only lip service to the implementation of Action Plan. Seminars/workshops were no doubt conducted in the states as follow up. In Jammu and Kashmir, a Committee of which I was also a member deliberated on the issues and made specific recommendation which as usual were immediately accepted their implementation, however was altogether a different matter. The only tangible gain from the 1997 resolution, it seems was the enactment and enforcement of the Right to Information Act. Surprisingly but happily a very significant and welcome movement forward was recorded in radical and meticulous programming, unwavering focus on integrity in implementation and complete transparency by many grass root level democratic institutions like Panchayats and Block Samities in some states. These have the potential of becoming models for development at the state and national levels. And once the people become aware of their right to demand accountability from the political class and the bureaucracy and that their Report Cards impact the future of governments, members of the parliament and state legislatures, and the administrators the entire political and administrative scenario in the country was bound to change drastically dumping the outdated feudal and imperialist concepts of governance of a long dead era in the dust bin of history.

There was an ongoing perception that public accountability in modern-day governance was in 'crisis', caused by globalisation and the increasing power of private economic interests. There was no doubt that key issues, such as public-mindedness, democracy and responsibility, and structures like bureaucracy, markets and transparency, adopt radically different and sometimes contradictory interpretations when viewed from different experiential perspectives. But underlying all this were core communities of experiences that bound these diverse interpretations and perspectives into a complex web of mutual interaction and influenced "opening up the path to harmonisation. "In any case there was no way the governments in present times could escape the responsibility to be fully accountable to their peoples and transparent in the use of public resources.

Governments, especially those democratically elected, were duty bound to respect economic, social and cultural rights of the people and discharge their obligations by delivering economies that were equitable and work for the poorest people, delivering quality universal public services and ensuring decent work for all and all be accountable."[7] Public Accountability indeed was universally recognised as the key touch stone of good governance in democracies.

References

1. Hand out titled "What is good governance?" issued by United Nations Economic and Social Commission for Asia and Pacific.
2. Citizen's Charter- Handbook. A Publication of Government of India, Department of Administration Reforms and Public Grievances, New Delhi.
3. *Ibid.*
4. Dr Sita Sekhar, Director Public affairs Foundation, Bangalore Presentation in Jammu on 17 December, 2009.
5. Paper presented by, Dejo Olowu in the VIIth World Congress of Constitutional Law, Athens, Greece. 11-15 June 2007.
6. Citizen's Charter- Handbook. A Publication of Government of India, Department of Administration Reforms and Public Grievances, New Delhi, p. 3.
7. Public Accountability: Designs, Dilemmas and Experiences Series: Cambridge Studies in Law and Society Edited by Michael W. Dowdl.

PART: 2

Coalition Governments in Jammu and Kashmir

Roots of coalition governments in Jammu and Kashmir can be traced to the experiment of Diarchy tried by Maharajah Hari Singh in 1945-46 under which he "inducted two men from public life, Ganga Ram from Jammu and Afzal Beg of National Conference from Kashmir into his five-member cabinet. Beg had more standing in the public and was better educated and more capable than Ganga Ram. Even so, Ganga Ram was given the portfolios of Home and Education. Beg got the much less portfolio of 'Construction.' "Despite these discriminatory practices Afzal Beg did not give up but whenever he drew the governments' attention towards certain welfare needs, he was promptly told there were no funds available," recorded Sheikh Mohd in his autobiography "Attis is-I-Chinar." Soon enough, he realised that the so called experiment of sharing power with the popular representatives was an eye wash. He asked us if he should resign from the cabinet. In March 1946, only a few months after his induction in office, Beg quit his post", the Sheikh concluded. Thus came to an ignominious end the first ever experiment in sharing of power by "peoples' representatives" under the autocratic dispensation. The fate that met coalition governments/support from outside in Jammu and Kashmir thereafter appeared to be following the same pattern.

The first such arrangement in the post-independence era where under the political power was handed over by the ruling Congress party to the National Conference Supremo Sheikh Mohd Abdullah pursuant to the Indira-Abdullah accord of 1975. It may be noted that neither Sheikh Mohd. Abdullah nor any of his colleagues who were sworn in to constitute the mini State cabinet on 25th of March 1975 were leaders members of the Jammu and Kashmir Legislative Assembly. The Congress-National

Conference relations soon turned sour. Apparently, the political expediency that necessitated the arrangement also triggered its demise. The arrangement, therefore, collapsed exactly after two years on 25 March,1977 whereupon Governors' rule was imposed. Elections to the state assembly in 1977 gave Sheikh Mohd. Abdullah and his National Conference a massive mandate. The Sheikh thus bounced back as chief minister of the state on his own strength. He ruled Jammu and Kashmir till his sad demise on 8th September, 1982. He was succeeded by his designated heir and eldest son Dr Farooq Abdullah. The State legislative assembly was dissolved on his recommendations dated 18th April 1983. The June election in the same year saw National Conference romping home on the crest of a popular wave with a huge majority. The success appeared to have emboldened Dr Farooq Abdullah to build bridges with the national opposition parties egged on by his bureaucratic advisors who were known to enjoy close personal relations with some of national opposition parties. The opposition conclave in Srinagar proved to be the proverbial last straw on the camel's back. Prime Minister Indira Gandhi made up her mind to ease him out of power.

The Farooq Abdullah government was overthrown in July 1984 through an inner party coup led by his brother-in-law G.M. Shah, who broke away from the parent organisation, the All Jammu and Kashmir National Conference and floated his own party called. The All Jammu and Kashmir Awami National Conference. Begum Khalida Shah, the eldest daughter of Sheikh Mohd Abdullah became the President of the party. G.M. Shah formed the government which was supported by the Congress party from outside. The Congress-Awami National Conference honey moon lasted for about one year and nine months, whereafter the former pulled the rug from under the feet of the government heralding another spell of Governor's rule.

Rajiv Gandhi was installed as Prime Minister of India on the assassination of his mother, Shrimati Indira Gandhi. On 31st October, 1984, the personal friendship between the sons of Sheikh Abdullah and Indira Gandhi was believed to have significantly influenced the repair of equation between National Conference and the Congress party leading to the inking of the Rajiv-Farooq Abdullah Accord of November 1986. Consequently, another round of experimentation in Coalition governance between the All Jammu and Kashmir National Conference and the Congress ensued. Dr Farooq Abdullah was back in power as the Chief Minister of the troubled state Jammu and Kashmir.

In both arrangements the Congress party played the second fiddle. In 1975 arrangement the Sheikh was too tall a leader for any Congress leader to even dream of competing with him. As far as Farooq Abdullah was concerned, his friendship with Prime Minster, Rajiv Gandhi effectively reinforced his position as the leader of the majority legislative party in the coalition. This, his detractors alleged vested him with almost despotic powers. But even they conceded that his friendly disposition, easy accessibility and spirit of accommodation largely blunted the attack of his detractors. I recall my conversation with a Congress cabinet minister who was cribbing about a particular decision of the cabinet. I asked him why did the Congress ministers not assert?. "Assert? Assert on what strength?" he shot back "You know, Farooq begins all important discussions in the cabinet with the declaration that he had already spoken to the Prime Minister and obtained his approval." Why didn't you go to the Prime minister? I persisted. He looked at me hard and said "You know, it takes me a week, that is when I am lucky, to get an appointment with the PM. Farooq, on the other hand just walks into his bedroom at will." There was no dearth of experts and common men who believed that the central leadership turning a blind eye to the goings on Jammu and Kashmir because of the personal relations between the Prime Minister Rajiv Gandhi and Chief Minister Farooq Abdullah largely contributed to the opening the Can of worms in the 1987 elections.

The Pak ISI planned, promoted, funded and operationalised full scale secessionist terrorism in December 1998 changed the entire scenario and upset all equations. There was a change of guard in Delhi with VP Singh taking over as the non-Congress Prime Minister. More importantly, Mufti Mohd. Sayed occupied the crucial position as the Union Home Minister in his cabinet. While Farooq was trying to come to grips with the enormous and vicious terrorist challenge, the Government of India decided to appoint Jag Mohan as the Governor of Jammu and Kashmir. This was like the proverbial red rag to the bull. Farooq Abdullah, already under tremendous stress resigned and Jammu and Kashmir once again came under Governor's rule which lasted till 1996. It was in that year the then Governor, Gen. V.K. Krishna Rao surprised his admirers and detractors alike by deciding to hold elections for the Lok Sabha and State Legislative assembly. Political Pundits and bureaucrats were unanimous in predicting a disaster, as according to them the situation was "certainly not conducive for such a massive exercise requiring public participation." Gen Rao, however persisted and with the support of his clansman Prime Minister

Narashima Rao brought about the miracle of successfully holding elections to both august democratic institutions. The Jammu and Kashmir National Conference won decisive majority in the election-1996 to the Jammu and Kashmir assembly. The leader of its Parliamentary party, Dr Farooq Abdullah was sworn in as the Chief Minister.

Rise and Fall of PDP-Congress Coalition (2002–2008)

Dr Farooq Abdullah led National Conference government that took office in 1996 completed its full term of six years in office as mandated by the Jammu and Kashmir Constitution. Elections to the Jammu and Kashmir Legislative assembly were thereafter held in year 2002.

The fractured verdict of election-2002 created a record of sorts. Jammu and Kashmir National Conference suffered first ever defeat in the history of elections in which it entered the fray. Even though it emerged as the largest party, the National Conference decided not to stake claim to the formation of the government. The deadlock in government formation was resolved through hard bargaining between concerned political parties which culminated in installation of a PDP-Congress coalition government in Jammu and Kashmir. The coalition was to be headed by the PDP and Congress nominees for three years each by rotation.

The Congress-PDP Cabinets whether led by Mufti Mohd. Sayed or headed by Ghulam Nabi Azad never functioned in the true spirit of coalition "Dharma." The principle of Joint Responsibility, the corner stone of cabinet system was the first causality. Right from chief ministers downwards, every one spoke in terms of our and their government. Comparisons in performance of the coalition government led by Mufti Mohd. Syed and that headed by Ghulam Nabi Azad Congress, not infrequently odious were routinely made in the media as well as on the floors of both houses of the legislature. Ironically, the cabinet ministers belonging to the party whose nominee was not the chief minister felt no hesitation in decrying the decisions to which they themselves were party.

The persisting feud between the coalition partners placed the bureaucrats across the administrative board in the most unenviable position. Senior officers in general and those posted in the secretariat in particular found it hard to find ways and means of staying the straight and narrow path without inviting the wrath of or ruffling feathers of ministers on either sides of the divide. Unfortunately, there was no dearth of time servers and morally deficient who chose to become partisan. The majority, however, took the soft option of inactivity or the barest minimum participation in decision making. This resulted in the administration performing at its lowest efficiency index. Good bye Good governance.

Mufti Mohd Syed, a shrewd politician and a smooth operator maintained a facade of unity and harmonious working relations with the coalition partner. Having been a Congressman for the major portion of his political carrier and enjoying personal rapport with most of the Congress leaders who mattered, it was easier for him to connect. His equation with UPA Chairperson Sonia Gandhi and Prime Minister Manmohan Singh significantly influenced the attitude and conduct of Congress ministers. Ghulam Nabi Azad, on the other hand was perceived as a virtual outsider. For some mysterious reasons, he appeared to be happy to be treated as such–a Delhi man. His style of working and the strategy of "maintaining distance even with cabinet colleagues" the distracters argued created further estrangement. Surprisingly some of his own frustrated party leaders in private called him "the Viceroy" from 'Delhi Durbar'. On the other hand, his bid to cultivate PDP leader Muzaffar Hussain Beig to spite Mufti proved a total disaster. The move appeared to be devoid of adequate preparation, anticipation of the reaction of the PDP leadership, sophistication and an element of finish in execution. To his and Beig's horror the PDP leadership struck back in an unprecedented harsh manner. Beig was not only withdrawn from the cabinet but also removed from the leadership of the PDP legislative party.

Period

The Coalition Coordination Committee put in place to preserve harmony and homogeneity between the partners proved a non-starter. The central leadership which brought about the coalition was expected to and should have effectively intervened in time to take all necessary measures to preserve the coalition and make it work sadly proved wanting. The rot was thus allowed to fester. It soon became obvious to all and sundry that the coalition ridden with unconcealed dissentions and indulging in open confrontation within the cabinet, the legislature and in the media was bitten by the suicide bug was only waiting for the last straw to break its back. The Amar Nath Yatra land row erupted as if in answer. And thereby hangs a tale.

The history of the pilgrimage to the holy cave of Shri Amarnathji situated in the high mountains of Pahelgam tehsil of Anantnag district in Kashmir region of Jammu and Kashmir state was rooted in the hoary past. Bhrigu Rishi, the legend had it, was the first pilgrim to have 'Darshans' of the ice Shiv Lingam at the Holy Cave. The cave thus came to be known as lord Shiva's abode and became a Centre of annual pilgrimage. Since then devotees thronged to the holy cave in the month of Sharavan (July–August) braving tough terrain and hostile weather conditions. This incredible shrine, where lord Shiva's image was formed naturally of an Ice Stalagmite in the form of a Lingam annually attracted devotees like a huge magnet. It waxed and waned in harmony with the cycle of the Moon.

The Amarnathji Yatra got disrupted because of violent political upheavals and waves of conversion to Islam under some bigoted Sultans of Kashmir. According to the folklore it finally stopped during the reign of Sultan Sikander (1389-1413 A.D.) also known as 'Butt Shikan' (The Idol breaker). Whom Sir Wolseley called "a ferocious bigot" (A Cambridge History of India, Volume 111, p. 280).

The credit for the re-discovery of this Holy Cave was earned by a Muslim shepherd named Buta Malik. Again, according to folklore, Buta Malik, while grazing his flock near the location of the holy cave encountered a Sadhu. The Sadhu blessed him and made over to him a bag full of Coal. On reaching his home, Buta opened the bag, and to his utter amazement found it full of gold coins. Overwhelmed with joy, he rushed back to express his gratitude to the Baba. On reaching the spot he found the Sadhu missing. Instead, he found a 'Shiv Lingam' in the Cave. He narrated his experience of the discovery of the cave and existence of the 'Lingam' there in to the villagers. As the news spread, the Hindu priests came into the picture, established the connection with reference to scriptures and the annual Yatra was restored. In recognition of his contribution Buta Malik and his descendents were allotted a share in the offerings made at the holy cave every year.

Since the days of the Dogra rule the yatra traditionally commenced from Hanuman Akhara, Srinagar. The Mahant led the yatris carrying the holy Mace of Lord Shiva which he did even now. The Yatra size initially was rather small in numbers but by 1966 it had reached six thousand two hundred mark. The Tehsildar, Pahelgam was designated as the Yatra officer. As the number of pilgrims continued to increase aggregating to twenty six thousand by 1981, the level of the Yatra officer was raised to that of the Deputy Commissioner, Anantnag. Significantly, the massive spurt in the pilgrim traffic occurred after the onset of militancy and heightened terrorist threat. Devotees surged from all corners of the country indeed the world towards the holy cave unmindful of the threats of the fundamentalist militants as if in defiance of terror Diktat. Even terrorist attacks that claimed number of lives failed to dampen the pilgrim enthusiasm. The ever escalating rush derailed all yatra schedules despite the commissioning of another route to the holy cave via Bal Tal bifurcation on the Srinagar-Leh road. In 2014, three lakh seventy two thousand and two hundred nine pilgrims had 'Darshan of the holy Lingum'.

The normal administrative apparatus burdened as it was with its own multifarious duties was in no position to adequately cope with ever swelling number of Yatris and the myriad of problems it generated. The need for creating a mechanism to manage and facilitate the Yatra, of course with the help of governmental agencies was acutely felt. Impressed by the excellent record of Shri Mata Vaishno Devi Shrine Board in managing an all the year around Yatra of a much bigger magnitude provided the inspiration for constituting a similar institution for the Shri Amarnathji Yatra. The State legislative assembly passed the Jammu and Kashmir Shri Amarnathji Shrine Board Act 2000 "in order to institutionalise the arrangements for the smooth management of the pilgrimage in the holy shrine of Shri Amarnathji." The Shri Amarnathji Shrine Board Act was notified by the state Government by SRO 54 dated 12/2/2001 which came into effect on the same date.

The Chief Executive officer Shri Amarnathji Shrine Board forwarded a Project report to the Jammu and Kashmir Government in the Forest Department in October, 2004 proposing, "the transfer of 3642 Kanals of land for seven halting places on twin routes to Shri Amarnath ji Shrine via Baltal and Chandanwari for the purpose of the smooth conduct and management of the pilgrimage. This innocuous proposal unfortunately became an issue of confrontation in an already divided coalition cabinet. The proverbial last straw on the camel's back was provided by the overenthusiastic and proactive intervention of the chairman of the Shri Amarnathji Shrine Board who also happened to be Governor of the state and a highly polarised bureaucracy.

The state government had spilled the beans through "A background note on the issue pertaining to the diversion of the Forest Land to Shri Amarnathji Shrine Board" which was released to the media on

24th of June, 2008." It convincingly advertising the fractured nature of the cabinet, exposed the manipulative nature of decision-making and the subservient and questionable role of the bureaucracy.

Even a cursory glance at the "Background note" gave the game away- the game to somehow abort the proposal for temporary/seasonal diversion of the land to Shri Amarnathji Shrine Board for facilitating the Yatra–a game plan which lacked both ingenuity and logic.

The first government order granting permission to Shri Amarnathji Shrine Board the use of the identified Forest land for constructing prefabricated structures for Yatra was issued on 29/03/2005. Thereafter the government discovered that a CMP filed in 2004 by "some people in the Jammu and Kashmir High Court agitating the matter" was subjudice. The position taken by the State government was completely false and untenable. How could the government be possibly unaware of the existence of CMP and the orders passed by the Jammu and Kashmir High Court with which were attached the Advocate General and army of Government Advocates to conduct numerous state cases on daily basis and kept a tight vigil in all such matters? As it is, the issue had evoked lot of public interest, provoked public controversy and was prominently discussed in the media. In fact, the issue had begun to dent the cabinet solidarity already under considerable strain. Still the narration of events sequentially gave the impression that knowledge about the CMP filed in 2004 was post- Government order of June 2005. The statement that "In the meanwhile it was learnt" spoke for itself. And what actually prompted the government to file an appeal when there was no conflict between the Government order dated 29 June, 2005 and High Court order of 15 April, 2005 ? In fact the interim direction of the Division Bench of the High Court was also basically on the same lines. The matter should have rested there. But a section of the cabinet had other ideas. The issue was clumsily dug up and controversy revived on the pretext of clarifying whether the land was allowed to be used by the Shrine Board free of cost or on royalty. The Principal Chief Conservator of Forests innocently referred the matter to the Forest Secretary. It may be recalled that the Government order of 29/3/2005 was passed after meticulous scrutiny and in depth examination. The note itself testified that "The matter was examined in the Forest department at various levels and the case was finally submitted to the Hon'ble Minister." No case had ever been finalised by the government department or the secretariat without settling the vital question of land allotment/diversion on royalty, free of cost or on rent and if so at what rate? The events that followed made it abundantly clear that a fraction of the cabinet had taken a conscious political decision to stall/abort the temporary/seasonal diversion of land to the Shri Amarnathji Shrine Board and assigned to pliable bureaucrats the task of finding ways and means of achieving the pre-determined objective. What transpired showed some service officers in very bad light. Their clumsy exertions lacked conviction and were devoid of honesty and logic. It adversely reflected on their moral fibre, service ethics and oath of independence and neutrality.

Interestingly, the commissioner secretary Forests instead of replying to the query raised by the Principal Chief Conservator of Forests determined that "the government order issued is not fully in the same spirit as the order passed by the minister "and same shall be withdrawn." Simple. No need to point out any particular infirmity from which the order suffered or in what manner did it violate the "spirit of the ministers' directions. The minister, who was perhaps waiting in the anti room to sign on the dotted line wasted no time in according the approval. At this stage the chief secretary was brought in, who "had received a complaint against the government order." Another oddity perhaps without any precedent. Certainly a path breaking excuse for an apparent bid to cover up "the lacuna left by the Forest secretary."

Two specific reasons were given for the cancellation of the order: (1) Unnecessary haste was shown to allow SASB to utilise the said land. (2) There were no compelling reasons for the Forest department to issue the impugned order. Both lacked any basis and were far from convincing. Remember, the Government order 148FST of 2005 was issued on 29th of March, 2005. It would obviously take time to be circulated and still more time to be implemented. As the preparations for the yatra commenced in the month of May, there was indeed urgency and enough compelling reasons for issuing the order.

The governor, also ex-offico chairman of the SASB sent a message to the cabinet under section 44(C) of the State constitution triggering yet another bout of evasion in classical 'Babu red tape'. The cabinet decided to circulate the message amongst all the cabinet ministers and then discuss the reference in the next cabinet meeting. The note amazingly recorded that "There is no record to indicate whether the matter came up before the cabinet for discussion as desired by it."

To cut the long story short, the land for the purpose was identified. However, a multi-discipline high powered committee which included all the senior officers of the Forest department met on 12/07/2007 and decided to seek the opinion of the Chief Wild Life Warden as the areas fell adjacent to the Thajiwar sanctuary. Interestingly the Chief Warden had already communicated his opinion a month earlier saying that "the proposed site for construction of Shri Amarnathji Shrine Board complex" is located on the right side of the Sindh rivulet. The proposed complex does not seem to have any significant effect on the ecology of Thajiwar Wild Life Sanctuary." He also described the apprehensions expressed by DFO Sindh and the Wild Life Warden as resulting from an "over cautious" and environmentally conservative approach." His opinion was on record. The Forest Advisory Committee was thus left with no option but to clear the diversion of requisitioned land to the Shrine Board on the prescribed terms and conditions on which there was no dispute. The matter should have ended there as far as the examination by the bureaucracy was concerned.

But the opponents of the proposal were not about to give up. The issue was tagged with a Supreme Court ruling of 2007 which related to the provisions of the central Act not applicable to the J&K. The file shuttled up and down finally stating the obvious that "the order dated 27/4/2007 does not have an applicability with respect to the state of J&K in as much as since the Forest Conservation Act of 1980 and the rules made thereunder are not applicable to J&K." As all concerned found the proposal acceptable, the file was submitted to the Forest Minister who approved the submission of the proposal to the cabinet on 3/1/2008. But the General Department (Under the Chief Minister) insisted on obtaining the opinion of the Law and Dy. Chief Minister (representing PDP). The Forest department then placed the matter before the Dy. Chief Minister who opined that "There is no material difference between the opinion of the learned Advocate General and that of law department. Law department by way of abundant caution seeks to obtain clarification of the Supreme Court (a master stroke to bury the proposal for long, long time). I concur with the opinion of the view of the Central Empowerment Committee and the learned Advocate General."

A few more time consuming hassles were to follow ending with reiteration of the terms and conditions already discussed with and accepted by the Shri Amar Nath Ji Shrine Board. At long last, the State cabinet in its meeting on 20/05/2008 approved the proposal of the Forest department for diversion of 39.88 hectares of Forest land (30.88 hectares at Baltal and nine hectares at Domel to the Shri Amarnath Ji Shrine Board for raising pre-fabricated structures for camping purposes of pilgrims only. It took almost four years for the State government to take a decision on the Project report submitted by the Shri Amar Nath Ji Shrine Board and received in the State Forest Department on 15/10/204 with its deliberations marred by controversies and acrimony.

It was interesting to note that the somewhat unique and long winded 'Background Note' was released on 25th of June, 2008 at a time when the parting of ways between the coalition partners had become imminent. The intention obviously was to place in the public domain the point of view of the then Chief Minister, Ghulam Nabi Azad in pursuance of the sterile game of one–upmanship. The objective was to convey that the Land Diversion order was "the handiwork" of the Forest Minister, a PDP nominee who submitted the proposal to the cabinet for diversion of the land and the Law Minister, also belonging to the same party who cleared it. No one bothered to pause and consider the fact that the Land Diversion decision was taken by the cabinet unanimously. Even otherwise, the cabinet system worked on the principle of joint responsibility. Each and every member of the cabinet was therefore severally and jointly responsible for the decision.

On its part, the PDP threatening to pull out its ministers from the government if the Land Diversion order was not withdrawn by 30th of June, 2008. The PDP contingent of Ministers, however resigned on 28th June, 2008 after it leaked out that the order may be withdrawn earlier than 30th June to rob them of the opportunity of "martyrdom." Later Mehbooba Mufti was to claim that what they could not secure while in government they achieved by sacrificing their ministries.

The withdrawal of the PDP from the coalition reduced the Ghulam Nabi Azad led government to minority. Azad claimed the support of the majority in the legislature and Governor asked him to prove it on the floor of the house. However, having failed to muster the majority support in the Legislative Assembly, Chief Minister Ghulam Nabi Azad tendered his resignation bringing to an end a government which had been at war with itself since 2005, when Azad succeeded Mufti Mohd Syed in pursuance of the power sharing formula between Congress and the PDP.

No tears needed to be wasted on either the break-up of the Congress-PDP coalition in Jammu and Kashmir or the somewhat ignominious demise of the Azad led dispensation. As it is, the ever-feuding coalition was doomed from the very first day of its conception. The real miracle is that the jugglers middlemen ensconced in the corridors of power in Delhi succeeded in keeping it afloat so long.

Over one and half century plus eighteen years of religious, cultural and administrative association and commonality of economic and developmental interests had laid a solid foundation for the composite state of Jammu and Kashmir. True, inter-regional strains had developed since 1947 and some garbage piled up during the past two decades of militancy. But neither of these posed insurmountable problems. Under the surface, the bonds between the civil societies and common people remained stout and enduring. All it needed was a dedicated and sustained effort and the edifice would have emerged strong and shining. The coalition partners not only missed the point but unfortunately displayed a lack both the vision and the requisite political maturity.

Performance Monitor

The mode of evaluation of the performance of Congress-PDP coalition in this study traversed a somewhat non-conventional route. The exercise commenced with a pre-election key note article published in the Fortnightly 'Main Stream' New Delhi, the acknowledged mouth piece of Indian progressive intellectual class. This brought into public domain the constitutional, historical and contemporary perspectives pertinent to democratic processes and happenings in the electoral arena. Under focus were positives and negatives including the subversive role of Pakistan and her local assets as well as the enormous interest the elections in Jammu and Kashmir provoked in the international community especially the United States of America. It placed on record the unprecedented public enthusiasm and commitment to participate in the elections and consequent formation of a democratically elected government in defiance of the boycott calls by terrorists and their overground proxies and unmindful of threats of grave consequences and even murder of candidates.

The performance audit of the coalition in general and its handling of specific problems, challenges and issues that cropped up was conducted on "As it happened" basis. It did not stop at identification of the instances of political waywardness of coalition partners and governance deficit but went on to suggest concrete corrective measures laced with warnings of probable consequences in the event of failure to act effectively and in time. In terms of periodicity, the performance of the coalition was even scanned after 222 days of its coming into being.

PUBLISHED ARTICLES

(1) J&K ASSEMBLY polls; Elections with High Stakes

The Jammu and Kashmir Constitution mandates elections after every six years. The four-phase electoral process, as decreed by the Election

Commission, had to be completed before October 17, 2002 when the six-year term of the present Assembly expires. It was significant that the October 2002 elections were to be conducted on the basis of Census-2001 that was carried out after a gap of two decades. In this election, fifty six lakh twelve thousand one hundred and 49 voters representing 55.73 per cent of the total State population of one crore 69 thousand, nine hundred and seventeen were entitled to exercise their right of franchise. Against this, around 49.34 per cent of about 70 lakh population only was qualified to vote according to the 1981 census. The next Assembly would therefore have the distinction of representing the largest number of voters in the State's history. This election arrived at a crucial juncture in the history of the State which was a victim of unprecedented, brutal and horrowing bloodletting for about fourteen years. The Pakistan promoted terrorism had inflicted extensive damage to its social, cultural and economic infrastructure. It put the clock of progress back by decades, and bred ethnic, communal and regional tensions. Pakistan continued to persist in pushing terrorists across the Line of Control (LOC). Our neighbour was doing everything to derail the electoral process despite, her "commitment" to fight terrorism worldwide as part of the US and assurances to the world community to stop cross-border terrorism in Jammu and Kashmir permanently.

President Mushaaraf of Pakistan openly expressed his own and Pakistan's full and complete solidarity "with All Parties Hurriyat Conference (APHC) in boycotting the sham elections being held under the shadow of 700000 (seven Lac) Indian military men." This solidarity was expressed on August 31st2002 in Islamabad during his talks with Sardar Abdul Qayoom Khan, the "President of National Kashmir Committee" floated by Mushaaraf himself. It may be interesting to note that the Hurriyat had, for quite some time not given any call for the boycott of the elections. The conglomerate only decided to abstain from participating in the elections. Yes, the election boycott was indeed dictated by Mohd Yusuf Shah alias Salah-ud-din, Chairman of the Jehad Council based in POK, a creation of the Pak ISI. He went to the extent of threatening the Hurriyat leadership with dire consequences if the Diktat was not complied with. The humiliating gesture was perhaps too much even for the Hurriyat leadership to swallow. Sajjad Lone of the People's Conference sharply reacted and publically questioned the right of "those hiding in Pakistan" to dictate the decisions to the Hurriyat. Mirwaiz Moulvi Farooq conveyed the same message in his usual polite manner. Even the Hurriyat president, Abdul

Gani Butt, known to be in cahoots with the Pak ISI felt compelled to record his protest. As recently as on September 4, terrorist groups like Hizab-ul-Mujahideen, Al Umar Mujahideen, Jamiat-ul-Mujahideen, Islamic Front and Jehad Kashmir declared that 'those joining the elections would he considered as traitors, who would not be spared'. The very fact that the terrorist outfits had to reiterate the warning earlier sounded by Salah-ud-din showed that the people of Kashmir were not impressed with these antics. The pro-Pakistan Jamat-e-Islami's associate Dukhtran-i-Millat had added a new dimension to the controversy, by accusing the APHC of a "sell out." Addressing a press conference, its underground head, Asiya Andrabi, blamed the Hurriyat Conference "for clearing the way for the conduct of elections by not issuing an election boycott call."

Richard Armitage, the US Deputy Secretary of State, declared in Islamabad on September 5th that 'violence free and broad-based elections in Kashmir' were an international concern. "The US feels that free and fair elections in the Valley would be an expression of the will of the people and may help a movement forward," he significantly added. This position of the United States, fully, supported by the European Community and other world powers is at the core of Pakistan's woes and stubborn resistance to fair and free elections in J&K. The option of a plebiscite in Jammu and Kashmir had since been buried. The United States had made her position on the issue clear. UN Secretary-General Kofi Annan had said this in so many words, The bi-lateral nature of the Kashmir dispute was internationally recognised. However, as a concession to Pakistan, the Western powers sought its resolution in accordance with the aspirations of the people of Kashmir. The question therefore arose as to who would be qualified to speak on behalf of the people of Jammu and Kashmir? Pakistan's proposition to push the Hurriyat as the sole representative of the people of Kashmir was too much even for her sympathisers to countenance. Credible and inclusive elections in Jammu and Kashmir therefore emerged as the only viable democratic option. Obviously, Pakistan had a serious problem with this option. She was fully conscious of her marginal popular support in the State. Even on the terrorist front the 'local' 'support' was vanishing. Figures of the terrorists gunned down on the borders during the period June to September 2002 speak for themselves. Out of 80 terrorists killed till date, 66 were foreigners. This explained the mulish stubbornness in sabotaging the elections 2002. The Indian leadership on the other hand, went out of the way to persuade the dissidents groups and even some militant elements to participate in the elections. The Prime Minister repeatedly held out an assurance of fair and free elections. Electronic Voting Machines were introduced for the first time in the State. The Model Code of Conduct was being vigorously enforced. A Deputy Commissioner and a number of other officers have been transferred on the direction of the Election Commission. A Minister of the Uttar Pradesh Government, who ferried BSP supremo Kanshi Ram to J&K, was asked to pay for the flight from his own pocket. Strict vigilance shall, however have to be maintained to ensure that 'the elections are transparently fair and impartial. This is obviously in the national interest.

The 'post-election scenario is sure' to witness exceptionally hectic activity. Some unique development have taken place this time around. All political parties in Ladakh have voluntarily lapsed into oblivion. A single political platform to struggle for the Union Territory status for, the district was contrived. Its, two nominees have been returned unopposed, to the J&K Assembly. The ruling National Conference had a change at the top. Omar Abdullah not only succeeded his father, Dr Farooq Abdullah, as the President of the party but also emerged as the Chief Ministerial candidate. Dr Farooq Abdullah opted out of the electoral contest. Two serving Ministers of State, Mohammad Hussain of Darhal, Rajouri and Qmar Ali Akhoon of Kargil, ex-Ministers and number of sitting MLAs were denied the party's nomination. Perhaps for the first time in the history of the National Conference so many long-time party loyalists were dumped and revolted. Some have been fielded by rival parties. Others are contesting as independents. Even Shafi Shaida, a political non-entity picked up by Farooq from nowhere and appointed as his Advisor with the status of a Minister of State, deserted. He resigned from the National Conference to contest as an independent. Almost all political parties worth the name have suffered defections. *Aya ram's and gaya ram's* are merrily floating around. Prominent political activists of the People's Conference have filed their nomination papers as 'independents' claiming the legacy of the slain leader, Abdul Gani Lone. Suspecting the hand of Lone brothers, Sajjad and Bilal, the Hurriyat went into a tizzy, decided to suspend them from the combine but hastily retraced the step for fear of repercussions. Even a prominent Jamat-e-Islami activist-was reported to be contesting.

The National Conference's Chief Ministerial candidate Omar Abdullah admitted that there was an anti-incumbency wave in Jammu and Kashmir. Before filling his nomination papers from Gandherbal constituency Omar told reporters that his party faced the toughest ever challenge since 1977.

"The anti-incumbency factor is strong. But we have to work hard and take measures to check it."

In Jammu, the RSS backed Jammu State Morcha entered the election fray on the issue of Statehood for the Jammu region. This further weakened the already depleted BJP vote-bank. It also compounded the confusion amongst its cadres, who were torn between loyalty to the parent organisation, the RSS, and commitment to the party ruling at the Centre, which did not openly support trifurcation of the State. All this obviously did not augur well for the party which had suffered grievous loss of credibility due to its coalition with the National Conference at the Centre while opposing the party in the State tooth and nail.

There was a striking contrast between the election scenes of 1996 and 2002. In 1996, candidates were scarce to, find, the campaigning was erratic and subdued. An overpowering sense of fear and apprehension generally prevailed. The unbelievable change that had taken place was viewed in the bedrooms the world over, thanks to the exertions of the ever present electronic media. There was little scope left for spreading falsehood and indulging in unabated distortions. According to independent press reports, Kashmir Valley seemed to be fully immersed in the election gush. People thronged public rallies of different political parties. The militants' threats to the public who attend the political meetings had no impact. Statistics corroborated this projection. More than three hundred and thirty three election rallies were held in the last one month across the State. There was an air of festivity with buntings and banners erected at prominent places inscribed with party slogans. Flags of various political parties were hoisted in large numbers, terrorist killings of candidates, attacks on Ministers and other contestants and their supporters notwithstanding.

The murder of an independent candidate, Sheikh Ghulam Rasool, his kin and supporters in the terrorism infested Kupwara district in fact galvanised to more vigorously participate only frustrated the terrorists. To their utter dismay the brutal strike, instead of generating fear, had raised the level of public anger against them. People were defying the boycott diktat in their desperate quest for peace through the ballot. The option of the bullet seemed to have been decisively discarded. The Kashmiri's defiance of terrorism was best illustrated by the rare assertion of unique political commitment, lion heartedness and extreme determination by the Butt family of Tral in the Pulwama district of Kashmir. This was an extraordinary story of a traditionally National Conference family written in blood. Mohd Shubhan Butt, popularly known as Zaildar sahib was a prominent National Conference leader and freedom fighter. He suffered privations and incarceration during the Maharajah's rule and later as a leader of the Plebiscite Front. Even at that point of time his faith in secularism and democracy remained undiluted. When terrorism was at its peak, he dared to defy the terrorists and was assassinated. His son who took up the cause, was similarly gunned down by the terrorist brutes. When the elections were announced, the second son was the front-runner for the Tral-constituency as a National Conference candidate. The terrorist threats failed to dissuade him from carrying the family legacy. Even before the party mandate could be granted, he was shot dead. Undeterred by the terrorist brutality and unbearable losses inflicted on the family for their political commitments, Dr Ghulam Nabi, another brave son late Mohd. Subhan Butt, decided to pick up the gauntlet. This was a saga of valour and unparalleled sacrifices that would do any family, community, party or nation proud.

The people of Jammu and Kashmir had convincingly, and firmly shown their faith in parliamentary democracy and preference for the ballot over the bullet. As the polls drew nearer, the Pak ISI and the terrorist goons strove hard to disrupt the elections through acts of terror. Targets euphonically described as 'soft' were mercilessly and repeatedly hit. The ball was now in the court of the State and Central governments. It was their duty and responsibility to provide the necessary security cover not only to the candidates but also to the voters at large.

The State machinery should take abundant care not to do or permit anything to be done that taints the free and fair character of the polls. The political, parties must rise, above petty party interests and help in ensuring the greatest possible participation in the elections. The credibility and level of voter participation in elections 2002 will have fallout far beyond the confines of Jammu and Kashmir. These could well determine the direction and movement forward in resolving the Kashmir tangle and firming up international support for the Indian position on the issue of Kashmir.

(12 October, 2002)

(2) Restoration of Vital Institutions; the foremost challenge before ruling combine in J&K

It is indeed ironic that Shiekh Mohd Abdullah, who successfully led the Kashmiri people's struggle for the overthrow of the dynastic rule in the name of democracy, secularism and socialism should have been the one to lay the foundation of an authoritarian political dispensation. The tallest amongst the Kashmiri stalwarts of the political upsurge, Qaid- I-Azim, Sher-I-Kashmir and the first elected Prime Minister of Jammu and Kashmir in independent India was no doubt the undisputed supreme leader. And he ruled as such. His word was the law.

The Shiekh became the role model for his successors—from Khlid-i-Kashmir Bakhshi Ghulam Mohd to Qaid-I-Sani, Farooq Abdullah. G.M. Sadiq was the only exception to conduct the affairs of the state as a "mere Prime Minister doing a job for which he was elected. And he did his job exceptionally well, established healthy traditions of cabinet system, banished administrative anarchy and established governance by laws and rules. The return of Shiekh Mohd Abdullah to power in 1975 following Indira-Abdullah Accord, however reestablished the institution of the supreme leader. It may, however be said to the credit of the Sheikh that he did not temper with the system, was just and fair in all matters except where he held strong personal views. Never the less, the government came to be run according to his perceived "whims and fancies" as the Supreme leader. My experience based on directly dealing with him as head of Jammu and Kashmir Prisons department and Commissioner Poonch-Rajouri Division was that the great Sheikh was amenable to reasoning and willing to even change his decisions only if someone had the moral courage and conviction to put the other options before him. On his demise, his eldest son Dr Farooq Abdullah took over. Except for a brief period when G.M. Shah became the chief minister, and spells of governor's rule the state was run by Dr Farooq Abdullah till the recent polls in which his party, the National Conference was out voted.

The environment under 'one man rule' was most conducive for manipulations and 'palace intrigues'. Host of sycophants, time-servers and manipulators amongst the civil servants inevitably warmed their way into favour of the political masters. They, at times rode rough shot even over the cabinet ministers, who found discretion to be better part of the valour. The single party brute majority in the legislature and an ineffective and rudderless opposition facilitated the degeneration of the constitutional democracy into a virtual dictatorship. At the political plane, a class of hangers on, brokers and blood suckers attached themselves to the men in authority. They doled out favours, jobs and contracts *et al*, of course for consideration. Justice, fair play and equality before law were just words in the dictionary to be recited for the benefit of the credulous. The recent election to the state assembly has brought about a revolution of sorts.

The fractured verdict and the electoral arithmetic hardly provides any scope for the continuation of the institution of the 'Supreme leader'. This presented an opportunity to cleanse the system of parasites and 'yes men', to herald an era of decency in public life and integrity and transparency in governance in the bloodied and battered state of Jammu and Kashmir.

The once mighty Jammu and Kashmir National Conference has been humbled at the hustling in a fair contest. It was not just a political party but a historical movement that under the leadership of Sher-i- Kashmir Sheikh Mohd Abdullah, awakened the people of Kashmir from centuries old slumber, welded them into a powerful people's movement fired with a secular, democratic and progressive political ethos. The credit for linking the fate of the Muslim majority state with secular India in preference to a theocratic Pakistan also goes to this party. The first National Conference government under the Premiership of Shiekh Mohd Abdullah ushered in unprecedented and till date unmatched revolutionary land reforms and Debt reconciliation measures freeing the tenants and poor borrowers held in bondage since centuries. How these enormous assets were squandered away is a subject of an independent and in-depth study. The National Conference, the largest single party with 28 members still had a strong presence in the assembly. Its leadership had, however done well to sit in the opposition and initiate 'serious and honest' introspection for ascertaining the causes of the electoral debacle. If the right lessons were learnt and necessary corrective measures taken, the party may be able to rejuvenate itself. In the meantime, its parliamentary wing should discharge the constitutional obligations of a constructive and responsible opposition acting as the watch dog for people's interests.

The Congress-PDP coalition which emerged as the alternative was committed to do away with the system aberrations and distortions that became the hall mark of their predecessors in power. Having contested the elections on a common anti-National Conference plank and hammered out a Common Minimum Programme, the combine should be in a position to seriously and determinedly work for its implementation. It needed to be emphasised that even though the popular verdict was fractured in terms of party preferences, it was categorical for change and the rejection of the then ruling party.

The electorate have a right to expect that the Congress-PDP combine provide a government with a difference–a clean, efficient and transparent government that really works. The genuineness of its commitment to the welfare of all the people of the state irrespective of regional, communal or ethnic considerations will be tested in days to come. The objectives of Peace, reconciliation and reconstruction should inspire its policy formulations and programme implementation. They have to make good the promises held out in the Common Minimum Programme to retain the faith and confidence of the people. People expect them not only to resist the temptations that come with power but be also seen to be doing so.

The role of the legislature, the cabinet and the public administration was critical to the proper working of the democratic and secular polity. Bringing back these institutions on the rails, infusing propriety, a sense of purpose, total commitment to the service of the people in their working and an unwavering adherence to the constitution should be on the top of the agenda of the coalition government.

Legislature

Unfortunately, the standard of performance in our law making bodies had suffered gradual decline over the decades. The down slide was primarily attributable to the dwindling values, falling standards of debate and scant knowledge/understanding of parliamentary laws, rules and practices. The ruling party and the opposition perceived themselves in an adversarial rather than a complimentary role. The first and foremost requirement, therefore was to adequately equip our legislatures with the necessary knowledge of parliamentary rules, practices and code of conduct. As a first step précis containing necessary inputs on parliamentary etiquette, code of conduct, the material concerning rules that were commonly invoked during debates in the house should be compiled and circulated by the Speaker's office. This may be followed by periodical interactions of the members with veteran parliamentarians of repute whether sitting or former members of the legislatures. Such exposure would enable the members to perform in the house with greater confidence, help raise the quality of debate and contribute more meaningfully and effectively towards issues of public concern and proposed legislations.

Both the ruling combine and the opposition will need to change their perceptions of roles and attitudes in and outside the House. The ruling coalition should respect the views, rights and privileges of the members of the opposition. Their perspectives and concerns should be received with an open mind and accorded due consideration. The opposition, on its part, should be responsible as well as responsive. It should be conceded and demonstrated by both sides that the house was a forum for informed, intelligent and serious debate on matters of public interest. The quality of arguments and not the exercise of lung and muscle powers or sheer weight of numbers should determine the outcome of debates. The opposition will be well-advised to put to gather a Shadow cabinet, which should be provided access to necessary information by the government on issues that come before the assembly. This will enrich the debate content, make the ministers work harder and significantly serve the public interest.

The Cabinet System

The founding fathers of our constitution opted for the parliamentary form of government with the cabinet system at its core. The system worked according to the cardinal principles of Collective responsibility, Intra-cabinet responsibility or cabinet solidarity and Political accountability. These principles and the universally acknowledged practices of cabinet system suffered in J&K severe violence during last two decades or so. As the gap between the stature of the chief minister and his cabinet colleagues widened, these principles began to be observed more and more in breach. The powers of cabinet got concentrated in the Chief Minister. More often than not, he preferred to act on the advice of a coterie of favourite bureaucrats rather than consult with his cabinet colleagues. Even policy decisions were at times announced by the Chief on his own. Whenever the Chief Minister pre-empted the cabinet decisions, the worthy ministers simply thumb-printed on the dotted line. In defence, it was argued that the ministers who retained their positions in the government only so long as they enjoyed the confidence of the Chief hardly had any choice but to toe the line. The senior ministers, however were compensated with freedom to run their department more or less as their fiefdoms. The Chief Minister seldom asked for their advice. The ministers thought it prudent not to offer any on their own. No wonder system paralysis and administrative chaos overtook the organs of governance.

The debilitating distortions that plagued the system had to be corrected without any waste of time. As it is, partners in the multi-party coalition were bound to insist on functioning according to the classical form of cabinet system of governance. Chief minister, Mufti Mohd Syed was on record that all interests would be involved in decision making. Now, it was up to the coalition partners to ensure revival of the system and make it tick. As a first step, the Rules of Business need to be reviewed and revised. The Business Rules that emerged after the review and revision in late sixties could perhaps serve as the basis. This exercise restored the cabinet to its original stature as the supreme policy making body and apex executive. It was universally recognised that the authority and responsibility had to go together. The cabinet ministers doing an onerous and demanding job and accountable to the people had to be empowered as per the tenants of the Cabinet system. And a system was as good as the men and women who worked it.

The Services

Of the many assets the British bequeathed to India at the time of independence, perhaps the most valuable were the Civil Services notably Indian Civil Service and Indian Police. These consisted of "a small aristocracy of highly educated, carefully selected by difficult competitive examination, remarkably adaptable; honest entirely free from corruption, extremely devoted to duty and perhaps more important of all, Pan Indian rather than regional or provincial in loyalties." The 'steel frame' was designed to be a link between successive ministries and the repository of principles and practices which endure while governments came and went. The expectations from the All India Services were aptly summed up by H.N. Kunzru, one of the most eminent parliamentarians that India has produced. While speaking in the Constituent Assembly he said that it was important "to secure for the state, efficient public servants, who will serve all the people equally well and will always watch over the interests of the communities and state as a whole."

The All India Services in the country, especially in our state hardly bear any resemblance to the model. Though extended to Jammu and Kashmir in 1958, these actually became a regular feature from 1965, when the first batch of direct recruits was allotted to the state. The 'outside talent' was of course tapped even during Maharajah's regime when integrity and efficiency were the norms. This practice continued even after the popular government took over. The real problem arose when direct recruits attained senior positions and some of them found it profitable to jostle for positions of proximity to and favours from the political masters. The emergence of the 'Syndicate' and 'Indicate' in the state bureaucracy post-Indira-Abdullah Accord and the mess they made of the administration was by now a part of the history.

The monopoly of power in one party reduced the state into a virtual monarchy minus its good features. In the ensuing environment those driven by raw self-interest and endowed with less stout moral fibre made hay. Oath to the constitution and ethics of service became irrelevant. Competent, self-respecting and officers of integrity were sidelined or 'shunted off' to Delhi on deputation. The proximity to rulers, the ability to please and eagerness to bend rules to comply with the wishes of lords and masters opened up doors to power and privilege. The situation seemed to merit the harsh judgment by U.B. Kulkarni who wrote, "India is thus burdened with a vast and financially ruinous army of government officials, most of whom ought to have pursued some other vocations instead of creating an illusion that they are capable of assisting their political masters in an era of socialism."

To be able to make good its commitments to the electorate the Coalition government would need civil servants of integrity, competence and courage who tender advice strictly according to law, rules and regulation freely and fearlessly without fudging the facts. Minions though good for ego trips were no substitute for officers of personal and intellectual integrity and invariably end up as a liability. Fortunately, there was no dearth of good officers in the state cadres. The government had only to look around for those who fit the classical profile. Once the overall administrative environment changes and services come into their own, the service of people will bounce back at the cantre of their concerns. This could well be the beginning of a new era of hope, justice, good governance and peace in Jammu and Kashmir.

(3) A coalition "Made in Delhi"

The Jammu and Kashmir Legislative Assembly election 2002 universally perceived as "free and fair" returned a stunning and fractured verdict. The fractures were multiple and messy altering beyond recognition destinies of parties and political leaders. Political equations and personnel profiles were badly bruised. It also marked the emergence of the fledging Peoples' Democratic Party, a brain child of Mufti Mohd Syed, a veteran of the Congress lineage. Mufti appeared to have finally carved out a political niche for himself in Kashmir valley with the aid of his firebrand daughter, Mehbooba Mufti and a select band of loyal workers who followed him wherever he went. The PDP surprised everyone- friends as well foes alike by grabbing sixteen seats in the Jammu and Kashmir legislature at the very first showing on strength of mere 09.04 percentage of votes cast in the election. The vote share of the party in the Kashmir valley, however was impressive 24.55 per cent. How and why did such large number of voters show favour for a just launched little party with a foreign sounding name and hardly enough time to even introduce itself properly to the electorate? This question had been baffling many political commentators and analysts. This miracle was brought about by Mufti Mohd Syed through the master stroke of picking up the election symbol. Of 'Pen and Inkpot' for his party. This was the election symbol of the erstwhile Muslim United Front in the crucial and "land mark' 1987 elections. Highly publicised and well-recognised all over Kashmir, the symbol also had a particular sentiment attached to it. It was widely believed that a fairly large number of voters pressed the button under this symbol believing they were voting for the new incarnation of the MUF. This was not to deny the fact that the PDP leadership especially its president, Mehbooba Mufti had made significant inroads into the rural areas and earned recognition through her aggressive campaigning against the security forces for alleged "repression and human rights violations." There was hardly a home of a felled 'militant' that she did not visit to show her sympathy and concern for the bereaved family. Mufti Mohd Syed's 'Healing touch' policy was making waves. The political thrust of the PDP was to occupy opposition space which had become the monopoly of the secessionist political fringe. After a long time someone known to be close to powers that be in Delhi was speaking a language that sounded good to a variety of people for equally diverse reasons. Something unprecedented was happening which incited both curiosity and hope.

The Jammu and Kashmir National Conference, the grand old party founded by Sher-I-Kashmir Sheikh Mohd Abdullah and led by him till his sad demise suffered its worst ever electoral reverse at the hustling. For the first time in its electoral history, the National Conference lost control of the legislative assembly. Moreover this assembly would have no member of the first family of Kashmir. Dr Farooq Abdullah did not contest the elections. Both Umar Abdullah, the party president and his uncle Mustapha Kamal were defeated. Its vote share fell from 65.5 per cent in 1996 elections to 28.3 per cent in 2002, and the tally of seats in the legislative assembly dropped from 57 in 1996 to 28. Notwithstanding all these setbacks, the National Conference still emerged as the largest party in the legislature with 28 members representing all the three regions of the state, Ladakh,

Kashmir and Jammu. Even in Kashmir region it maintained its lead by securing 35.52 per cent votes against 24.55 per cent gained by its new challenger, PDP which was said to enjoy quite backing of various elements not directly participating in the electoral process.

The National Conference leadership wisely opted out of the government formation and decided to sit in the opposition even though as the largest party in the legislature, it had the right to take the first crack in government formation. The leadership, particularly the younger element led by the Party President Omar Abdullah strongly felt that the debacle had occurred not because of shrinking of public support but resulted from the weakness in the party machine which over the decades had degenerated into an adjunct of the government. The manner and seriousness with which National Conference played the role of a responsible opposition both inside and outside the legislature earned praise from independent observers and the people. The quite commitment with which young Abdullah went about cultivating cadres, restructuring and revamping the party set up and boost the morale of the grass root level workers infused a new life in the oldest political outfit of Jammu and Kashmir. But the strategic endeavour to revamp and fine tune the party machine was in the realm of future. The process of government formation was the most pressing imperative of the post-election era.

The Bharatiya Janta Party was the other important loser. Its representation in the assembly violently dipped from eight in 1996 to one in 2002 even though the voter support by an large remained stable-12.13 per cent in 1996 to12.15 per cent in 2002.

A somewhat surprising but strong performance was that of the Panthers party which not only won four seats and clocked 07.02 per cent votes but managed to create a strong and solid support base in a block of four adjoining constituencies of Samba, Ramnagar, Udhampur and Chenaini in Jammu region.

The prospects of the Indian National Congress were rated somewhat bleak as the workout for the hustling 2002 got underway. The party, however got a big shot in its arms when the Congress high command assigned the Union Parliamentary Affairs Minister, Ghulam Nabi Azad to Jammu and Kashmir as President of Pradesh Congress Committee. Azad wasted no time in devising a workable poll strategy primarily aimed at addressing the sense of alienation in the minds of the people of Jammu, party's main constituency. It recognised the strong feelings of discrimination particularly in fields of development, representation in the legislature and share in political power. Pursuant to this, demands for a Jammu Chief Minister, appointment of the delimitation commission, implementation of the wazir commission recommendations on creation of new districts, (three in Jammu and one in Kashmir), constitution of a Finance commission and setting up separate Development Boards were concretised and forcefully and loudly projected during electioneering. This strategy clicked. Party workers were soon galvanising into action with renewed vigour their morale soared and dissentions, a perennial Congress curse brought reasonably under control. Consequently, Congress performed well in the elections 2002 winning 20 seats against seven of 1996. Its vote share increased from 20 per cent 1996 to 21.38 in 2002.

As far as smaller parties were concerned the CPM won two seats against one seat it 1996, BSP dropped three seats and its representation was restricted to only one in 2002, JK Awami League retained one seat, Congress (T) neither existed nor contested the 2002 elections and a new outfit called Democratic Movement (DM) won one seat. The independents did very well in 2002, securing 13 seats against only two held by them in 1996.

The Congress high command in its attempt to forge a workable coalition was confronted with a herculean task. The post-election scenario of 2002 was studded with the baffling line up of independents and parties, each conscious of its importance and determined to exact their pound of flesh in a hard bargain. Apart from the need to provide a viable government in the state, the central leadership of the UPA was keen to quickly cash the international approbation through recognition of the 2002 election as credible. Many watchers of the Kashmir political scene were convinced that the concerns for international approval was the overriding consideration that drove the frantic ministry making exercise. Mufti Mohd Syed, the PDP supremo was fully aware of this soft spot in Congress game plan. He bargained hard and that too from a position of strength. So the scene of Ministry making that had shifted to New Delhi saw UPA chairperson Sonia Gandhi and Prime Minister exerting all their influence and skills to put together a workable coalition Thus, began series of mid-night goings and comings, demands and barging chips rolled across the political green table and intermediaries found themselves overworked. Amongst the serious and tense parlays at one point of time, Bhim Singh, the leader of the four member Panthers party neither a member of legislative assembly nor Council threw in his hat for the chief ministership introducing an element of comedy thereby relieving some of the tension.

Finally, Sonia-Man Mohan Singh efforts and influence yielded a coalition arrangement which had some unique features. The chief ministership was to be held on rotational basis, the Congress party and the PDP taking turns for three years each. Even though PDP was the minority partner, Mufti Mod Syed got the first shot at the top slot. In addition the central leadership succeeded in bringing on board diverse political elements Panthers party, CPM, Awami League, and independents, many of whom had formed Fronts during the parleys obviously for a better bargaining position. A Common Minimum Programme was drawn up which "accommodated" acceptable elements of the election manifestoes of the coalition partners. An 11-member Coalition Coordination Committee was constituted under the chairmanship of Congress leader Ghulam Nabi Azad. This committee was designed to oversee the functioning of the coalition and sort out any issues that may crop up.

The CMP appeared to be an impressive accommodative document. It attempted to provide space for all the constituents of the coalition but essentially addressed PDP concerns highlighted by Mufti Mohd Syed. Prominent features of the PDP agenda, the "Healing touch policy", unconditional wide ranging dialogue mainly targeting the secessionist fringe, promoting return of the militants belonging to the state to "their families", review of the cases of detainees held for long periods without trial, review the operation of special laws (relating to militancy) Rehabilitation of the families of deceased militants and revocation of POTA were included in the CMP. The Jammu-based parties notably Ghulam Nabi Azad led Congress and Bhim Singhs' Panthers party succeeded in including setting up of the Finance Commission, due consideration for the recommendations of the Wazir Commission, setting up a Delimitation Commission, and inclusion of Dogri in the eighth schedule of the constitution in the CMP. Significantly, not to speak of a commitment there was not even a mention of Good, Transparent, Responsible and Responsible governance as the goal of the Congress-PDP government though some related elements like equitable devolvement and resource distribution between the three regions of the state, curbs on corruption and provision of the basic minimum needs etc did find mention. The usual promises and regular homilies like greater employment opportunities, empowerment of Panchyats, and acceleration of development works were all there. The CMP did not forget the "aspirations" of Ladakhis, Gujjars and "Paharis." Yes, the CMP sounded like panacea for all the terrorism-related problems that "impacted the society", human rights, relief and rehabilitation of the victims of terrorism "encourage" and return of those young men from the state who have resorted to militancy to return to their families and the main stream." Of course, it spoke of some important Jammu sensitive political issues as enumerated above. To discerning eyes it looked too good to be true.

The divergent political goals of the major partners, their conflicting party and constituency stakes and above all long-term competitive political interests hugely mitigated against any serious and focussed implementation of more important commitments made in the CMP. There could be no doubt that the worthy men and women at the top of the national political pyramid who drafted and approved the CMP were aware of the problems and difficulties, which in some cases were transparently insurmountable. These difficulties notwithstanding, the rising political stakes and mounting international pressure impelled them to go for the early installing of a duly elected government in Jammu and Kashmir so as to justify the international acclaim for holding free and fair election in the troubled state of Jammu and Kashmir. The hard work that went into the putting together of the PDP-Congress coalition paid off. The US endorsement was quick to come. K. Alan Kronstadt Analyst in Asian Affairs Defense, and Trade Division of the US Congress wrote.

"The United States welcomed the successful October conclusion of 2002 elections in the Indian state of Jammu and Kashmir, where nearly half of the electorate cast ballots." The elections resulted in the ousting of the long-dominant National Conference party and its in the national coalition-the Bharatiya Janata Party, thus bolstering the credibility of the process and dampening criticism that the elections were flawed or "farcical."

The opposition Indian National Congress and the regional people's Democratic Party (PDP) won a combined 36 seats in the state assembly, and Congress leader Sonia Gandhi agreed to a first-ever power-sharing coalition. PDP leader Mufti Mohammed Sayeed has assumed the office of Chief Minister vowing to bring a "healing touch" to state politics. His "common minimum programme" includes controversial policies including the freeing of jailed political prisoners that have been lauded by some and criticised by others. The new government's seeming moderate image has brought renewed hopes for peace in the troubled region."

(4) 222 Days of Mufti Government

The Congress-PDP coalition rose to power on the crest of waves of high hopes and great expectations. A disillusioned and traumatised citizenry was waiting for someone to promise even the slightest hope of light beyond the dark tunnel in which they were trapped for about a decade and a half. The PDP in Kashmir and the Congress in Jammu promised exactly this as Elections 2002 came by. The voters eagerly grasped the opportunity and voted these parties to power. It was an act of faith on their part and measure of their confidence in the electoral promises held out by the leaders, Ghulam Nabi Azad and Mufti Mohd Sayed. And let there be no doubt that the people were going to hold these leaders to account. Most analysts agreed that it would only be right and fair to allow a spell of at least six months in power to the Congress- PDP coalition before drawing a balance sheet of their performance. This period has since elapsed.

It may be said to the credit of the Congress-PDP coalition that a somewhat bumpy ride and occasional hiccups notwithstanding, it has succeeded in maintaining the climate of hope and expectations amongst the people. It fact, its installation and policy pronouncements had the effect of enhancing people's yearning for peace and development. The unexpected strong peoples' participation in the Republic Day celebrations in the valley including Srinagar and Kargil bears testimony to the changed popular mood. Mufti also succeeded in bringing the pressing problems of the state to the centre stage and compel attention of the Government of India. Through sheer persistence he secured higher financial allocation extended and enhanced project specific financial support and promises of more such aid in days to come.

The Prime Minister chose to mount yet another peace initiative and extended the hand of friendship towards Pakistan from the soil of the troubled state in a well attended public really in its capital. This single event attracted worldwide attention. The conclave of the chief ministers of the fifteen Congress ruled states presided over by Sonia Gandhi, Srinagar lent the national focus. A well attended public meeting in the northern town of Baramulla addressed by leader of the opposition in the Lok Sabha, Sonia Gandhi sent a powerful message that the situation in Kashmir was on way to normalcy. Chief minister Mufti Mohd Sayed went around almost all major centres in the country inviting tourists to Kashmir. The cumulative result of these exertions can be seen in the spurt of tourist traffic in the valley. Those returning from Kashmir testified to a 'sea change' not only in the security environment but also in the common Kashmiri's behaviour who today feels free to extend his usual warmth and hospitality to visitors from the other parts of the country. The impressive

Khir Bhawani Mela in which about fifty thousand devotees were reported to have participated added yet another feather to the cap of the coalition government. For obvious reasons, the Congress-PDP coalition deservedly got the credit for the dramatic turnaround in the situation. And with credit came the enhanced responsibility to preserve peace and order and ensure that no one was allowed to disturb or reverse the process.

The State apparatus had, however been largely resistant to the change. Many ministers, senior as well as juniors were believed to be unable or unwilling to shun the inherited 'despotic mindset'. The fascination of playing pals with obliging bureaucrats, it was said made them blind to the woes of the common man. The army of officials and party functionaries that accompanied them on frequent tours and the mode and sources of entertainment were, it was said no different from their ousted predecessors. The benefits of change in government for the common man were few and far between. There were also disturbing reports of fresh bureaucratic groupings dispensing favours and indulging in nepotism. Given the history of Service Pressure Groups right from the early eighties when the 'syndicate' and 'Indicate' played havoc with the administration. The development was certainly not auspicious for the Mufti government. The Chief Minister and the Chief Secretary would be well advised to watch out and quickly and firmly stem the rot.

Of course, there were bright patches in the large administrative canvass. Among the Ministers young Harsh Dev Singh, the Education, Minister had distinguished himself by directly and effectively addressing the basic policy parameters, infrastructural shortcomings and quality deficiencies in our educational system. The measures devised should begin to show positive results soon. To Health Minister, Lal Singh went the credit of inculcating the much needed sense of discipline in the Health Care System. Even the rural areas were reported to be witnessing solid improvement in care and comfort of the patients. The hospital premises across the state were reported to be less untidy and the hospital linen refreshingly clean. The hospital staff wore uniforms and name plates. They were also more attentive and responsive. The common man expected him to carry forward the campaign with renewed vigour. It was, however generally felt that the Minister should take note of the 'resentment' against his alleged use of 'harsh language' with medical staff especially the senior functionaries and that too in public. One could surely be firm without being rough. Urban Development Minister Mir deserved the credit for the removal of unauthorised constructions on the highways, streets and public land. These ugly structural intrusions were causing hardship to the common man, marring the aesthetics of the landscape and environmental pollution. The Beatification drive could hardly be painless. There was bound to be resistance from the vested interests and the short sighted. Regrettably, the operations in Jammu after the initial thrust became halting and somewhat sporadic. The outcome, in Jammu-therefore did not match the extent and standard achieved in Srinagar.

Mufti's healing touch policy primarily focused on providing succour to the victims of terrorism and release of militants and other detainees held in prisons for long without trial. The initiative taken by him to personally deliver the relief amount and letters of appointment to one member of the family of each victim on the spot earned popular approbation. This people friendly gesture was in clear contrast to the callous attitude of the political executive and bureaucratic overlords and lent visible content and credibility to promises made during electioneering. It should, however not be forgotten that though welcome and praiseworthy as a short term measure, this mode could not be a substitute for the system rejuvenation. Sooner than later, the task had to be performed by the Deputy Commissioners of the concerned districts for which the government should prescribe a time frame and set up a credible monitoring system. Experience showed that most of the delay occurred in the prescribed documentation. The claimants already under shock and acute mental distress were further exposed to the humiliation and torture of running from pillar to post. The delaying tactics on the part of the government functionaries made victims' families vulnerable to corrupt practices. The state government should itself assume the responsibility of completing the documentation formalities. For this purpose, the concerned officials in each Tehsil/Block should be pre-designated. The victims' heirs should only be required to sign the Performa to be produced by the official at his or her residence. The relief should be available to the deserving family member within a month from the date of the tragedy. A committee comprising of the Dy. Commissioner of the district, a member of the Rehabilitation Council and the local MLA should review the progress once every quarter. In the event of sizeable backlog, special teams drawn from various departments should be constituted to clear it in go. The continuation of the present practice of the Chief Minister distributing the letters of appointments etc. personally could soon become subject to the law of diminishing returns.

The Common Minimum Programme made it incumbent upon the PDP-Congress coalition to review the cases of certain category of *detainees* being held without trial for long periods. This particular PDP electioneering plank had attracted criticism from the opponents right from day one. The party was accused of being 'soft' towards the militants. It was, therefore, only to be expected that the protests will grow shriller as the policy reached the stage of implementation. It had to be conceded that the opposition to the policy of releasing 'militants' also came from some non-party sources and concerned citizens.

In a narrow sense, the PDP really had no problem with such allegations politically. It did not hurt its political interests in its constituency which was practically confined to Kashmir valley. The BJP was using the alleged, pro-militant stick to beat the Congress in rest of the country especially in Gujarat where the electoral stakes were very high. The Congress party should therefore have responded with convincing and forceful counter-offensive for which ample material existed. The state leadership of the party was perhaps too busy in celebrating the miracle of its return to power but what about the party 'brain trusts' at Delhi? This lapse was said to have cost the party very heavily in Gujarat. Knowledgeable sources estimate that the "release of militants in J&K, the terrorist attack on the Raghunath Temple in Jammu coupled with the similar assault on Akhshar Dham in Ahmedabad" cost the Congress, party 15 to 20 seats in Gujarat Assembly.

The institute of Public Opinion organised a Seminar at Jammu only couple of days after the formation of the coalition government, and well before the releases were ordered Speaking on the subject, I suggested a course of action and certain measures that would not only address the genuine concerns but also deny vested interests the opportunity and rationale for exploitation of the coalition decision to release certain categories of militants detained without trial for long. "Such releases" I had suggested "must be decided with care and caution according to a fair, equitable and transparent criteria without compromising the security of State." A multi-disciplined Screening committee was recommended to be constituted for an objective and through examination of each case taking also into account the behavioural pattern during the period of detention and conduct of the individual during the period of detention. Special focus was suggested upon the detainees proximity to the hardened and notorious terrorists confined in the same prison and the likelihood of catching the 'Jehadi' infection. In such cases the length of the period of detention should not be the determining factors for release. I had further suggested that Village/Ward Committees should be required to-stand guarantee for the "good conduct" of the first offenders after release. Detailed and clear cut guidelines were urged to be issued for regulating the functioning of the Screening Committees so that the entire process be transparent and criteria bound.

The release of political détentes was a matter of political judgment. The political leaders had been in and out of jails in the Governors' rule as well as under the elected governments. The CMP promised "to encourage those young men from the state who have resorted to militancy" and simultaneously declared that the state government will fully co-operate with Government of India in combating cross-border militancy originating from Pakistan. The question of release of foreign militant therefore did not arise. Those under detention were suggested to be placed in three broad categories:

1. Those picked up on suspicion, on flimsy grounds or having given shelter to the terrorists on solitary occasion.
2. Those who harboured militants, joined the militant ranks' out of sympathy for the 'cause' or wielded gun for power and kicks. They would fall in 'grey area' requiring lot of care and caution on the part of Screening Committee. Only those found to be actually repentant or mellowed enough to be trusted may be considered for release. Obviously such individuals would need post-release psychological treatment and surveillance.
3. The fanatics, committed, and hardened variety should continue to be detained till they earn the reprieve. The period of incarceration and the offences for which they were held should not be a consideration in their cases.

The cases falling in category (1) were proposed to be reviewed first and so on the review, it was suggested should become an annual feature so that more and more people were motivated to earn release for good behaviour and genuine change of heart. These suggestions were apparently ignored. The State government began the process from the wrong end. Instead of taking up cases of least involved and most deserving whose release would have been generally welcomed and generate goodwill for the government and cause no serious concern in about the country, the state government opted for release of prominent leaders thus providing ammunition to the political opponents. To compound this blunder, the government made the disastrous slip of describing one of the 'militants' by his assumed name as 'General Musa.' The media lapped it up. The reaction of a voter in a distant constituency of Gujarat who learnt from the media the release of a terrorist 'General' by the coalition government in which Congress was the major partner was predictable. On the other hand, if the real name of the detainee, Ghulan Hassan Wagey or whatever had been given out and clearly stated that the individual was neither a 'General' nor the 'Musa', the impact would have been completely different. Reference to his current status of irrelevance in the terrorist network would have conclusively clinched the issue. Non-application of mind to details could and did many a times prove very costly.

On the home turf, the release of the first batch of detainees caused disappointment and anger amongst the parents and relations of the first and casual offenders. The parents and relatives who were eagerly awaiting the return home of their dear ones on the Eid day were understandably disappointed and hurt. The effect of-Mufti's "healing touch" in this crucial area thus ran aground. Since the first wrong turn, the process of releases lost both momentum and focus. In addition the state government had to pocket 'the humiliation' of being 'forced' to accept a Union government nominee on the Screening Committee, who was said to have his own brief. The embarrassment would have been averted and process moved forward without any serious hitch if the advice had been heeded.

The seriousness and urgency with which the coalition government initially addressed the complex and critical problem of electric power procurement and distribution earned instant popular-gratitude. Even though many amongst the elite and intellectuals nursed a sneaking hope that the bonanza would somehow prolong, the common man was convinced that the good time would last only till about the end of the month of Ramzan. He was right. After all "Public, Hai Yeh Saab Janti Hai." The frequent and unending electric supply cuts, some scheduled others unscheduled had since become routine. Lives of the Jammu city dwellers were rendered miserable. The situation sometime was worst than before. As it is, Jammu power supply remained subject to fair weather. A little breeze and the power supply was shut down. The electric lines were loose and swing at the fist whiff of breeze causing 'short circuit'. The good old 'separators' had been dispensed with but no substitutes provided. The trees along the electric supply lines were not pruned causing avoidable hassle. Vast majority of Transformers had no proper switch boards attached. 'Naked wires' hanging loose were 'fused' to provide the connection. The immediate area around the Transformer, was virtually a death trap. No wonder many Transformers 'exploded' almost as a routine. All these and many other problems were easily curable. Whenever contact was established with the PDD authorities, they conceded the problems but expressed helplessness due to non-availability of funds. However, Finance Minister Beig had literally thrown a bomb shell by announcing in the state assembly that out of the amount provided to the Jammu PDD, an amount of Rs 3.20 crores was surrendered. This was clearly scandalous. The young and energetic Power Minister must identify the culprits and take them to task.

While the complex and multi-dimensional problem of regular power supply was no doubt daunting there were clearly identifiable areas susceptible to quick remedies. It should also be remembered that sizeable number of employees in the PDD were good, efficient and honest. Most others would in any case fall in line if malpractices were considered taboo in the department and merit and integrity recognised and rewarded. This would isolate the minority of incorrigibles who could be tackled – with a firm and heavy hand. Painting the entire department black was neither helpful nor desirable. In fact, it was bound to prove counterproductive.

The above analysis merely covered a part of the political and administrative scene in the state—post-installation of the coalition government. Naturally it could be only illustrative and not exhaustive. Looking ahead, the Mufti government needed to build upon the popular good will and the persisting environment of hope and expectancy. This uphill task could be accomplished only through a radical change in the mindsets of both the political executive and the bureaucracy. This change had regrettably not come about in the desired degree and to necessary extent so far.

The administrative machine generally continued to be slow, tardy and irresponsive. Delays that breed malpractices are still the order of the day in government offices and the secretariat. Good governance could become a reality only through transparency, accountability and time bound programming. The citizen satisfaction, access to the government functionaries at all levels was a matter of right while freedom from harassment, extortion and humiliation constituted the acid tests for the Congress-PDP government in days to come. The PDP-Congress government will have to come up to their expectations if it aimed to preserve its popular acceptability. *(June 19, 2003).*

(5) Good Governance; How Many More Miles to Go?

Chief Minister Mufti Mohd Sayed claimed the other day that the verdict in the state assembly election-2002 was for good governance. No one quarrelled with this assertion. It was obvious that if the people were satisfied with the performance of the predecessor administration, they would not have voted the National Conference out. Moreover good governance and peace, the other dominant issue in the elections were inseparable.

Welfare of the people constituted the very soul of Good governance. It was neither an act of compassion not benevolence on the part of rulers of the day who were empowered to govern for a given period under a democratic dispensation. But then good governance could perhaps more easily and more effectively be provided by despotic and authoritarian regimes. Attributes of transparency, accountability and responsiveness integral to a democracy distinguished it from other forms of government their efficient and effective performance clout notwithstanding.

The performance of the coalition had so far been a mixed bag. Peace prevailed in the tourist corridor in the valley during the season providing great impetus to be tourist influx. Tourist season over, the terrorists were back in action with a bang. The significance of the renewed terror lay not only in its reach, but also in the selection and quality of targets. The assassination of Kuka Parrey, the man who piloted the turn round in the terrorist situation in the dark days of nineteen nineties and sent most of Hizab men scurrying into the Pahelgam forests on his own home ground represented the high mark in return of the terror. It would be a grave mistake to treat the current spate of terror as sporadic incidents. The sweet refreshing appetising inputs of peace and the economic benefits that flowed there from made the common man in Kashmir rediscover his vested interst in peace and accelerated economic activity. He would do everything possible to promote and sustain the climate the peace. That explained the sharp and angry reaction to the resumption of terrorist strikes particularly in the city of Srinagar. Now it was up to the parties in power and the government in Srinagar and Delhi to build on this positive sentiment.

The Amarnath Yatra passed off without any incident. The terrorists, however succeeded in mounting an attack on the yatra en route the Holy cave of Shri Mata Vaishno Devi. It was another matter that faith decisively prevailed over the terror and the yatra goes on leaving it to the government to plug loopholes in the security set up from Katra to the holy Shrine. The prospects of harvests looked good. The coalition government had announced number of people friendly measures. The latest being the extension to the population located on the international border all the benefits so far restricted to those residing on the Line of Control (LOC). The people were sceptical because the coalition government was perceived as long on declarations but short on implementation. For instance, one of the earliest and most widely welcomed decision to remit the old age /window pensions through money orders was yet to be fully implemented.

Even the increase in the rate of pensions sanctioned for this category was not well publicised. Large number of beneficiaries were unaware of the exact extent of benefits accruing there from opening up avenues of malpractices. There was, therefore an urgent need to set up a permanent monitoring mechanism so as to ensure speedy and complete implementation of all decisions especially those concerning people's welfare.

The common man continued to be exploited by the administrative minions. Hardly anything moved in the government offices without greasing some one's palm. Rates for various 'services' ranging from addition of a family members' name in the ration card, issuance or renewal of a Ration card, grant or permanent Citizen Certificate for the offsprings of a permanent resident, obtaining of variety of forms and certificates routinely prescribed by the government required to be attested by Gazetted officers were 'standardised'. Cuts were levied in respect of financial transactions with an element of subsidy. The Revenue department, however, took the cake. An amount of Rupees five thousand per Marla was reportedly being extorted just for certifying that the ownership, location of a piece of land and its survey number. Records required for sales deeds of land, fetched much higher bribes depending on the value of the land in question. The list was endless. And shameful as it might sound, the society was reconciled to these malpractices. The people were convinced that the administration was a massive corruption racket integral to the democratic system. Many find it much more convenient and economical to pay and have the job done rather than be subjected to numerous 'Hazris' and humiliating waits. Bureaucrats and politicians were believed to be hypocritical in their so called fight against corruption. A villager asked "Have you ever heard of a Minister or an officer asking people not to pay bribes to the Patwaris?" "Has any Chief Minister or

Minister warned the Revenue officials against rampant corrupt practices in the department in numerous Revenue officials conventions they so proudly addressed with huge garlands purchased (with money extorted from the citizen) around their fat necks and rose petals sticking all over their attire?" "Don't the Ministers and senior officers know that most of 'Revenue officials' had engaged private personal assistants to attend to their official business while they serviced seniors on shining Taxis engaged on permanent basis, "No, Nan", then why do you want us to hit our heads against a solid stone wall and waste time in seeking cure for an incurable disease? he demanded. Will someone from the government respond?

If the coalition government was proving a disappointment, their declared good intentions and many positive exertions notwithstanding, the fault primarily lay in the failure to ensure matching change in the mind-sets of the ministers and the bureaucrats. The system was just not working. Many ministers preferred to ignore, "useless shackles of cumbersome rules and regulations." Moreover, public felt the ministers were merely pontificating not performing. They mostly ran around in circles like the proverbial 'KOHLU KA BAAIL' dragging the field officers along leaving little, if any time for them to attend to their public duties. The officers were not only expected to remain in tow on tours but also be in attendance at the residence. On number of occasions many senior officers were undeservedly humiliated by the senior ministers for their sin of HAZRI at the residence of the junior minister when he should have been in attendance in their Durbar and vice versa. As if by some kind of telepathy, both required his presence at the same time. This problem was particularly prevalent in ministries where the junior and senior ministers belonged to different parties. A story making the rounds described embarrassment of a ahead of the Department accompanying the senior minister on tour in one of the district of Jammu when he received Fax summons from the junior minister demanding his presence at Srinagar the very next morning.

Hordes of petitioners can be seen in the secretariat and the residences of ministers awaiting their turn for audience. The position during the tours of ministers was even worst. The petitioners chased the Ministers' car clutching applications tightly hoping to catch the eye of the dignitary to hand over their bundle of woes drafted by someone else for a price. Even those lucky to make contact were in for disappointment as their petitions more often than not went untraced.

The redress of public grievances and responsiveness to citizens concerns constituted the foremost responsibilities of the democratically elected government. Arrogance of power in dealing with public had no place in our system of governance. The politicians in power enjoyed delegated authority and were required to seek popular mandate after the expiry of the prescribed period. Despite this reality, power turned the heads of many ministers, whose attire, mannerism, gait and even hair style underwent sudden but drastic changes. Either they did not bother to go though their mails or did not consider it necessary even to acknowledge the receipt not to speak of sending a reply. This malady afflicted even the Chief Minister's office.

In 1996-97, great emphasis was laid upon effective, transparent and responsive governance at the national level. As in the rest of the country, a national level seminar was held in Jammu in pursuance to the deliberations a Committee for "Framing an action plan for Effective and Responsive Administration" was constitutes in April 1997. I was also on the committee. The recommendations of the committee were accepted by the government but not implemented.

On the subject for redress of public grievances, the committee drew attention to Government Order No. 256-GAD of 1993 dated 18-03-1993 that laid down that public grievances would be heard by the Deputy Commissioners on every Wednesday and in case Wednesday be a holiday, the public hearing be held on the next working day. "Wednesday should be observed as a public grievances day by ministers, administrative secretaries and heads of departments as also by officers at all levels and there should be no touring on this day as otherwise the schedule drawn up by the lower level functionaries can get adversely affected. Ministers may like to hear the grievances of the public at their residence, so that large number of people are not required to come to the secretariat on such day" recommended the committee. It further suggested that:

The receptionists, security personnel and peons should be given suitable instructions about the meetings so as to allow the members of the public to meet officers without appointment. This should be enforced also in attached officers (e.g. J&K Academy of Art Culture and Languages, Red Cross Society etc) and public agencies under the supervision of the government.

A locked Complaint Box should be placed at the Reception and opened every day followed by expeditious action.

Each grievance petition must be acknowledged within two weeks of receipt along with an indication of the name, designation, and telephone number of the employee who is processing the case.

Wide publicity should be given about the Grievance Redress machinery created in the departments/public sector undertakings/autonomous organisations.

The grievance column of the newspapers should be regularly examined by each department/Agency of Government for picking up cases which relate to it and quick action should be suo moto taken for their redress on a time bound basis 'The action taken' should be publicised.

Booklets/pamphlets may be made available to the citizens at easily accessible contact points containing information regarding procedures, name of authorities concerned waiting lists, for various jobs.

The committee also recommended the establishment of a Multi-tier grievances cell for citizens so that these were addressed "at point where they arise instead of getting thrown up to the highest level as a result of non-performance at the grass root level." A Grievances Redress Department at the state level in the Secretariat directly under the control of the Chief Minister was proposed. Every departmental secretary was to nominate a senior officer of the rank of Additional Secretary as the Department Grievances Redress Officer.

All Heads of the Departments, Divisional heads, district chiefs right down to the Block level were to nominate their immediate subordinates to be the Grievance Redress Officers in their respective offices. The committee made detailed recommendations regarding establishment of their authenticity through preliminary enquires and then earmark and assign them to the concerned officers for full formal enquires and report within a specified time frame. If the grievance was referred by the Minister, Administrative secretary, the HOD, the divisional or District heads, the reports will be furnished to them. The committee did not envisage the creation of any additional staff for the purpose and recommended that special mention be made in the APRs of the good work done by the officers in disposing of grievances and adverse entries made in case of failures. The entire data relating to Grievances Redress was to be computerised and necessary software got prepared for operation at various levels.

Recommendations of the committee included Mass Contact Programme by government functionaries at all levels and ministers along with team of officers. Such tours were to be widely publicised in advance. All applications/grievances received by the minister were to be classified department-wise, entered in a register and then forwarded to the State Government Redress Officer for disposal. The oral representations made to the minister, to be reduced into writing by his PS and forward to the SGRO under the signatures of the minister.

A non-functional system created a vacuum in which the time honoured and delineated spheres of authority and responsibility between the political executive and the permanent civil services got badly blurred. Instances of lack of harmony, eruption of differences and ego hassles were making rounds not only in the corridors of the secretariat but also in the Lal Chowk, Srinagar and Raghunath Bazar, Jammu. Bureaucratic pressure groups had resurfaced at the higher echelons to the detriment of discipline in the services. Regimes and rulers might change but not faces of appendages. These unsavoury darlings of political masters formed coteries and kitchen cabinets, held men in power hostage playing on their preferences/weaknesses who acted as if mesmerised. It was indeed amusing how politicians changed. When out of power they were most vociferous in roundly condemning the 'evil' but eagerly promoted and patronised the same evil when catapulted into power. Even more baffling was their propensity to shut their eyes to the obvious and enormous damage to their own credibility and integrity and that of the government to which they belonged.

The favourite faction bred centres of extra-constitutional authority, indulged in the disastrous game of palace intrigues and promoted favouritism and nepotism. More often than not they also succeeded in thwarting the reform process.

The Mufti government was expected to become wiser after the fate of its predecessor but seemed to have failed to grasp the lessons. The severe public criticism of recent transfers and posting ordered by the government illustrated the point. Moreover, in a small state like J&K hardly anything remained a secret. All connections, relations and combinations were public knowledge.

A good, responsive, transparent and effective governance focused on the day to day problems of the people still appeared to be a somewhat distant dream. It would indeed be a tragedy if the coalition were to adopt an ostrich like policy on these vital issues and finally get devoured by the proverbial cat.

(September, 19, 2003)

(6) The Bus Service Across LoC

The Srinagar-Muzaffarabad Bus Service is on. The first Bus was slated to roll across the LoC on 17th April, 2005. This was announced by Pakistan foreign minister, Khurshid Mahmud Kasuri in a joint statement read out by him to the media in Islamabad on 16th February in presence of his Indian counterpart, Natwar Singh. The agreement came after numerous diplomatic turns and twists lasting a little less than a year and half of Indo-Pak negotiations. These were reinforced by back channel diplomacy and intense pressure from international community as well as the civil societies from both sides of the divide. The success of the venture was billed as the "path-breaking" confidence building measure on the contentious and complex "core" issue of Kashmir that carried a huge potential for acceleration of the ongoing Indo-Pak peace process and opening up vast vistas of cooperation between the two estranged neighbours.

Predictably, there was mixed reaction in India and Pakistan. The Pakistan Peoples' Party Chairperson, Benazir Bhutto welcomed the decision and claimed it was vindication of the Indo-Pak friendship vision of her party "which was now being owned even by those, who had dubbed her and her party as security risks." Qazi Hussain of Jamaat-e-Islami Pakistan, who was also the MMA chief, opposed the bus service and termed the agreement as "a ploy to ignore the Kashmir problem." Pakistan Muslim League (Nawaz Shrief) secretary general, Iqbal Zaffar Jhagra went to the extent of saying that "the service would be stopped after the change of government in Pakistan." Visibly upset about the development the United Jihad Council chief Salah-ud-Din condemned the move. The 'Jaish-e-Muhammad' terrorist outfit threatened to disrupt the bus service, and called it a "conspiracy by India to weaken Jihad." The Jaish spokesman, Mufti Abdul Rauf said "it tantamounts to the betraying the blood of the Mujahiden in Kashmir." The Hizabul Mujahideen termed the bus services as "cosmetic" step and a non-issue. The vast majority of people in Pakistan as well as in POK, however welcomed the move.

Back home, the BJP and the Sangh Parivar were vehement in opposing the starting of the bus service without proper passports and Visas. They apprehended increase in antinational activities and acceleration of ongoing secessionist terrorism in the disturbed state. According to Hurriyat (G) supremo, Ali Shah Geelani, "there was no justification for any bilateral talks unless India declared Kashmir as a disputed issue, get the forces back to barracks and abolish the Disturbed

Area Act." "We are not offering sacrifices for opening the road but for the solution of Kashmir issue as per the UN resolution." He also told the BBC that "its (the Bus Service) projection would sideline Kashmir dispute." Dukhtran-e-Milat chief, Syeda Asiya Andrabi described the reopening of the road as an attempt to send the Kashmir Issue to the cold storage. She alleged that the development had damaged the nature of Kashmir issue. GM Bhat, general secretary of Awami Action Committee led by Mir Waiz Umar Farooq, on the other hand claimed that "any step taken by Pakistan would be in the interests of the Kashmiris and the same has been depicted from time to time."

The mainstream parties in Jammu and Kashmir, the Congress, the National Conference and the Peoples Democratic party, on the other hand hailed it as a giant step towards peace and unity of the divided people of Jammu and Kashmir. Only former PCC chief Mohd Shafi Qureshi struck a discordant note by describing the bus service as a "gimmick." People across the socio-religious spectrum enthusiastically welcomed the thaw in Indo-Pak relations and the opportunity of contacts with their brethren on the other side of the LOC. The real jubilation was, however evident amongst the divided families. Choked with emotions, many were unable even to express themselves. Others danced with joy and burst crackers. They likened the day the bus service commences with Eid. The over whelming approval of the bus link up had isolated the extremist fringe and created panic in the ranks of terrorists.

Historically, the demand for opening "the Rawalpindi road" was as old as the Kashmir issue itself. The opening of the Jehlum Valley road was to begin with projected by the pro-Pak elements in Kashmir as the symbol of union with Pakistan. The establishment rejected the demand. In fact, come independence and accession with India, Shiekh Mohd Abdullah had the pro-Pak leadership shipped over to Pakistan to enjoy the fruits of the 'Mumalkat-i-Khudadad'. However, Dr Farooq Abdullah, who accompanied his father to Pakistan in 1964 when he went there as an emissary of Pandit Nehru, claimed that Sheikh Mohd Abdullah had taken up the issue with Gen. Ayub Khan in his presence. It was not known whether the Sheikh had the approval of Pandit Nehru to explore the possibility or he had made the suggestion on his own. The corroboration of Sheikh Abdullah's views did come in July, 1992 from Syed Mohd Abdullah Bukhari, president of Jammu and Kashmir Muslim Association (POK) who remained General Secretary of the Muslim Conference for seven years. He claimed that during his visit to Kashmir in 1980, Sheikh

Abdullah told him that he had proposed the restoration of traffic on Srinagar Muzaffarabad road "thereby bringing together fractured Kashmiri families living on both sides of the LoC." The proposal was vigorously opposed by Sardar Abdul Qayoom Khan, the Prime Minister of PoK" the Sheikh was reported to have confided in Bukhari. Qayoom felt at that time, as some in Pakistan do even today that the restoration of road link across the LoC would "change the international status of the border thereby adversely influencing the struggle of independence from the Indian yoke."

It was around 1996 that the focus in the demand for bus service across the LOC shifted from the political to humanitarian and the destination from Rawalpindi in Pakistan to Muzaffarabad in Pakistan Occupied Kashmir. This not only changed the context but also the rationale which struck a sympathetic cord in the west as well as the human rights activists the world over. As the Indo-Pak peace process gained momentum, the bus service emerged as the first step towards softening of borders and addressing the problem of divided families living across the LoC. The agreement to restore the service represented the first and the most important CBM on Jammu and Kashmir. Interestingly, even Qayoom Khan, a former POK 'Prime Minister' earlier opposed to the proposal had come around to support the bus link up. He now considered the proposed bus service as a very positive step and a pragmatic breakthrough. "There is no justification for opposing the bus service and my message to the hard-liners is that please do not subject the Kashmiris to further trials and tribulations", he said in Muzaffarabad on 21st February.

Now that the hype over the bus service was yielding space to practical reckoning and the spell of credit grabbing seemed to be coming to an end, the over politicisation of the issue must stop. The mainstream parties and the establishment must concentrate on not only putting their act together but also resolutely to counter the vicious whispering campaign that Muzaffarabad was merely a stopover and the ultimate destination was Rawalpindi. The implications of this canard were obvious. No one should be allowed to distort, sabotage or highjack the vital step towards peace and amity.

In essence, the resumption of Srinagar Muzaffarabad bus link was a small but highly significant step. It was pregnant with tremendous scope for softening the borders, enhancing people to people contacts and if handled sincerely and careful may one day prove the harbinger of peace and cooperation between India and Pakistan. Like in all pregnancies, care and caution were the watch words and avoidance of too much excitement and bumpy rides essential. It would therefore be desirable and sensible to proceed gradually and cautiously in the matter. Initially the focus may be on bringing the divided families together,. permitting people to discharge their social and religious obligations without avoidable hassles. In fact, a time limit for the permit needed to be prescribed and scrupulously adhered to. Those detailed for frisking etc., at the LOC check points should be specially selected, properly trained, thoroughly briefed and closely supervised to ensure that the visitors feel comfortable and welcome.

It had to be recognised that sizeable number of people in the state and the country were apprehensive about the cross LOC bus service. In the prevailing security scenario it was understandable. It was argued that Pakistan government had not altered the policy on Kashmir. President Parvez Musharraf continued to insist that the terrorists in Jammu and Kashmir were conducting the "struggle for independence to which he would continue to render moral and diplomatic support." The terrorist training camps in POK and Pakistan were intact and so were the launching pads on the borders. The presence of terrorists in Jammu and Kashmir was an established fact, only the estimates of numbers varied. Frequent terrorist strikes tellingly demonstrated their capability.

We live in a world that was fast shrinking into a global village. There was no way any country could charter her course ignoring the concerns of the rest of the world. The imperatives of the prevailing world order, the geo-political compulsions and above all our national vested interests demand that we resolutely fight the proxy war in Jammu and Kashmir and remain willing to negotiate with Pakistan, the source and promoter of the proxy war. Strategically, the thrust of negotiations should be directed at the Pakistan civil society which had, begun to assert. Moreover, the civil society alone had the power to persuade the parents not to let their sons be drafted for slaughter for a nonexistent cause as also the clout to dissuade the young men from joining the ranks of terrorists.

Of course, the security concerns cannot be wished away and need to be addressed squarely. Firstly, the apprehension that the bus service would or could in any way facilitate the infiltration of armed terrorists was totally misplaced. In real terms, the movement across the LoC would in no way be different from the one taking place at Wagah or any other authorised point of entry on Indo-Pak border. Secondly, the grant of permit by the designated authority in Muzaffarabad was subject to prior clearance by the designated authority in Srinagar and vice versa. Thirdly, the existing vigilance network on the ground would naturally be strengthened to take care of any odd undesirable person managing to secure entry. In short, the starting of the Srinagar-Muzaffarabad bus service posed no insurmountable security problem. Our security forces and the Jammu and Kashmir police can be relied upon to take the development in their strides. This was fortunately a win-win situation for all parties and a bonanza for the divided families. All must bend their full energies to make the experiment a success. That would facilitate exploration of other positive avenues like duplication of cross-border access at other points similarly situated providing momentum for further movement forward.

(*February 25, 2005*)

(7) Coping with Earth Quake Fall Out

Lot has been said and written about the devastating earthquake that shook the mountains and wrought havoc in vast tracts of the hilly areas of Uri, Tang Dhar in Kashmir and Poonch in Jammu on the black Saturday, the eighth October 2005. The areas across the LoC falling in Pak-occupied Kashmir were the worst effected. By now we have a fair idea of the intensity and extent of devastation, the loss of lives and limbs, damage to and destruction of property and developmental infrastructure. Which were both massive and unprecedented.

The quick and purposeful response marked by exemplary solidarity, boundless compassion and generous aid and assistance by the Indian state and people across the socio-political spectrum was worthy of a free society and a democratic polity. Prime Minister Manmohan Singh, Sonia Gandhi, the ruling UPA chairperson flew in to Kashmir along with hosts of other dignitaries to express sympathy, support and provide succour to the victims of the catastrophe. The Quake was declared a 'national Disaster', large amounts of funds were sanctioned for relief and an assurance publically held out that any amount of money needed for the relief and rehabilitation of the effected people would be forthcoming. Ghulam Nabi Azad, then a union minister camped in Kashmir to co-ordinate and personally supervise the relief and rehabilitation operations. But sadly and somewhat surprisingly, neither the Prime Minister nor the UPA chairperson, found time to visit similarly quake ravaged Poonch triggering public resentment in Jammu against this "discriminatory treatment." The hurt feelings have somewhat been assuaged by Chief Minister Ghulam Nabi Azad's recent visit to Poonch. On this visit he also announced that Poonch will be treated at par with Uri in respect of additional grant of Rs 30,000 for constructing temporary one-room shelters and the cash reward of Rs 5000 to those who complete their abodes on or before 30th of November, 2005. Good. Very good. The question, however arises why Poonch was not included in the scheme in the first instance? Who goofed up? The chief minister will do well to go into this and take suitable action.

The Indian army earned an enormous fund of goodwill and gratitude of the afflicted people by launching relief and rescue operations within minutes of the tragedy. The officers and men got on with the job wiping their tears at the loss of their own comrades, many of whom were buried alive. SMA Qadri (K.T. Nov. 8, 2005) summed up the scenario in following words: "In this precarious hour when everything was going topsy turvy, when the residential houses were crumbling down and the inmates coming under the debris crying for help, when the old ones breathed their last due to horror of the quake, when the children were getting nervous due to sudden sharp pulls of the quake, raising hue and cry and calling their parents in one voice, facing crude death one after the other and when the survivors were beating their chests in anguish only the army came hurriedly, forgetting their own sorrows and death of their colleagues to wipe out the tears of shock striven people. They pulled out victims from the debris and thereby saved the lives of lots of people, took survivors to safer places and dispatched the injured to various hospitals in helicopters and took immediate relief measures for the victims. In this way they played a very commendable role and proved as angels for the very unfortunate people." According to him "They have reached such areas which were quite inaccessible and where the civil administration cannot imagine to reach especially when the roads were cut off and landslides take place the people of these areas speak very highly of this force who have really performed miraculous job for them." This was supplemented by Vajr Division of the army by handing over two 1OKVA micro Hydel Power Projects each with the capacity to light up 50-100 houses to the natives of over 54 villages in the north and south of Shamashbari hills in Kupwara on the Eid Day. Their homes were thus lit for the first time thanks to the army. There was no doubt that the army had made the precious and praiseworthy in puts in relief operations. It is now up to the governments, the political class and the NGO's to built on these assets. Of course, the army will need to carry forward the mission of winning the hearts of the people of the state and be perceived as the peoples' army dedicated to their protectors and security.

The last Eid was special for the residents of the devastated areas in more than one ways. It was a day for praying for the departed souls and thanks giving for survivors. It became even more special for the people of Tang Dhar as Chief Minister Ghulam Nabi Azad arrived to celebrate the Eid with them. The gesture to be with the quake hit fellow citizens away from his own home and family on the auspicious day was highly commendable and widely applauded. This single act of intense sensitivity and compassion qualified to be rated as one of the most significant instance of the 'healing touch' policy.

The difficult task of relief and rehabilitation of the victims of the unprecedented Earthquake was compounded by its unfortunate timing. It hit at a time when the winter pregnant with icy winds, rains and snow was just around the corner. The authorities barely had couple of weeks (precious five weeks having already passed into the limbo of history) to at least provide suitable shelter to the shivering and apprehensive homeless. Their responsibility was greater in respect of Teethwal and Tang Dhar located across the Nastachun Pass. In this task the state government had the full backing of the union government. The prime minister wrote a blank cheque for the relief and rehabilitation of the sufferers. There should also be no doubt about the political will to provide speedy and timely succour. The litmus test, however lay in the capability of the establishment to conceptualise a time bound programme of action to lick the daunting problem, construct dedicated and reliable mechanism for the purpose and identify and employ personnel capable of efficiently achieving the physical targets well in time. In essence, it was now the turn of the policy-makers and their field agencies in J&K to deliver. On their performance hinged the fate of thousands of quake sufferers spread over large chunks of difficult hilly terrain in Baramulla, Kupwara and Poonch districts.

The current speed and direction of R&R measures unfortunately do not inspire much confidence. For instance, Chief Minister Ghulam Nabi Azad on his visit to Poonch .on 12th of November found that 200 engineers detailed for relief duty had failed to report in villages nearly a month after they were ordered to do so. The chief minister threatened them with suspension. Great. But what about chain of superiors placed in supervisory role? Were they not accountable for this scandalous state of affairs? Was this not an instance of system failure? The chief minister will have to come up and come up fast with credible and effective measures to rejuvenate the administration and spur it into some kind of disciplined performance? Here was another howler. Many allegations in relief distribution were reported in the press against a Niab-tehsildar posted in Uri on the job of relief distribution. The man happend to be a local. How come, he came to be posted on this sensitive duty in his own hometown? Did this posting not violate the government rules and standing orders? A Sikh lady from Tang Dhar appeared on a national TV channel and narrated her tale of woes. She ended up by saying "I hope and pray the government will come to our rescue." Why was she ignorant of all that the state was doing or planned to do for sufferers like her? More worrying in the report (Hindu, November13, 2005) that "The worst – hit this time are women and children. A number of children are suffering from severe cold, pneumonia and other respiratory diseases." A PHE Executive Engineer was reported to have declared that the water supply to villages in quake - hit areas falling in his jurisdiction would be restored only after the road becomes traffic worthy. What nerve? Surprisingly, no one seemed to have taken notice of the press report and asked the Engineer and his staff to start footing the distance. In any case the water pipes did not necessarily run along the roads and the labourers who were to do the actual repair job were not as handicapped as the boss.

Devoid of innovation, deficient in initiative capability and trapped in stereotypes, red-tape, outdated and outmoded rules and regulations that only constrict thinking and performing processes, the establishment appeared ill-equipped and/or apathetic. Too much time was wasted in preliminaries and formalities. To put it bluntly, any evidence of comprehensive analysis of the specifics and dynamics of the quake fall out, adequate recognitions of the compulsions of the terrain, vagaries and cycle of weather and the widespread nature of the effected population in highly low density populated problem areas on the brink of cruel winter was yet to materialise. For instance, it should be obvious that while the immediate shelter could be providing under canvass, undertaking construction of temporary shelters was the only short-term viable answer to the pressing problem of shelter. Except in rare cases where the mother earth decided to swallow habitations and the unfortunate inhabitants, Earthquakes only shake and pull down structures. The debris constituted material capable of being salvaged and reused. This was exactly what some resident of worst effected village of Khairi Kamarra in Poonch district had started doing on their own. The motivation came from compulsion of circumstances and after more than one month of excruciating wait for help from authorities. The initiative was taken by Mushtaq, an ITBF cop. "Since I have to report back to my duty, so I cannot wait for long for the government relief to trickle in to resume the reconstruction work" he told daily Kashmir Times, Jammu on 12 Nov, 2005. This spoke volumes and provided evidence, if any were needed of great fortitude and resilience of our people to come to grips with the disasters and hard times. Apparently, the administrative system and officials failed them in the hour of extreme distress. The feudal and slavish mindset of the bureaucracy was in fact at the bottom of the problem in a free democratic society where citizens were not merely notional fountainhead of power, they were the masters of their destiny. It would therefore be sensible and realistic to treat them as the most precious resource for problem resolution and defer to their 'rustic common sense'. In the ultimate analysis they were the best judges of what was attainable and in their best interests.

The speed of distribution of relief was obviously unacceptably slow and tardy. This was unfortunately inherent in the system. I am aware of the official phobia of 'misuse' of funds. Who would accept responsibility for the 'leakage and misappropriation of fund'? Who will answer the vigilance? These were the question bandied around when any innovative measures were suggested or implemented. Interestingly those who indulged in corrupt practices were the first and foremost in raising such objections. It was axiomatic that apprehensions of delay in receipt of relief money promoted bribery. As the State Relief and Rehabilitation Commissioner after the 1971 war with Pakistan, I was faced with such a dilemma. Prior verification, I was told was mandatory for release' of 'Cash Doles' in favour of the uprooted populace. That would have naturally delayed distribution causing avoidable hardship to the displaced persons. I decided that all those applying for registration as Displaced persons should be registered but each applicant would give an undertaking that he would not only accept the financial liability if his claim was found to be false but also be liable for prosecution. In any case, I told my staff, we cannot deny or slow down distribution of relief to lakhs of displaced persons merely because of the apprehension that a few hundred unscrupulous persons may take undue advantage. At the end of the day some fake Displaced persons were detected and dealt with, but their number in terms of percentages was less that half of those detected in relief distributed after 1965 war even though at that time 'painstaking and thorough screening' was claimed. And when officers of integrity transparently distribute the relief on spot, the chances of fraud were definitely minimal. In any case, traumatised people in agony hurrying up to construct shelters for their families all the time staring at the threatening skies and drenched in pouring icy rain water were less likely to worry about pinching few thousand rupees. It is only when corruption becomes the order of the day, justice and fair play are given a go by and a general climate of permissiveness prevailed that unscrupulous element in the civil society and the administration found it convenient to join in the loot. I should know because I am speaking from experience of not only providing relief to the effected population all along the borders with Pakistan/POK but also handling the unfortunate and volatile population of Chamb-Khour areas in Jammu districts, for whom the 1971 displacement was third in the row.

This was not the time for writing critiques. There would be enough opportunity for such exercise in future. The highest priority today should be to urgently and quickly accomplish the task of distributing cash relief and providing material and physical support for constructing roofs over the heads of people rendered homeless by the earthquake. Two dimensions of the Relief and rehabilitation problem needed to be addressed urgently :

Problem analysis, Policy frame, strategy determination, implementation mechanism and Monitoring progress of field operations.

Chief Minister Ghulam Nabi Azad talked about the setting of Disaster Management Authority. This was an overdue measures and should be taken up on priority. In the meantime, there may be merit in constituting a High Powered Committee comprising of administrators, technocrats, and R&R/Disaster management experts drawn from a pool of serving and retired officers under his chairmanship. This committee may act as the Think Tank, programme constructer, strategy formulator and programme implementation monitor Engineering a Field Support System to attend to the essential needs of human resource and material management for R&R. In this context following steps recommend themselves:

(a) Building material like corrugated tin sheets, complete with nuts, bolts etc, cement, and allied material be transported/airlifted to designated locations on top most priority. This is especially important for Teethwal-Tangdhar as the Nastachun pass may close to traffic any day due to early snowfall.

(b) The requirement of masons, carpenters and other artisans be immediately worked out, if not done already and their services procured from neighbouring areas and made available on fixed daily wages.

(c) Timber be provided through Forest Department depots established in the vicinity of the effected localities. Saw Mills owners or entrepreneurs be motivated and encouraged to set up or shift such mills to the earmarked locations. If this did not work the Forest Development Corporation should chip in.

(d) In remote areas where our people have honed Survival techniques utilising local material mostly wood and mud should be provided hassle–free timber and cash assistance on spot.

(e) The real damage in an Earthquake was to the foundation which could not be quantified. This made so-called 'through verification' of the damage meaningless. It might be more appropriate to classify the dwelling as follows:

Class I. Mud dwellings. These should be treated as total loss.

Class II. Brick and mortar structures. If walls had developed cracks and roof suffered over sixty per cent damage total loss.

Class III. Brick/cement concrete buildings be treated as per the existing norms.

Before construction or reconstructions of permanent structures was authorised experts should certify the suitability of the location and building material with reference to earth quake vulnerability.

The J&K Bank should provide on the spot banking facility in accessible areas where unavailable. The facility be located at central and within reach locations. Mobile Banks in adequately protected vehicles may also be pressed into service.

Even though the population effected by the earthquake was not too large, its spread in difficult terrain and inaccessibility made the task of relief and rehabilitation tough. In any case the object should be to rehabilitate the effected population in a suitable manner without wasting time. The question is whether the government would take the welfare oriented and forward looking route and contribute to the enhancement of the quality of life of the victims through better and upgraded access to education, healthcare and means of livelihood. Or recreate symbols of poverty and backwardness replicating patched and leaning mud houses, pock mark cracked brick walls and leave the inmates in a condition worst than before to curse their luck, nurse their wounds and grieve for their dead. The Congress leadership that had come to power in Jammu and Kashmir after three decades was faced with its first major test. It could not afford to fail.

(2005)

(8) Time to Stop Quarrelling and Start Governing

Ever since President Musharraf of Pakistan began firing salvo after salvo of "ideas" promoting his brand of the out of the box solutions of "the Kashmir problems", the PDP-Congress relations came under heavy strain. The parties not only adopted conflicting positions on the issue of 'demilitarisation' but started the suicidal blame game segregating Mufti's three years tenure as the chief minister and leader of the Coalition from Azad's current tenure in violation of the principle of joint responsibility under the cabinet system. This suited the opposition National Conference strategy of showing the PDP in bad light in respect "of human rights violation record", a vital issue in their common Kashmir constituency.

The demilitarisation mantra began to be chanted from Islamabad to Srinagar by secessionists, their over ground faces, the Hurriyat, the opposition National Conference and the PDP. It found its strong echo in the state legislative assembly. Chief Minister's outburst in the Legislative assembly on 5th February, 2007 could be directly linked to the constant nagging. "Don't make statement to appease the public" admonished Azad. He went onto throw a challenge "If you assure me in writing that you are not concerned about your personal security, I assure you on the floor of the house I will write to the Government of India recommending the withdrawal of forces as the state does not want the security paraphernalia." He had a point but made it in a wrong place and wrong constitutional forum. There was no doubt that the overall security environment generated the threat perception on the basis of which personal security and its scale was determined by the authorities. During normal times say prior to 1987-88, the number of Protected Persons could be counted on fingers. Who needed security and at what level was to be determined by the authorities. The person concerned had little, if any say in the matter. More importantly, PDP ministers, Members of the Parliament and the state legislative were clearly on the receiving end of the admonition as well as the challenge. In any case, these were sensitive issues for a well considered and collective view by state cabinet of which PDP was a constituent. The chief minister threw the gauntlet to the coalition partner including colleagues in the cabinet. One would have preferred to treat this indiscretion as an off the cuff remark in the heat of debate if he had not made the same statement earlier. It appeared that Azad did not have the benefit of advice either from his political colleagues or the bureaucrats with requisites political sense. It was not his style to hold wider consultation involving even knowledgeable and experienced members of the civil society. That was perhaps why no one cautioned him about the implications and consequences of his stand.

Not to miss the opportunity, Mufti Mohd. Syeed took a dig at Azad, in his balanced and well drafted letter dated 6th February, "It had on occasions been reported that you have linked the acceptance of these suggestions (gradual reduction of Central Security Forces and withdrawal of Armed Forces Special Power Act) to personal security arrangements for politicians who demand it...But we always thought this could not have come from the chief minister." While reiterating the demand for gradual reductions of security forces from the state with greater involvement of the state police and withdrawal of Armed Forces Special Powers Act, he requested Azad to "Please withdraw my personal security and that of Ms Mehbooba Mufti MP with immediate effect." This position was immediately endorsed by the PDP ministers and legislatures. On 7th Feb., 2007, Finance ministers Tariq Hamid Qurra demanded that Azad must honour his commitment of approaching the central government for withdrawal of the troops from the state within 24 hours. "We have responded in a humble way by asking him to keep his word", he pleaded. The knives appeared to be out albeit still under the sheaths. The events thereafter indicated mellowing down of the pitch by PDP so far as the stability of the Coalition was concerned. The party would, however persist with calculated and controlled brinkmanship-on the political front drawing maximum mileage from the discomfiture of the Congress Chief Minister.

In his reply to the demand of grants for the police department under his charge Azad reeled off figures of human rights violation separately for the period when Mufti was in the driving seat and his own tenure. This showed PDP in bad light. Here again he was ill advised. In fact it would have been a far better strategy to present relevant statistics for period before and after the formation of the Congress-PDP government which would have established that the graph of human rights violation was consistently going down ever since the coalition took office. This would have raised the stature of the chief minister and firmly established him as the leader of the coalition and not only that of the Congress party.

The main source of the current difficulties of the coalition could be traced to negation of fundamental principles and time honoured practices integral to the parliamentary democracy with the cabinet system at its core. Under this system the governor named a person as the chief minister who enjoyed majority support in the legislative assembly and could provide a stable government. The governor appointed or sacked ministers allocated or shuffled portfolios on chief minister's advice. The CM presided over the cabinet meetings. Even in a single party government this was where CM's pre-eminence ended. The system was designed to work according to the cardinal principle of Intra-cabinet responsibility or cabinet solidarity and political accountability.

In a coalition based on power sharing formula under which the government was to be led by the Congress and PDP by turns for three years each, Mufti was placed on the pedestal first. As soon as he took the oath of the office of Chief Minister, ministers, legislatures and others began to compete in singing his praise to gain favour. But Mufti was a clever and seasoned operator. He insured that the praises showered upon him were appropriately laced with loud endorsement of his policies especially that of the 'Healing touch'. Of course, there were hassles during Mufti's stewardship of the coalition but he managed to take the Congress team along. The Mufti ensured that his relations with the Congress Deputy Chief Minister Mangat Ram were not only cordial but were also seen be so.

True to the tradition when Azad came at the helm, he was crowned as the 'supermo'. A record breaking spell of sycophancy since held sway. Azad's term, however began with a controversy about the induction of Muzaffar Beig as the Dy. Chief Minister representing PDP. Apart from Beig's problem within the PDP leadership, his closeness with Azad queered the pitch. Beig was overnight divested of the leadership of the PDP legislative party and withdrawn from the Cabinet. Azad resisted. In an open confrontation Azad had to blink first. His tenure as the chief minister of the coalition government thus took off on a sour note. Since then news of differences regarding political perception as well as the management of the affairs of the state were making headlines. The "ham handed and extra - constitutional meddling" by the Chief Minister's office especially in the placement of senior officers without even routine consultation with the cabinet ministers concerned further thickened the atmosphere of resentment and mistrust.

On the political front the contradictions between the coalition partners sharpened as the Indo-Pak peace process moved on and Pak President Musharraf focused on the internal politics of J&K. The opposition National Conference and the PDP hitched their wagons to Musharraf's 'self-rule' formula. On the issues of demilitarisation and withdrawal of Armed Forces Special Powers Act, these main stream parties and the Hurriyat spoke with one voice. Human Rights violation today top the popular agenda. The Pak agencies were expectedly taking full advantage of the much trumpeted human rights violations. The central and state governments were on the defensive. Pakistan was thus one up in the on-going psychological warfare thanks to the extraordinary behaviour of coalition partners that made a mockery of the Cabinet system.

The Congress-PDP combine was installed in power to provide a government with a difference a clean efficient and transparent government that really worked. These expectations were not fulfilled. The genuineness of its commitment to the welfare of all the people of the state irrespective of regional, communal or ethnic considerations had yet to pass muster. The state was nowhere close to the achieving the objectives of reconciliation and reconstruction. People were understandably sceptical about the future. The feuding partners would do well to remember that people were watching. Moreover, they had to face the voters next year. To retain the confidence of the people the Congress-PDP alliances had to be seen to be making genuine, sincere and concerted efforts to fulfil popular expectations during the little time left at their disposal. It would therefore be only sensible for the ruling combine to begin to function as a genuine coalition strictly according to the principles and practice of the cabinet system dedicated to the Common Minimum Programme. In this connection the resolution adopted by the PDP executive meeting on February in Jammu assumed importance. It stated "the PDP notes the fact that its alliance with Congress is based on goals set out in the Common Minimum Programme. It sincerely wants to pursue this relationship in the interests of secularism, democracy and peaceful settlement of the problem of Jammu and Kashmir.." The PDP further resolved that "it would take all reasonable measures consistence with its agenda and policies to ensure that coalition government translated its Common Minimum programme into reality for the welfare of the people."

I wish the Congress leadership were to raise their hands in prayer and say "Amen."

(*16 February, 2007*)

(9) Transforming Administrative Chaos into Good Governance

The season for conventions, conferences, rallies and statements bordering on slanging matches had commenced. Political leaders of all hues had jumped into the fray selling their agenda at the top of their voices, ironically to impress contrived gatherings and paid audience. The people found the hectic almost feverish "bhag dour" by politicians entertaining and amusing. The labourers and unemployed, however never had it so good. Daily wages doubled when competition became intense and free transportation to and fro, free meals and booze to boot for "Mates" (in case of Jammu) came as bonus just for shouting slogans and breaking into applause on cue.

The people had great fun and enjoyed on-stage comic performance of the leaders. The turnout in the rallies gladdened the hearts of leaders, the perspective leaders as well as the have been. The people disappointed no one. It would, however be sensible for the leaders not to read too much in the size of turn out in their public meetings. The people had learnt from the leaders the art of subterfuge and double speak. Remember, "JANTA Hai Yeh Sab Janti Hal." At one stage it looked as if the panic button was triggered in anticipation of early elections to the state assembly. But who knows?

Chief Minister Ghulam Nabi had, according to one reckoning, spoken more words in last two months than he uttered during five years in power or power sharing. It must, however be said to his credit that his public speeches, addresses to officials and workers meeting were quite focused on the agenda, his own as well as that of his party. Azad seemed to have selected different political issues for Jammu and the valley keeping in mind the sensitivities and the popular mood of the time. In Jammu, it was the challenge to the security and integrity of the state not the demand of demilitarisation. "I am responsible for the security of my people", he declared in a public meeting and demanded, "How can I hand over the state to the terrorists on a platter?" Brave words, well chosen and effectively delivered. That the position was perilously close to that of the BJP line did not bother him. Nor was he concerned about the premium it would provide to the PDP in Kashmir. Of course, in the valley he recited the peace and development mantra and alluded to the achievements of his government including the creation of four new districts, which incidentally no one had demanded.

Azad addressed district officers meetings in both divisions. His advise, exhortations and admonitions made sense. Addressing meetings of district officers of Poonch, the chief minister made two significant points. Firstly, he enjoined upon the government functionaries "to make public service their motto because their devotion and performance was pre-requisite for translating development schemes into reality." Secondly, he announced that "from June 1, Public Grievances mechanism would be institutionalised where under district, tehsil and block levels officers will hold public hearing sessions. A calendar would be drawn for such "Durbars." In separate meetings held at Jammu and Kathua, Azad impressed upon the officers to re-double their efforts to accomplish works well "in time and bring about attitudinal changes and inculcate missionary zeal to achieve the desired goals." "Personal interest in implementation of projects should be the guiding force to ensure delivery of benefits", he emphasised." "Time has provided us an opportunity to progress, as such, exemplary performance by administration at all levels is a must. Functionaries at all levels are equally important in the development process therefore it is important that everyone of us perform optimally", he said. According to him, "rapport with public is imperative to formulate and successfully implement area specific development projects, address grievances and ensure people's participation in the process of development." The Chief Minister made it mandatory for the officers at block, tehsil and district levels to devote two hours for public hearing everyday. He also announced that city and village committees to monitor works would also be put in place. "I have come to Jammu and Kashmir with a mission to develop it and restore peace", concluded Chief Minister, Ghulam Nabi Azad who sought whole-hearted support from public and unblemished performance by the administration. Come from where? Is he not rooted in this soil? Why did he have to project himself as an outsider with a transient agenda beats me?

His exhortations to the people and the public were straight from the text book. In fact he had been talking in the same vain ever since he assumed the leadership of the coalition and occupied the "Gaddi" of the Chief Minister. There was no valid reason to question his sincerity. So why all his exertions were not producing any significant impact on the administration and spurring the bureaucrats and their minions in to compliance, a response which came natural to them? Why do the ground realities not square with his claims of radical improvement in the performance of administration? How was it that he was unaware of the prevailing rampant corruption especially at the cutting edge level persisting apathetic attitude of majority of the officer class and unending exploitation by political "Kharpanchas"? How many of his colleagues in the cabinet and ministry were genuinely committed to the standards of integrity he was preaching and change in 'mindset' so loudly proclaimed from the official pulpit? These and other similar questions and their obvious unpalatable answers of which he surely could not be ignorant would worry the chief minister if his feet were firmly on the ground. Critics even go to the extent of alleging that he was operating in a vacuum and living in a world of make believe. This may be somewhat uncharitable assessment arising out of an extreme viewpoint. Nevertheless, Azad could not evade resolution of these contradictions any longer. For the success of his campaign he had to either discipline or dump his ministers and executive aids who failed to fall in line. I am afraid, he was left with no soft options if he really meant business.

All policies and programmes formulated by the political executive had to be implemented through the public services. It was indeed a tragedy that even after sixty years of independence there was no comprehensive and concerted effort to convert the so called "steel frame" of the Raj into a public service of a democratic polity. The police continue to function as the "coercive instrument" used and misused by the party/parties in power. The same applied to the rest of the official class, high or low. The character of the administrative machine remained wedded to feudal and colonial ethos that spawned and sustained a slavish mindset in relation to the rulers and an arrogant and ham handed in dealing with the common man.

Let us begin with addressing some basic questions. Were the government functionaries, of today equipped, oriented and motivated to render the kind of public service mandated in a democratic dispensation? What was the prevailing level of devotion to duty and what would need to be done to secure and optimise this primary ingredient of public service?

The unpleasant ground reality was that except for few honourable exceptions, the officials as a class are woefully deficient in attributes of public service in a democracy. It would, however be both futile and unfair to lay the entire blame for this sorry state of affairs at the doors of the "government servants." After all they were mere instruments in the hands of the politicians catapulted into the positions of power and authority by the people. The truth was that once the political leaders got in to the driving seat they fell in love with the mould and the style of governance adopted by their royal predecessors. As a matter of fact the new 'Rajas', their hordes of clansmen and hangers on happily embraced all the ills of the autocracy shamelessly discarding its positive features. This set in motion the erosion of the moral and ethical ethos of the freedom movement. Lack of integrity in public life and services in due course spawned a lethal nexus between crooked politicians, pliable and self-serving bureaucrats and crime mafias. The institution of the 'supreme leader' that has not only survived the vagaries of times but grown and thrived was perhaps the strongest stumbling block in the path of transition from the feudal mindset to a democratic temper. The moot question was whether Azad was prepared to give up this status which enabled a special ego trip of a Chief Minister of Jammu and Kashmir? And when and how would the ruling elite develop a democratic temper and the public servants imbibe the public service mindset?

The road to the transformation of the prevailing chaotic and unprincipled dispensation into a truly democratic governance undoubtedly had to pass through a minefield of vested interests, rouge political elements in the political establishment itself, the mafias and other assorted blood suckers of the vulnerable sections of the society. But men of grit, determination fired with missionary zeal backed by an aware, mobilised and strongly motivated public opinion were known to be capable of exploding or demining the minefields and reach the summit of success. Only stout political will and courage of conviction to take the bull by the horns would bring about that miracle. *(June 29, 2007)*

(10) An Economic Survey; Congress Forced on the Back Foot

The Fifth 'India Today' Annual State of States Report could not have come at a more awkward time for the Congress led coalition in Jammu and Kashmir. The survey conducted by economists Eiek Debóroy and Laveesh 'Bhandahri has consciously preferred performance criteria to that of perception which suffers from the fatal fault of subjectivity. The study wisely relied on the data from the central government sources. For the purpose of comparison between the states they identified eight heads ranging from Budget and Prosperity to Law and Order. "Each of these" said the economists "includes six-eight key variables that track the performance of states. These range from percentage of population above the poverty line, inflation, from area under cash crop to loans extended to farmers." With application of such methodology and reliance exclusively on authentic sources the findings were bound to pass muster with the political parties, think tanks, civil society and politically aware voters. The influence of the findings on the public perception and consequently the voting options could be significant. For this reason alone the Report interested the political parties and their leadership whether in power or in opposition.

In the case of J&K, the analysis of the report had to be tempered with the reality of uniqueness and waywardness that characterised the functioning of the PDP- Congress coalition in Jammu and Kashmir. This combine neither adhered to the 'Coalition Dharma' nor respected the principle of Joint Responsibility, the very soul of governance under the Parliamentary system in a democracy. The only practical course open therefore was to divide the period covered by the Report between the Mufti Mohd Sayeed era (2003 and 2004) the Ghulm Nabi period (2005).

Subject	*2007*	*2006*	*2005*	*2004*	*2003*
Budget and Prosperity	2.05(7)	6	7	7	9
Agriculture	0.71(16)	25	15	15	12
Primary Health	1.60(7)	7	5	4	1
Investment Environment	1.35(14)	12	10	9	10
Primary Education	2.89(8)	10	8	7	7
Infrastructure	2.44(12)	11	8	10	8
Law and order	0.44(15)	17	17	12	13
Consumer Market	1.007(8)	8	8	7	6

The projections made in the report for year 2007 which was still rolling were not taken into account for the purposes of analysis. Moreover it was assumed that the data cited referred to the calendar years. As may be seen from the above table, out of the eight key variables settled for tracking the performance of the state seven recorded a downwards slide in the - years 2005 and 2006 when the Congress led the coalition. During the PDP's stewardship of the government a parity was maintained in the case of Primary education. The performance during the first year (2003) in power was better than the succeeding year in other sectors. It was significant to note that performance level in Agriculture and Primary Health, two key sectors badly slipped from 12th position in 2003 to 25th in 2006 and from number one position in 2003 to 7th in 2006 respectively. This was perhaps the most damning indictment of the Congress - PDP coalition. Interestingly, the Agriculture portfolio was held by PDP's Abdul Aziz Zarger while the Primary Health was headed by Congress ministers. In the context of the forthcoming elections, National Conference could claim that the party left the state in a better economic health in 2002 which the successor dispensation failed to even sustain. It was only in the Budget and prosperity segment that the coalition had excelled consistently improving from 9th position in 2003 to 6th in 2006. Credit for this could, however easily become a bone of contention between the coalition partners as the finance portfolio was held by the PDP minister Muzafar Hussain Beg and Tariq Hamid Qara and no one dare accuse the coalition of adhering to the "principle of joint responsibility." It surely was intriguing that a state that witnessed unprecedented blood bath, suffered almost total loss of economic and social infrastructure and victim of near collapse of governance had listed a rising graph of prosperity during the period. Has the 'India Today' survey established that terrorism is indeed the most thriving industry in Jammu and Kashmir? Or did it in fact point towards the injection of huge amount of funds into the "economy" by agencies indigenous as well as foreign?

It was only logical for the opposition to utilise the Report Card and the position that finally emerged from the study of the report to put the ruling coalition in the dock. The party in power would, on the other hand attempt to parry the assault by questioning the very basis and accuracy of the findings by the India Today Report. The president of the main opposition party, Omar Abdullah had already triumphantly waived it before the media, as the evidence of Congress-PDP's "disastrous rule." This was repeated in public rallies. The media lapped up the sensational findings. The daily Kashmir Times, Jammu carried the banner line in its issue of 27th September "Coalition has failed: NC waved Survey report in governments' face." Similarly. The Early Times, Jammu headline of the same date screamed "Coalition claims fall flat: Survey says J&K in reverse gear." Embroiled in intense infighting, the ruling combine seemed to be still wrestling with options for a public response. However, in not too private gatherings the PDP was also making full use of the 'survey finding'. Even though elections were still about a year away and there were no reliable indications of a mid-term poll, the valley had been virtually in the grip of the election fever for the past couple of months. The preparations for the poll appeared to have reached a fairly advanced stage. A friend from the Valley told me the other day that apart from holding public rallies and conducting a high-voltage pre-election campaign, the parties have even booked groups of local "Bhands" to entertain the voters.

(*19 October, 2007*)

Performance Evaluation

The thirty one point Common Minimum Programme hammered out in Delhi with the blessings of Congress President, Sonia Gandhi and Prime Minister, Dr Man Mohan Singh was the sheet anchor of the PDP-Congress Coalition. The document embodied the solemn commitments made to the people of Jammu and Kashmir by the coalition partners underwritten by the Congress President and the Prime Minister. To what extent and in what measure the coalition government succeeded in delivering on these promises would be revealed only by an objective, impartial and a realistic survey and scrutiny of its performance.

The goals of the Coalition Government enunciated in the CMP were broadly addressed by the coalition government. It translated into "the Healing touch" policy pursued by the state government and the Round table conferences promoted by the Government of India. While the main stream political class responded positively even though some had reservations, the separatist leadership was not persuaded. Even multi-channel desperate attempts by Government of India agencies and interlocutors came to naught as these were bound to. The reason was simple. The government of India, in its wisdom worked on the premise that the Hurriyat and other separatist outfits were in a position to respond to its invitation for dialogue on their own. This was a totally unrealistic and misplaced expectation. Any one, even with a nodding acquaintance with the history of separatist movement in Jammu and Kashmir and its Pak Islamic terrorist manifestation knew that the Kashmir separatist leadership was tied to the apron strings of PAK ISI and that the ISI would not permit such contacts at the back of Pakistan. It was an open secret that belligerent neighbour was committed to only and only a tri-part irate engagement involving Pakistan, India and the Hurriyat, which was touted as the "sole authentic voice of Kashmir (read Jammu and Kashmir)" a totally absurd proposition. Restoration of peace in the state therefore remained a distant dream. The rejection of their boycott call of the 2002 election in which people voted in large numbers fully exposed its real popularity index and limited relevance. The curse of terrorism, however continued to take its toll of human lives and disrupt people friendly developmental activities.

Progress was discernable in the release of detainees held on "non-specific charges" and payment of ex-gratia grant at the enhanced rates. However, the impact of these and similar measures was at the best marginal. As far as the return of "misguided youth" to the state and the main stream, the crossing over of the very first batch created so sharp a reaction that the project had to be dropped like hot potatoes. Welfare measures for the families of militants killed in action and rehabilitation project for surrendered militants, however received serious attention of the government so much so that it was perceived as discriminatory towards the unemployed youth of Kashmir who struggled under the system. They often complained that it paid to become a militant simply by acquiring an AK-47, and pairs of Jeans and sneakers, the militant accoutrement and then surrender to obtain benefits of the Rehabilitation Scheme rather keep on running from pillar to post clutching sheaf of certificates in the never ending futile search for jobs.

(1) Return of 'Kashmiri Pandit' Migrants

It was in 1999 that the microscopic minority of peace loving, non-violent, hopelessly outnumbered terrorised Kashmiri Pandits trapped within the confines of high mountain ranges were forced to migrate to the hot burning plains. Series of gruesome murders, abductions and rapes were committed to lend substance to the threats simultaneously broadcast on high decibel loud speakers fitted in the precincts of places of worship. An impotent state, a paralysed administration and a terrorised citizenry abetted the horrendous crimes both by acts of commission and omission. Lakhs of innocent men, women and children were thus forced to flee the land of their birth in search for a place under the Sun where they could survive in honour and safety.

The Kashmiri Pandits who took pride in being the extension of the great Indian nation were horrified and bewildered when the succour and support from Delhi that they expected as a matter of right failed to materialise. The rulers in Delhi and their agent, the governor of Jammu and Kashmir who straddled the state apparatus like a potentate with unlimited powers disgraced themselves and the nation by miserably failing to discharge their constitutional duty and moral obligation to protect and rescue the miniscule minority during the worst crisis in their history. Generations of Indians will bear the stigma of this national let down.

The Common Minimum Programme of the coalition government affirmed determination to secure the return of Kashmiri Pandits as "an essential ingredient of Kashmiriat." The policy frame and initiatives deigned to translate this determination into action, however lacked realistic comprehension of the complexities of the problem, extent of the social divide and enormity of human sufferings that triggered the migration. Instead of making concerted efforts to win the confidence of the migrants, motivate the Kashmir civil society to demonstratively participate in the endeavour to heal the rupture and ensure them security, the government adopted the disastrous short cut of tasking "some notables" to "win over" even small segment of the community to begin the trek back, a ploy in tune with the imperialist policy of "divide and rule." The vital issue of return and rehabilitation of the migrants which should have been addressed with sensitivity, care and caution was thus trivialised. Engaging in such loathsome tricks to execute by hook or crook the plans prepared by the government was certainly not an option. The migrants and their wide awake leadership could not have failed to see through the game. They not only withheld cooperation but comprehensively exposed the intermediaries as "agents" of the establishment.

The inadequate and unrealistic, perhaps motivated plans of rehabilitation sponsored by the establishment were, to a large extent the product of the flawed appreciation of the motivation and objectives of entire fundamentalist operation. Unfortunately, an Army of so-called experts on Kashmir and scores of policy-makers erroneously assessed the migration as incidental to the secessionist militancy. The state responses were therefore inherently flawed. The truth was that the exodus of Kashmiri Pandits from the valley was not incidental but central to the Pan-Islamic Fundamentalist–Pakistan axis plan to convert Kashmir into a 'Talibanised' society. The return of Kashmiri Pandits to the valley and restoration of 'the Kashmiriat' should be viewed in this context. Only then would it become possible to engineer a multi-pronged plan of action and achieve the objective.

As soon as the terrorist were perceived on the retreat, voices of restoration of peace, normalcy and composite social were raised by saner element of the civil society. Even though their credentials and motives were suspect, the political elite of different varieties joined the chant of "Kashmir in complete without Pandits" mantra. Taking advantage of these positive trends the government undertook repairs to the holy shrine of Mata Shri Kher Bhawani. This proved to be a welcome signal for resuming the pilgrimage after a gap of more than twelve years.

Then there was the all important issue of guarantee of the safety and security of the migrants on return home. This involved two elements–the government and the civil society. Realistically speaking, neither of them was in a position to give any credible guarantee at that point of time. Even though the level of "militancy' had come down, the terrorist retained the capacity to strike at will. They had convincingly demonstrated this by enacting incidents like Wandhama'. The helplessness of the civil society was articulated by a Kashmiri Muslim friend who when asked why were they showing reluctance to reassure the migrant Kashmiri Pandits if they were really sincere countered "How free and secure are we ourselves"? The government, on its part had nothing substantial to show by way of seeking the cooperation of all elements in the society to create an atmosphere conducive to their safe return. Their failure to address the problem in a mature and strategically appropriate manner to generate a socio-security environment conducive for the return of forcibly displaced Kashmiri Pandit minority was palpable.

It was conceded by all that the migrants should and would return to Kashmir as soon the security situation was brought under effective control and peace restored in the valley. However, whether the situation was indeed conducive for their return can only be determined by the migrants. Their satisfaction was the prerequisite given the horrowing trauma they gone through. At stake were their lives and honour. It must therefore be recognised that no amount of cajoling, pressurising, or propaganda would help. Practical wisdom demanded perseverance and patience. Lot of dedicated effort would have to go into the endeavour to heal the wounds of hurt and curing of the scars of the recent past. Seeking back the rhythms of harmony was going to be a uphill task.

The return home in safety, dignity and freedom was the dream which all Kashmiris cherished. But this would only be possible when Kashmiriyat, its ethos of communal amity, cultural homogeneity and social harmony re-asserted dominance over the hearts and minds of the Kashmiri people. Essentially, the Kashmiri Muslim society had to make a conscious, decisive and open statement of rejection of Wahabi fundamentalism and reassertion of the glorious traditions and ethos of the Sufi Islam. Even though, the option had to be exercised by the community itself, it should, not be forgotten that the sway of the 'Wahabi cult' in the hay days of terror was propelled and sustained through the might of the gun. The vast majority of Muslims at that point of time, in fact had little or no choice but to retreat into in their shells.

There was enough evidence to suggest that common Kashmiri Muslim though silenced into submission remained wedded to his liberal traditions, pluralistic ethos and teachings of brotherhood. Obviously, it was necessary to create an environment free from fear and threat of the terrorist gun to enable him to exercise his option. It was the duty of the State to create the necessary environment. The mainstream political parties, community leaders and enlightened citizens should shed ambivalence and mount a powerful and sustained campaign to arouse and concretise the common man's will to restore the age-old ethos of the traditional 'Kashmiriyat' and bury the unwanted Wahabi baggage of the black days of terrorist ascendancy. However, If the state and the political class continued to dither and the civil society chose to remain un-concerned, the Kashmiri Pandits community may never be able to return to Kashmir. In that disastrous eventuality the Pan Islamic Fundamentalist would have accomplished the 'Final solution' of 'the Kashmiri Pandit question'.

The migrants had to wait till 2008 for a worthwhile initiative on the relief-rehabilitation front to materialise. This also happened to be the year in which the term of PDP-Congress coalition was to expire. A comprehensive package "for return and rehabilitation of Kashmiri migrants who wish to return back to Valley" (Package for return and rehabilitation of Kashmiri migrants, Appndx D), the first of its kind was announced by the Prime Minister on 25.4.08 during his visit to the state. The Rehabilitation assistance was provided under the following heads.

Housing

- Transit Accommodation
- Continuation of Cash Relief
- Scholarships to Migrants: Students
- Waiver of interest on loans
- Assistance to Agriculturists/Horticulturists
- Employment.

The vast majority of migrants arrived in Jammu only with the clothes they wore and the small change they had in their pockets or available at homes. Unfortunately, the response of Governor Jagmohan's administration to this humanitarian problem of huge dimensions was insensitive, causal and irresponsible. At a time when they deserved sympathy, support and succour, the government of the day dithered even in arranging bare necessities like rations and accommodation. Their misery was compounded by the intolerably adverse weather conditions and totally inappropriate nature of the temporary accommodation when it was provided. The coming up of two migrant colonies constructed under the Package in Jagti and Missriwals-Purkhoo villages in Jammu district therefore came as the much needed and overdue relief to the migrants families who had suffered avoidable hardship for about nine years.

The state government claimed that by the end of December, 2008, 811 migrant families had expressed willingness to return to Kashmir as per declaration in forms (Expression of Interest) circulated. The administration had also collected bio data of Kashmiri migrant youth numbering approx. 13500 who expressed their willingness to serve in the valley. However, the first concrete step for implementation of Prime Minsters' Rehabilitation Package aimed at securing the return of the Kashmiri Hindu migrants to their homes in the Valley was taken by Jammu and Kashmir government in December, 2009, more than a year and half after the Prime Minister announced the Package. The state government approved reservation of 3,000 government jobs for migrant youth in the Departments of Education, Social Welfare, Relief Organisation, Engineering, Finance, Tourism, Health and Revenue in Kashmir Division. It may be pertinent to mention here that the PDP-Congress coalition government had fallen in July, 2008.

Lured by the prospects of government service the migrant youth sought and obtained employment under the package. Major slice of jobs was in education department. They were posted in rural areas where schools had no hostels and the only option was to hire accommodation locally. The houses in the rural Kashmir were compact designed for family use. Many basic facilities were common. This created problems especially for the female teachers, many of them unmarried. The experience of the Migrant employees of this variety was somewhat mixed. Some migrant employees were welcomed with open arms and treated as part of the family. But many had, to put it mildly unpleasant experience. A few preferred to quit their jobs and return to Jammu. There were even some allegations of forcible conversions.

The working conditions in many rural schools were also not conducive for the migrant teachers. Reports suggested that the classical methodology of schooling had been substituted by the Jammat-Islami code and pattern. Any suggestion to adhere to a century old system followed in government schools was frowned upon and provoked sharp rebukes, even threats. As per reports this problem was posed by a school teacher before the lady member of the team of interlocutors. "Learn to adjust" was her wise and "practical advice."

The Prime Minister's Package was well intentioned aimed at facilitating the return of Kashmiri Pandit migrants to the Valley so as to restore the social, cultural and ethnical cohesion of the Kashmir society. Though well meant the initiative was premature as the required ground work had not been done either at the government or civil society. The Government of India to which numerous intelligence agencies reported had no business to rely upon the patently insincere and hypocritical utterances of politicians. Predictably, the project failed to take off. Having said this, it must be conceded that Package had made migrants life somewhat easier and addressed many of their grievances. This was a positive input benefit where from may accrue in future.

(2) Peace Process

The search for confidence building measures through Indo-Pak dialogue produced the agreement on resumption of the trans LOC bus service, billed as the "mother of CBMS" between the two feuding neighbours. This was the green signal for re-establishing road connectivity between Srinagar and Muzaffarabad, the POK capitol terminated since October 1947 when a sizeable portion of the territory of Jammu and Kashmir state was forcibly occupied by Pakistan army through military aggression camouflaged as "tribal invasion." The avowed objective was to enable separated families forced to live on either sides of the Krishen Ganga river, the URI mountains and the meandering LOC in Poonch sector of Jammu region to come together. This was a significant humanitarian initiative. Surprisingly, the resumption of the Srinagar-Muzaffarabad Bus service evoked vehement opposition from the indigenous pro-Pak elements who had for decades consistently agitated for the opening of the "Srinagar-Rawalpindi road" trotted as the symbol of their "historical linkage" with Pakistan. This volte-face established beyond any doubt their total subservience to and helplessness before the Pan Islamic fundamentalists diktat. The PDP-Congress coalition government in Jammu and Kashmir could legitimately claim the credit for consistently pursuing and forcefully pushing for the confidence building measure.

The first passenger bus rolled across the Aman Sethu, the bridge constructed for surface transportation on 7th September, 2005 undeterred by the terrorist attack on the Srinagar Tourist Reception centre, Srinagar. The central and state governments decided to stick to the announced schedule ignoring terrorist threats of similar strikes en route. The maiden convoy of busses did reach the destination safely without any untoward incident. The novelty of the Bus service soon wore thin. It did not take much time to bring out the truth that there were not many really divided facilities in the Kashmir theatre. A special category of separated families comprising of the kith and kin of Hindu and Sikh migrants left behind in POK in 1947 who had embraced Islam escaped notice of powers that be as the problem was viewed through tainted glasses of religious denominations. The call of blood proved stronger than 'the divisive pull' of religion. Highly emotionally charged Hindus and Sikhs lined up for Permits to meet their long lost relatives in POK. Many senior citizens not in too good health wished to visit the land of their birth before saying good bye to this world. Their keenness to embrace blood relations trapped in POK was matched by the eagerness and excitement of would be hosts. Those who managed to obtain Travel Permits and reach their ancestral villages were fondly and effusively welcomed on arrival in the POK by their Muslim relatives. But as the ill luck would have it, area was hit by a devastating earthquake at about the same time. Some of them were fated to be united only in death.

The resumption of cross LOC traffic cross Aman Sathu and Poonch-Rawlakot route led to demands for throwing open other traditional routes in Jammu and Ladakh–Kargil regions. The Indian initiatives in this behalf had so far met with evasion and lukewarm response from Pakistan. Apparently they were apprehensive about the political fall out of exposure of our people held in bodge in occupied territories to the intoxicating fragrance of freedom, security and huge strides taken in fields of economy and infrastructure development, road and rail connectivity, power generation education and health just to name some. They were bound to compare this with the miserable conditions on their side of the LOC in which they were forced to endure. So the matter remained "under discussion", the classical ploy for evasion. Why was Pakistan, the country that swore by human rights and shed crocodile tears for human right violations day in and day out stubbornly resisting to the purely humanitarian demand of facilitating the very minimum contact between the separated families? They may understandably have a problem in the case of Kargil-Askardu route. How could Pakistan establishment permit a contact which would enable the Shias from Kargil to see with their own eyes the conclusive evidence of the persecution, atrocities and massacre of their blood relations and other Shia brothers and sisters in Gilgit-Baltistan ?

For obvious reasons, the 'opening' of the Chakan-Da-Bagh route in Poonch in Jammu region for trade and passenger traffic to and from POK proved a success. For one, the number of divided families in that area was much larger and many lived just across the LOC at less than shouting distance. The Bus route was short and transportation quick and comfortable. More over ethnic bonding worked as the magnet pull. Against this, the people living in Muzaffarabad and beyond in POK were Paharis, of a different stock from Kashmiris who inhabited the valley of Kashmir.

The trans LOC traffic had exploded the myth propagated by pro-Pak elements, the Hurriyat Conference and its fellow travellers. It was vehemently argued that all problems relating to supply of consumer goods to the valley and export of perishable goods like Apples would be instantly and happily resolved when the traditional Jhelum valley road linking Srinagar with Muzaffarabad was thrown open to traffic. A comparison was often drawn with its all weather character and the temporary disruption of traffic on the National Highway that occur during a small part of winter season due to inclement weather conditions. The argument was further buttressed by citing the brief disruption of traffic on the National Highway between Pathankot and Srinagar during the "Bum Bum Boley"agitation in Jammu ignoring the fact that the people of Jammu suffered the very same deprivation. They went to the extent was accusing the agitators of 'Economic Blockade'. To press the point a massive "Muzaffarabad Chalo" march was organised in August 2008 originating from Srinagar thereby provoking a confrontation with the security forces resulting in avoidable loss of precious lives. And then to their utter surprise Srinagar-Muzaffarabad route was thrown open to traffic. The venture proved a non-starter as far as trade was concerned. The trial supply of Apples sent to Muzaffarabad was a business disaster. No marketing facilities worth the name were available. There was not enough space identified and made suitable to off load goods-perishable by the very nature. The POK on the other hand had almost nothing to offer for export to Srinagar in the category of consumer goods. The trade through the Chakan-Da-Bagh, on the other hand started off well and was growing steadily. In fact, the delegation of AJK Chamber of commerce which visited both Srinagar and Jammu made it abundantly clear that they were mainly interested in building and expanding trade relations with Jammu. The lesson that the fanatics must learn was that compulsions of logistics, geographical contiguity, ethnic affinity and above all profitability were the most powerful drivers of trade and commerce. Forcible injection of religion in an essentially secular domain was doomed to fail.

The political process which received a boost with the formation of the coalition government had a chequered history. The Indo-Pak dialogue floundered on the rocks of insincerity, duplicity and dishonesty. While India made sincere efforts at improving relations between the two neighbours on the basis of mutual benefit, common interests and good neighbourly relations, Pakistan engaged its declared "enemy number one" in negotiations to extract whatever advantage she could. In the dialogue process, track one or track two, she heavily relied on arm twisting the USA to put pressure on India simultaneously persisting with strategically spaced terror strikes across India in pursuance of its policy of "inflicting thousand cuts." Critically dependent on Pakistan for successful conduct of operations in Afghanistan, the USA understandably obliged.

The 26/11 Mumbai atrocious, vicious and audacious terror strike planned, provisioned and launched from her soil by Lashkar-i-Toiba, a known Pak army strategic asset, proved a game changer. Despite declaration of the Lashkar as terrorist organisation by USA and worldwide condemnation of its nefarious activities, Pakistan continued to shelter Hafiz Sayed, its chief and his fellow criminals specifically wanted in Mumbai carnage. Consequence the Indo-Pak dialogue process suffered a lethal blow and remained suspended to the discomfiture of the Kashmir separatist and a section of the so-called mainstream leadership.

(3) Education

The coalition government had undertaken to draw a new scheme with a view to universalise access to elementary education. Large number of schools were accordingly sanctioned but without matching or even elementary infrastructural facilities. In the absence of built in accommodation many schools functioned in the open causing hardships to the boys and girls of tender age. The situation became particularly intolerable during the inclement weather. The so-called "new scheme" launched by the coalition government became a subject of ridicule and generated popular resentment. Even basic study tools like "Black boards" were reportedly unavailable in many schools in rural areas. In some villages teachers were said to have resorted to the novel method of trapping and tying Black Buffalos under the trees and utilising their hides as substitute for standard black boards. Not to speak of proper mid-day meals, there was no arrangement even for potable water. Children were detailed to fetch water from the nearest source whatever its quality and distance. School uniforms were generously promised but miserly provided.

Number of colleges were sanctioned through upgradation of Higher Secondary Schools without provision for required built in space. Consequently, Higher Secondary Schools doubled for colleges for half the day. Moreover in the absence of libraries and laboratories as well as adequate and competent staff these newly sanctioned colleges proved to be cruel joke. The proficient teachers avoided postings to locations outside Jammu, Srinagar and other district headquarters as residential accommodation was scarce or just not available. Many colleges were alleged to have been sanctioned to accommodate influential MLAs without any concern or considerations for the needs and welfare of students and teachers. The quality of education witnessed an all time low particularly after the departure of Harsh Dev Singh from the ministry. Number of government schools achieved record breaking results including 100 per cent failures. Ironically, government schools had an array of highly qualified teachers. Some of them did maintain some islands of excellence in the sea of failures and mediocrity. Adequate funds, it was given out were available and the deficiencies would be made good in due course of time. What would be the span of this "Due course of time" was any body's guess.

(4) Discrimination against Jammu

The Kashmir centric promises incorporated in the Common Minimum Programme received due attention of government right from the commencement of the first three year coalition under the stewardship of Mufti Mohd Syed of the PDP. Two major and crucial commitments in the Common Minimum Programme of vital interests to Jammu relating to the constitution of the Delimitation Commission and the implementation of the Wazir Commission Report were, however kept in the cold storage. This was not only a case of blatant discrimination but also smacked of less than honest intent. As the matters stood, the constitution of the Delimitation Commission was not in the realm of possibility. This was known and still the promise was made in the Common Minimum Programme apparently to hoodwink people of Jammu region. Moreover, an intrinsically political and constitutional matter that squarely fell in the domain of the legislature was dragged to the courts thereby sealing its fate. I distinctly recall inquiring of the then chief minister, Mufti Mod Syed after one of our infrequent meetings, "Wazir Commission Aur Delimitation Commission Ka Kaya Socha Hai."? He stared at me and replied with a grin "Jaldi Bhi Kaya Hai." I knew then and there that he had no intention of touching these two burning but highly controversial issues. As a matter of fact, his strategy appeared to be to defer action on all contentious issues especially those pertaining to Jammu region perceived to be inimical to the interests of his own constituency in Kashmir. My own reading was that he hoped to continue in the saddle for full six years and probably planned to utilise the first three years to build bridges with a section of Jammu leadership with whose good will "via media" may be worked out and presented to a divided Jammu leadership some sops during the second half. In such a situation the opposition from Kashmir would also be diluted.

The Wazir commission was appointed to address the complaint of discrimination against Jammu region after three districts of Budgam, Kupwara and Pulwama were arbitrarily and suddenly created in Kashmir without adhering to any rational criteria. The Commission, after taking all relevant factors into consideration recommended the creation of three new districts in Jammu and one in Kashmir. Azad, who ascended the GADI of the Chief Minister on the Jammu ticket found a unique method of assuaging the hurt feelings of his constituency. He sanctioning four more districts for each region (on what criteria, he alone knows) thereby in effect perpetuating discrimination. Interestingly, the people of Kashmir were satisfied with the Wazir commission recommendation to create an additional district of Bandipur. There was no immediate reaction in Jammu because the leadership of all political parties was 'managed'. Do not ask how? The issue was, however far from dead. People had begun to discuss the enormity of deceit in the drawing rooms and social gatherings. No one bought the senseless argument that "Jammu got four districts it demanded then why bother about what happened in Kashmir?" Jammu had to bother because the development funds were allocated districtwise. This very same reason prompted opposition to the creation of three districts in

Kashmir in the first instance. Moreover, any attempt to box public concerns about the vital matters of the state administrative in regional cocoons symptomatic of a dangerously divisive mindset was fraught with highly potent and dangerous consequences. Of course, whatever happened in Kashmir was of deep concern for Jammu and vice versa especially for those committed to the integrity of the state. The Congress party would be well advised to ponder over long-term implications of impregnating such like divisive ideas in the public mind.

(5) Drive against Corruption

The coalition government had promised to accord "top priority to ridding the State administration of corruption and nepotism, especially in the award of government jobs and contracts and placement in institutions of higher learning." Moreover, the selection process to all those positions and institutions was to be made "fully transparent."

In the early euphoric days of the coalition, chief minister Mufti Mohd Syed appeared to be serious about combating corruption. He personally intervened to recall the services of RV Raju, a senior IPS officer of the Jammu and Kashmir cadre on deputation to Government of India. Raju had earlier headed the state vigilance organisation with distinction and enjoyed great reputation for integrity and efficiency. The officer had gone on deputation to Government of India only recently and had a stable and important assignment in a premier central government organisation. He was reluctant to return to the state. Mufti personally invited him to Jammu so as to persuade him to join in what he called "the crusade against corruption." In fact, Raju with whom I enjoyed close personal and professional relations met before calling on the chief minister. My advise to him was "to keep an open mind." His induction as chief of the vigilance organisation was obviously meant to induce the public perception that Mufti was indeed determined to combat corruption and eager to be seen to be moving meaningfully in that direction. "That to begin with, you will be given a free hand and supported in the anti-corruption drive to enable you to produce 'some spectacular results' in that field could who felt be taken for granted. But how his political compulsions would play out and impact future was anybody's guess", I told him. During their meeting Raju was impressed by Muftis' sincerity and returned to take over as chief of Jammu and Kashmir Vigilance organisation. The arrangement worked satisfactorily till the state government began to "reluctantly" ask him to go slow in "politically sensitive cases." The matters came to a pass when pressure was mounted on him "to accommodate" in a corruption case involving a powerful businessman cum politician who indicated willingness to switch over to the ruling party if shown "desired consideration" in the case proved against him by the Vigilance organisation. From then on the relations soured. Raju, who had personally supervised the investigation and piloted it to successful conclusion would not compromise on principal and refused to budge. Irritated by the mulish stubbornness of a mere police officer, the state government ordered his removal from the Vigilance organisation. And yes, the businessman cum politician did change sides.

There indeed was significant impact on the corrupt amongst the bureaucrats for about first three or four months of the Mufti regime. Then juicy stories of some ruling politicians "making money" and that too not very discreetly began to make rounds. Their bureaucrat minions were soon in the loop. The bund broke. And leadership chose to bend before "compulsions of coalition" at the cost of solemn commitments in the Common Minimum Programme and the oath of allegiance to the constitution sworn in the name of God.

Culpable lack of concern for the fate of the common man asphyxiated by the all prevailing corruption at the grass root level was the most disappointing feature of the coalition performance. As the time passed hopes of a government with a difference were shattered. The common man, however was not surprised. He had already accepted the institutionalised corruption as part of "the democratic" system of governance. Rates for every "favour" by the revenue officials for instance were not only known but openly advertised. Most Bank officials deducted a certain percentage at the time of cashing government cheques be it a case of subsidy, sanction of loans or even compassionate relief. The rot was no doubt inherited by the PDP-Congress coalition.

Having voted for a change the electorate took the promise of good governance and a corruption-free people friendly government more seriously than perhaps was intended by the coalition government CMP. Their hopes for a fair and clean dispensation were fortified by the substantive moves made by Mufti in early days of the coalition. This explained the enormity of popular resentment and anger when, to their horror they witnessed the revival of old corrupt and immoral methods by some ministers and a section of bureaucracy. Even the flicker of hope of good times for the man in the street disappeared.

(6) The "Roshni" Act

In the days of Maharajas Jagirs and Murrabas (chunks of land) were granted to the minor royalty, courtiers and senior level military and civil officials for loyal, meritorious or gallantry services at royal pleasure. In principle, all land in the domain was owned by the rulers. Land grants were also made in favour of Temples, mosques and other places of worship or charitable trusts like Dharamarth Trust floated by Maharajah Ranbir Singh. These were either outright grants or leases for a fixed period. The State reserved the right to resume land on termination of lease period or renew the lease for specified period as it pleased. However, leases in favour of those still enjoying patronage were renewed in routine. Rest were decided on merit on case to case basis strictly in accordance with law. Notices would be issued and served well in time and cases processed and decided expeditiously. It may be mentioned here that under Maharajah Hari Sigh's regime there was zero tolerance for corruption.

The standard of integrity in services was by and large maintained during the first tenure of Sheikh Mohd Abdullah as the Prime Minister of the state. Thereafter sprouted a new and expanded crop of political royalty and flocks of their not so scrupulous henchmen. What we witness today was the cumulative effect of politico-administrative waywardness, moral decline and institutionalised corrupt practices of varying degrees that thrived and were perfected by their practitioners over the decades. The State Nazool Department officials who dealt with leases of Nazool land were known to enjoy an intimate and mutually beneficial equation with lease holders. They had devised a near perfect mechanism to go around and bend the rules to serve the interests of Lease holder. It was cranked into action as dates of expiry of leases approached. The lease holder concerned quickly got in touch with the Nazool official responsible or serving the notice of eviction to strike the preliminary deal. This done, the case moved step by step at a leisurely pace. Neither of the parties was thereafter in a hurry. I happened to get the picture from a junior field officer of the Nazool department during the course of an inquiry into charges of corrupt practices levelled against a former Prime Minister. When pressed, he disclosed that they were mere tools and minions in a game in which politicians and number of top bureaucrats were the real and major players. "Sir, they have complete list of prime properties on lease as well as all relevant information including dates of expiry. They prefer to strike deals directly with lease holders over the heads of department officers," he moaned. Given this knowledge, it should not be difficult to read between the lines in The Jammu and Kashmir State Lands (Vesting of Ownership to The Occupants) Act (Appendix-E) and gain insight into its many 'Avtars'. It would also help in deciphering the hidden agenda that prompted number of amendments to the Act as well as the framing of "scandalous" Roshni Rules (Appendix –F).

The Jammu and Kashmir Legislative Assembly enacted Act No. XII of 2001 in the Fifty–second Year of the Republic of India which received the assent of the Governor of Jammu and Kashmir on 9th November, 2001. It was notified in Government Gazette dated 13th November, 2001. The declared objective of the act was "to provide for vesting of ownership rights to occupants of State Land for purposes of generating funds to finance Power Projects in the State." The legislation was mired in a fierce controversy from the very first day the bill was introduced in the state assembly. The motive behind the move was suspect. The mild critics called it ill conceived and irresponsible. Those on the extreme fringe dubbed it as unethical, intended to benefit politicians, senior bureaucrats and sharing booty with the all powerful land mafia with which they allegedly had cosy relations. Another school of thought contended that the political leadership having lost the will and forfeited the authority to eject the land grabbers and criminals hit upon this "brilliant idea" to resolve the impasse once and for all to the benefit of all concerned and in the bargain raise funds for financing power generation projects. Either ways the state was the loser. Its authority and prestige devalued, it opted for a bargain that favoured criminals and rich and mighty manipulators. The act, legalised surrender before the vested interests at the cost of public good. The criminals, trespassers, Mafias and violators of rules instead of being proceeded against under law were rewarded thereby making a mockery of the rule of law. The criticism though harsh was not without merit.

The beneficiaries of the legislation, broadly fell in following categories:

(a) Those in lawful possession of land prices whereof had sky rocketed and were ever escalation and for which ridiculously low rent was being charged.

(b) Lease holders whose lease had expired but continued to retain possession with the connivance of authorities.

(c) Small size holdings illegally occupied by committing the offence of trespass either in respect of the entire holding or part whereof was legally allotted and part trespassed upon.

(d) Huge tracks of land forcibly and illegally grabbed by Land Mafias, government officials and politicians.

Most Occupants falling in categories (a) and (b) above were rich and powerful. The rich were willing to make mutually beneficial "accommodation." The powerful were fraternity-politicians and bureaucrats.

Category comprised of favoured clans or the crucial vote bank.

As far as the Land Mafia and Siyasi–Sarkari land grabbers were concerned, the state appeared to be either privy to their nefarious activities or otherwise felt constrained to look the other way. Having said that it may be conceded that provisions of the Act of 2001 by and large conformed to constitutional norms and propriety. The government of the day also showed sensitivity to public criticism and refrained from framing Rules under the act in haste.

The Jammu and Kashmir State Lands (Vesting of ownership to the occupants) Act, 2001 mandated selling or regularising of the occupied State Lands at market prices to both, authorised and unauthorised occupants and also provide for auctioning of the vacant state lands publicly. The act was first amended in 2004 when Mufti Mohd Syed headed the PDP-Congress coalition. That the amendment was meant to serve the vested interests may be illustrated by following instance;

1. According to Section 2(C) of the original act "available State land means any State land, which was "not in possession of any person or which has been encroached upon by any person." The words "or which has been encroached upon by any person" were deleted by 2004 amendment.
2. In terms of Section 3(c), the provision of the Act were not to apply on certain lands which included those earmarked for a specific purpose in any Master Plan. This subsection of Section 3 was also deleted by 2004 amendment. Master plans embodying long-term development perspectives were vital sacrosanct documents drafted by experts after in depth study, tremendous research and eliciting public opinion. That the protection provided to land assets earmarked for public good was lifted by the coalition to benefit vested interests was beyond any shadow of doubt.
3. The 2001 Act provided for sale of State Land through public auction with predetermined Reserve Price. This was strictly in

accordance with the general practice and the law as laid down by the Supreme Court. The amendment to the Act and provision in the Roshni Rules shedding the option of public auction and fixing prices of different categories violated or rather defied the above mentioned cardinal principal repeatedly reiterated by the Supreme Court.

4. Section 10 of the Act contemplated creation of a separate fund under a proper account number in the J&K Bank in each district or to allot an account head in which cost of the land realised under this act should be deposited. No such Fund or Account was created. Instead amounts were deposited in Treasuries. The revenue authorities didn't even bother to conduct any reconciliation with concerned Treasuries. The CAG report lamented that in status report in respect of Jammu district showed a collection of Rupees 9.35 Crore but the treasury receipts attached with the application forms indicated receipt of only Rupees 8.33 Crore. An amount of more than one crore was un-accounted for.

5. Section 5(b) of the Act, passed in 2001 provided that only such occupants seeking transfer of ownership were eligible to apply who had been in actual physical possession of the land during the period from 1 January, 1990 to the commencement of the Act in a particular area. Thus the original Act (2001) limited the benefit of the scheme only to the long-term occupants. Under the 2004 Amendment to the Act, all those occupants who were in actual physical possession of the land, either personally or through their authorised agents, on the commencement of the 2004 Amendment Act were made eligible to apply, irrespective of the length of period of occupation. This opened fresh flood gate for feverish land grabbing especially by those who had failed to do so earlier. Their nefarious designs were further facilitated by allegedly deliberate delay in the publication of the amendment in the government gazette by about two months. Even though the Governor had given his assent on 19th March, 2004, the amendment was published in the gazette on 21st May, 2004. The act was to come into force on the date of its publication in the government Gazette.

Roshni Rules- The Mother of Scams

The act stipulated that rules for the proper implementation of the act would be framed by the executive and required no ratification by the legislature. The Government notified The Jammu and Kashmir State Land (Vesting of Ownership to the Occupants Rules) on 25th August, 2005 about four years after the enactment which were amended on 23rd November, 2006 and again on 5th March, 2007. Even a cursory reading would reveal that the rules framed under the act for its implementation were repugnant to the parent act and violated its stated scope and objectives. For instance, the Roshni rules authorised the transfer of agricultural lands free of cost, which was beyond the scope, objectives and mandatory provisions of the act. This, according to CAG report enabled a large portion of non-agricultural land, 3.4 Lakh Kanals to be precise, being dubiously shown as agricultural which was "gifted" to favoured occupants for obvious consideration. The government claim that 19 lakh cultivators would benefit from the rule was not only absurd but a down-right lie. Jammu and Kashmir state had less than 16 lakh cultivators and only 16.27 per cent of them were known to have encroached upon government land.

Principal Accountant General Dr Pandey also made the following startling disclosures quoting CAG report in an unusual press conference on 1st March, 2014:

(a) Irregularities in transfer of encroached land to occupants in Jammu and Kashmir from 2007 to 2013, saying the state government realised just Rs 76 crore against a target of Rs 25,448 crore.

(b) The legislature's rights have been violated because law has not been followed by the state government.

(c) Substantial deviations in the rules from the Act happened in 2007. The govt acted beyond the authority given by the Act and violated it.

(d) Mutation of title in revenue records should be carried out only after the transfer deed has been duly registered. Audit noticed that this was not being done and the State Exchequer was put to loss not only on account of transfer of lands free or below the price fixed by the committees but also on account of non-collection of stamp duty.

Asked whether the rules of state government were made to help land mafia, he said according to the CAG, the list "includes some businessmen, politicians, bureaucrats and journalists."

The CAG had filed the detailed report with regard to Roshni land transfers in the High Court, and hoped "for action."

As already pointed out, the act envisaged lands to be sold at market price but the rules provided for differential pricing and various kinds of rebates thereby benefitting the land grabbers and the rich and the mighty. The "authorised occupants" owning residential structures on government land of upto 2 kanals were required to pay only 25 per cent of the land value, and those living on plots of up to 10 kanals were required to pay 40 per cent. For "authorised overstayed" and unauthorised occupants, the rates were fixed at 35 per cent and 50 per cent of the land value, respectively.

In the commercial category, authorised, authorised overstayed and unauthorised occupants had to pay 30 per cent, 45 per cent and 60 per cent, respectively.

In case of institutions (educational, religious, charitable, social, trusts, societies) and political parties, the rates were fixed at 15 per cent and 25 per cent, respectively. That the public exchequer was thus made to suffer unnecessary and unacceptable huge losses appeared to be of no concern to the government.

Yes, rebate was indeed a common practice in marketing when the demand slumped to an unacceptable level or dried up. The aim was to salvage whatever was possible in an adverse demand and supply equation. Could there be a more blatant, scandalous and dishonest act by the government than to grant rebates in respect of the scarce, inflexible and precious land assets for which there was huge and enduring demand ?

According to CAG, "Among the beneficiaries of the illegal and irregular deals under the Act were the National Conference's Nawai Subah Trust and the Congress's Khidmat Trust. While 7 kanal, 15 marlas and 84 sq ft of land were transferred to Khidmat Trust, 3 kanal and 16 marlas were given to Nawai Subah at Zero Bridge in Srinagar." "The land, under commercial use, was transferred to the two trusts at concessional rate applicable to land under institutional use. The statutory committee under the Act fixed market rate of the land at Rs 1.10 crore per kanal in case of the Khidmat Trust and Rs 1.20 crore per kanal in the case of the Nawai Subah Trust. Both were given 85 per cent rebate, with land valued at

Rs 13.10 crore transferred for only Rs 1.97 crore." (Nation, March 10, 2014). Grant of Eighty five per cent rebate on the most sought after prime land which would fetch a fortune in an open auction at these commercially strategic locations that too on arbitrarily calculated low prices surely qualified to be termed as mother of scams and worst instance of Spoil Sharing System?

The Roshni rules would go down in the history as the most blatant breach of trust reposed by any legislature in the executive by openly and officially authorising misappropriation of public assets and criminal complicity in the promoting a scam of unprecedented proportion. "Possibly, yes" replied Principal Accountant ant General Pandey to a question in the press conference whether Roshni Act could be the biggest scam in the state. "The state government has estimated such lands for Rs 25,000 crores in 2006. Today you can yourself think of the value of this land." (Roshni Act Biggest Scam in J&K: Kashmir Observour, March 09, 2014).

To add insult to injury, the Roshni Rules authorised the Government to "devise and notify a policy of granting rewards and incentives to such officers administering the scheme who show excellent performance in implementation of the scheme." Pray what was the criteria the powers that be had in mind according to which the level of excellence in distributing and sharing the "loot" of public assets was to be determined and rewarded?

Incidentally, the instances cited above were merely illustrative not exhaustive.

The CAG had pushed the matter into the court of the Raj Bhavan where it awaited attention and action.

Before departing from the subject, it may be pertinent to list some of major commitments made in the Congress-PDP Coalition Common Minimum Programme that remained buried in files:

1. Construction of Permanent Shelters for persons living close to the Border/LOC.
2. Appointment of Commission for Police Reforms.
3. Appointment o f Delimitation Commission.
4. Take effective measures to check unplanned and unauthorised growth of towns and cities.
5. Appointment of Minority Commission.

(7) Fiscal Management

The funds from the centre flowed to Jammu and Kashmir as never before. According to Finance Minister AR Rathar "In 2003-04 the plan outlay allocated to state government was 2500 crore rupees, in 2004-05 the plan allocation was 2700 crore rupees which rose to 3000 crore in 2005-06, 3500 crore rupees in 2007-08, 4000 crore rupees in 2007-08 and 4500 crore in 2008-09." During 2008-09, Jammu and Kashmir had got plan allocation of Rs 5,512.97 crore, including Rs 1,012.97 crore of PMRP" said Chief Minister Omar Abdullah. "The state, however, could not spend all the money allocated to it under the plan outlay. It spent Rs 4,773.54 crore last fiscal year (2008-09)." This unprecedented feat was the outcome of coalition misadventure, persistent in-fighting in the cabinet, paralysis of governance resulting in absence of decision making.

The Congress – PDP Coalition, the first experiment of its kind in the strife ridden and terrorism infested state was bound to have problems. The on-going terrorist nightmare had made the management of its complex affairs even more daunting. The challenges of taming if not eradicating terrorism, infusing a sense of security and confidence amongst the populace and promoting re-construction and reconciliation were indeed formidable. The spirit of accommodation and unity of purpose which marked the putting together of the coalition with the efforts of the Congress President and the Prime Minister needed to inform the functioning of the coalition.

The situation mandated extreme care and caution as multifarious problems in running the administration under a coalition of this peculiar character and reconciling the diverse political stances of the partners were no doubt anticipated. It was, assumed that senior party leaders would show sensitivity to the grim complex situation. Conscious of the serious nature of responsibilities they were expected to smoothen the rough edges and sort out problems in the larger interest of the nation and Jammu and Kashmir. It was also expected that the Congress high command which had brokered the coalition would closely monitor the working of the arrangement and intervene as and when necessary. These assumptions unfortunately proved misplaced and expectations from Delhi were belied by subsequent developments.

The functioning of the PDP-Congress coalition under Ghulam Nabi Azad was reminiscent of the Interim government formed in undivided India at the fag end of the British rule with Nehru as the Prime Minister,

Patel as the Home Minister and most significantly, Liaqat Ali Khan as the Finance Minister. The PDP Finance Minister, Taraq Hamid Karra proved a tough nut to crack. He used his powers to the fullest possible extent to serve what he perceived to be in public interest and blocked, what he chose to describe as "not conforming to codal norms." A fuming Azad was known to have even complained to Prime Minister Manmohan Singh and UPA Chairperson Sonia Gandhi that Karra had made the working of the government impossible but failed to make the allegation stick.

The performance of the PDP Coalition could be best summed up in the words of Chief Minister Ghulam Nabi Azad himself. He was reported to have told the media that he headed a cabinet "half of which (PDP contingent) did not function and the other half (his own Congress party colleagues) were incapable of functioning with the result that he had to run the government single handedly." Further comments were superfluous.

It was a matter of gratification that all the deficiencies and drawbacks notwithstanding, the people's faith in democratic system amazingly remained unshaken. The level of peoples' participation in the elections-2008 provided convincing evidence of this. May be, consciously or sub-consciously they compared even the PDP-Congress variety of the democratic functioning with a 'Talibanised' dispensation and were horrified by the prospects of later becoming their fate.

The above survey flagged few achievements and numerous failures of PDP-Congress coalition in Jammu and Kashmir, a marriage of convenience primarily driven by party vested interests which managed to place public good low in their list of priorities. As it turned out even ideological commitments and political goals of the two parties were not only diverse but conflicting.

The Congress high command engineered, packaged and blessed the arrangement with open eyes and full awareness of its contours and likely consequences. Some Kashmir watchers argued that the Government of India after having successfully conducted free and fair elections was desperate to install a government, any government with a view to earn open and unqualified approbation from the international community especially the USA for her democratic credentials and recognition of voters faith in the Indian constitutional system. This, they argued was in national interest. Others contented that with National Conference having jumped on the BJP led NDA band-wagon, there was hardly any space left for manoeuvring. The debate on the issue was bound to go on. In any case, We were too close to the events to pass any objective judgment which was best left to the posterity. However, it should and could be hoped that the next government would learn lessons from blunders committed by their predecessors in office and consciously avoid pitfalls. And the ruling alliance in Delhi would, for once defer to peoples intense desire and urgent need for good governance in the blood soaked state of Jammu and Kashmir reeling under cross-border terrorism unleashed by Pakistan backed by Pan-Islamists and target of intrigues at the national and international levels.

PART: 3

Governor's Rule

Governor N.N. Vohra accepted the resignation of Ghulam Nabi Azad government and immediately initiated the process of consulting leaders of various political parties and groups in the Assembly to arrive at a firm assessment whether any of the parties were inclined to and capable of forming a stable government. He, however reached the conclusion that no party was in a position to do so. The Governor therefore issued a proclamation, in exercise of powers conferred upon him under Section 92 of the Constitution of Jammu and Kashmir, whereby he dissolved the Legislative Assembly with immediate effect (11th July, 2008) and assumed all the functions of the state government. This was to be the fourth spell of Governor's Rule in the state, the others being in 1977, 1986 and 2002.

By the time the PDP-Congress coalition came un-struck and Governor's Rule imposed in the state, both regions of Kashmir and Jammu were afire. The mischief mongers were vigorously pursuing their divisive and anti-national agenda, indulging in what came to be known as Street Terrorism and provoking confrontation between communities. The situation was rendered highly explosive as the Noisy riotous and emotionally charged street action was intensified in Kashmir at the behest of Pakistan ISI. As if on cue, her local collaborators and mainstream mentors began to shout "Intifada" predicting imminent exit of India from Kashmir. The assertion was backed by images of shrieking violent youth and threatening mob on the TV screens beamed in drawing rooms and bed rooms across the country. This ploy was first tried in the early days of militancy in early nineties. The 2008, Kashmir situation fraudulently contrived on the ridiculous allegation that India was trying to change the demographic character of Kashmir by establishing "Palestine like" Jewish settlements on 38.88 hectares of land diverted to Shri Amarnath Shrine Board for use during the Yatra period appeared to be tailor made for a second try. Even after the people of Kashmir had seen through the dirty game, the ISI lover boys persisted in their war cry proclaiming eruption of "Intifada." The Indian state, they demanded must quickly accommodate the demands of the agitators if it intended to preserve even a semblance of foot hold in Kashmir otherwise start packing up. The self styled ultra liberal fringe in our society, always eager to join the dooms day lobby chipped vigorously generating kind of panic in segments of the political class. Mercifully, the Government of India remained unfazed. The prime minister asserted that Jammu and Kashmir was an integral part of India and that resolution of internal difficulties shall have to be found within the framework of the Indian constitution. This unambiguous position made nonsense of the Panic brigade's raving and ranting and poured cold water on the "Quit Kashmir" protagonists.

An all parties meet was followed by visit to Kashmir by an all party delegation for on the spot assessment of the situation. Non-political interlocutors were named to conduct comprehensive and in depth assessment and submit their report who got on with their task in right earnest. During their visits to different parts of the state they interacted with all segments of the society. The separatists led by Ali Shah Geelani rejected the initiative and called for boycott of the Interlocutors. The other factions, placed as they were had no option but to nod agreement. Significantly, the interlocutors declared that they were interested in interacting only with those desirous of participating in the process. "We will not knock on the doors of those unwilling to meet us" said Dilip Padgaonker, the leader of the interlocutors group.

The battery of "Kashmir experts" were quick to project the Pro Pak hardliner Syed Ali Shah Geelani, the patron in chief of Hizb Ul Mujahideen as the "undisputed leader" of the Kashmir Muslims and therefore the one with whom Indian state shall have to do business. They had no time or inclination to observe the transparently vicious sadistic and brutal game plan of enticing, alluring and otherwise motivating innocent Kashmiri youth to march towards security forces bunkers raising anti-national slogans and generally act in a manner that created an environment of intense violence aimed at provoking the Security forces to resort to use of force under attack. The man, Musarat Aalam being eulogised as the messiah was in fact using the youth as sacrificial goats to serve his Pakistani masters petty political interests. Ironically, Mohd Yusuf alias Syed Salahuddin, the Hizab supremo was the first to raise his voice against Geelani's misadventure. Geelani's supporters even burnt his effigy in Sopore. The ISI bosses wasted no time in asking the UJC chief to shut up. The Council's Muzaffarabad based spokesman, Syed Sadaqat Hussain was drafted to issue a statement on his behalf saying that "The ongoing movement is identified with Syed Ali Shah Geelani. For, the sacrifices offered by him are countless and everlasting.... To cast aspersions on him is but foolishness."

Period

By the end of August 2008, Geelani's misadventure had caused so much of misery and distress in the socio-economic life of the people that Shiekh Ghulam Hasan, the Jamaat-e-Islami Amir felt compelled to publically join issues with Geelani. He pointed out that the prolonged strike had paralysed the normal life in valley and hit its economy hard. Those dependent on daily earnings to keep body and soul together were at the verge of starvation. The closure of educational institutions had deprived students, the future of Kashmir avenues of study, upset their preparations for examinations and marred their future prospects. He asked the "leadership" to understand the broader dimensions of the prolonged strikes and 'Bandhs' and reminded that the struggle for Azadi was a long drawn out battle "whose result cannot be seen overnight." The frustration and anger against insensitivity towards the plight of common man by Geelani and his PAK mentors was so over powering that in protest the petty shopkeepers indulged in counter violence. The students of Gandherbal took out processions demanding opening of schools. Anti-agitation demonstration was held in Kokernag constituency represented by Congress education minister Peerzada Mohd Sayed. These were unmistakable signs of the fizzling out of the grand design. In fact the Geelani led fake "Intifada" never enjoyed popular sanction as made out by its mainstream fellow travellers and India baiting ultra liberals. On the ground, the students got busy catching with their studies, the rural folk got busy with agricultural operations and labour and shopkeepers were trying hard to get their life back on the rails and prepare for the gruelling demands of winter. Only politically captive and paid elements were available to do Geelani's bidding.

The loss of support had badly rattled the tin dictator. This was conclusively born-out by, Geelani's Oct. 29 call for intensifying the protest programmes. "Those who show any laxity or violate the protest programmes in these days" he said " will not only commit treason with the martyrs' blood but also do an irreparable damage to the collective cause of nation" and threatened that, "the pro-freedom young generation will not tolerate such traitors and they will be dragged to the people's court for adjudication." Undisputed leaders of "Intifada" command respect and willing obedience of the masses. Surely they do not have to use the language of threats and violence to those not heeding the call.

(1) The Bum Bum Bholey Upsurge

Generations to come will find it hard to comprehend how an innocuous decision of the Jammu and Kashmir government to "divert" (Not transfer, sell or lease) a mere chunk of 38.88 hectares of forest land for a period of about three months every year to provide temporary (read collapse- able) structures like shelters and toilets facilities could incite such high voltage passions amongst people of the two-main regions of the already bleeding state ?

Remember the 'diversion' of this land was spaced on two different routes-Baltal and 'Domail-for the yatra that brought lakhs of pilgrim tourists each year to the valley thereby injecting crores of rupees annually in to the otherwise impoverished economy. There could be little doubt that the history would judge harshly the guilty men, rulers or others for enacting this tragedy for their petty political and parochial interests. But that was in the realm of future. Speaking of the relevant period, what about the unbearable agony and perpetual mourning of those who lost their loved ones in the orgy of violence and hundreds others whom the trauma of mental and physical injuries would haunt for the rest of their lives? The loss to the economy and the public property had acquired astronomical proportions.

The bumbling and blundering Congress-PDP Coalition let things come to such a disastrous pass through culpable acts of omission and commission. The vertically divided State government and its clueless administration even failed to build upon the bonanza which accrued in form of the categorical and comprehensive order of the Division Bench of Jammu and Kashmir High Court identifying the specifics of the issue and effectively dealing with all implications of the diversion of the State land to Shri Amarnath Ji Shrine Board. This could and should have helped settle the issue to the satisfaction of all concerned once and for all. But it did not because the coalition partners were too busy playing blame games and conspiring against each other.

The world of electoral politics recognised no rules, rationale or principles. It was solely fuelled by ambitions of the politicians and perceived petty party vested interests. It should therefore have surprised no one when the perpetually feuding PDP-Congress coalition after having taken the unanimous decision to order diversion of 38.88 hectares of land to the Amamath Ji Shrine Board Yatra got into the confrontation mode on the very same issue. The childish acrobats in which the parties nonchalantly indulged would have been comic if it did not concern a public issue of a highly sensitive and explosive nature.

It occurred to no one that while the two parties were wasting their time and energies on a sterile shadow boxing, the over ground faces of secessionist terrorists were busy forging a strategy that would destabilise the State struggling to recover from the trauma of terrorism. In pursuit of their diabolical design the secessionists conspired to incite local passions on the concocted but highly emotive issue of threat to the demographic integrity of Muslims of Kashmir. The conspiracy theory would have then believe that Indian government planned to establish Hindu settlements on land diverted to Shri Amarnath Shrine Board by the J&K government on the Israeli model of Gaza Strip settlements with a view to alter the demographic character of Kashmir (Muslim population). Never mind, the land in question measured merely 38.88 hectares (about 100 Acres) spread over an area of around 42 kms in inhospitable environs and was to be made available to the Shrine Board only for the duration of the Yatra. The High Court directive stipulated and the State government order further required that the prefab structures mainly Shelters and Toilets be folded up after the termination of the yatra each year.

The Kashmiri Muslim mindset was vulnerable on the issue of any threat to their demographic supremacy. "Apprehensions" were also fuelled by some right wing Hindu zealots on the lunatic fringe who did at times project such a courses as the solution of the "Kashmir tangle." This almost always was part of their tirade against Jawahar Lal Nehru whom they accused of a pro-Muslim bias. That such a wild suggestion was always laughed away as crankiest and rejected out of hand was of no consequence to them.

The plot was superbly executed in the classical Gobelian style. Hundreds of emotionally charged and motivated storm trooper suddenly appeared on the streets of Srinagar shouting highly provocative slogans proclaiming danger to Islam and the identity of Kashmir Muslims. As was the wont, the bystanders and sympathisers joined on the way swelling the size of the crowd. The secessionists of all hues badly sidelined for last many years gleefully jumped on the band wagon. The National Conference and the PDP fiercely jostling for the anti-establishment space vacated by a shrinking and fractured Hurriyat wasted no time in making sympathetic noises. These were predictable developments. But the response of Ghulam Nabi Azad, the then Chief Minister who was in total command after the exit of PDP contingent of ministers was baffling. He had an unassailable and iron clad case and simple and convincing arguments which if submitted before the bar of the public opinion would have blasted the false and fragile foundation on which the mischievous propaganda blitz rested. Azad surprised both his admirers and detractors by omitting to do so confining his exertions to a feeble and tentative offer of an all party meeting, which was predictably promptly turned down. This lent both legitimacy and authenticity to the fake and fabricated allegation of "Indian evil designs to alter the demographic profile of Kashmir." Thus, if Gillani and Co committed the offence of igniting fires on both sides of the Pir Panchal, its handling by Azad exposed him to the accusation of abetting the crime through omission. The cancellation of the Land diversion order completed the surrender. The victory celebrations led by Ali Shah Gillani were well earned and well deserved. In the bargain the Indian state suffered loss of prestige and a severe setback in the ongoing process of weaning the common Kashmiri away from the terrorist stranglehold. Tragically, New Delhi and the Indian political elite in its wisdom or lack of it substantially facilitated the gains made by the secessionists in Jammu and Kashmir. Will someone in the South Bloc dare to calculate the cost of this disaster?

The short sighted and naïve political bosses manipulating the levers of power in New Delhi and their bureaucratic minions wasted no time to pat each others' back for successfully "defusing the crisis in Kashmir." It was height of naivety. They were soon to be jolted to face the harsh reality that they had too hastily yielded to the mere recitation of the script dictated from Islamabad. The real drama in Jammu and Kashmir was yet to unfold.

The central government and political leadership miserably failed to gauge the intensity of people's feelings in Jammu on an issue which touched the most sensitive chords of faith and rudely scratched equally raw wounds of discrimination of six long decades. Jammu reacted strongly to the assault on their faith. Winter capital towns and villages shut down, the volcano of protests erupted and the crowds began to pour into the streets across the length and breadth of Jammu region shouting religious slogans. The government led by the first ever Chief Minister from Jammu responded with raw force. Large number of protesters and policemen sustained injuries. Even fatal casualties occurred on account of police firing. Curfew orders were imposed. At this point of time, Azad and his ministers descend upon Jammu. Azad astounded every one by his clairvoyance and callousness which evidenced monumental lack of comprehension of the sensitivity of the issue and enormity of the collective outrage. No word of sympathy for the families who had lost their loved ones. None for the injured groaning with pain. In fact he rubbed the proverbial salt on the wounds making it appear that he had done something great in favour for the people of Jammu by cancelling the land allotment order for Shri Amarnath Ji Yatra. Carried away by his self generated euphoria he exhorted them to distribute 'Ladoos' and dance 'Bhangra' in celebration of the great event. This added insult to injury, sealed the fate of Azad as leader of Jammu and put a serious question mark on the future of Congress party in the region.

What started as a protest movement under the aegis of Shri Amarnath Ji Shangarsh Samiti, a combine of religious and social groups bloomed into a massive public upsurge. While the collective resentment against prolonged discrimination in all fields and frustration with the political leadership, were no doubt vital elements that facilitated the movement, the sole focus remained on the demand for restoration of the 38.88 hectares of land in Domel and Baltal sectors to the Shri Amarnath Ji Shrine Board for providing facilities for the yatra. The cancellation of the order was universally perceived as an assault on their faith.' AASTHA PAR AKRAMAN'. This made it imperative to address the core issue of land use on the yatra routes on top priority. Other contentious issues no doubt important were consciously deferred for another day. The best way to resolve complex and complicated issues was to break them down into essentials and address the core first.

The tone and tenor of protests in Kashmir set by extremist separatists led by Ali Shah Geelani's men made Jammu reaction severely vulnerable to machinations of the local communalist elements. It was also pregnant with regional virus. The initial thoughtless and ham handed response of the government machinery further queered the pitch. Tempers were running high. The public mood was defiant and aggressive. The explosive situation demanded that voices advocating sanity, reason and harmony needed to be raised and raised loudly and consistently. As a first step, I broached the subject with some like-minded civil society notables. They agreed with the analysis but advised against any initiative as the reaction against any one, any one, it was emphasised was bound to be violent and unsparing. It made sense. But the stakes were too high. I decided to take the plunge. Immediately warnings began to be sounded. However, contacts with friends and well wishers amongst the agitation leadership and detailed discussion with them led to some softening of attitudes. Thanks to the local Take One TV channel this view began to be articulated during almost daily panel discussion. I argued that there was no reason or justification for either blaming Muslims or Kashmiris for the revocation of the land diversion order. In fact, people of Kashmir had dumped the mischief mongers and Jammu Muslims were sympathetic towards the objective of the movement. Violence in public protests was, in any case a weapon of losers, those denied majority public support. It was a crutch for the minority. More over, a violent public agitation was historically short lived and administratively easier to crush. It was heartening to note that as the days passed more and more opinion makers convincingly supported this projection. It must be said to the credit of the Sangharsh Samiti leadership that they did unequivocally declare the movement as non-political, non-communal, non-violent and certainly not anti-Kashmiri. And they strictly adhered to this commitment, whenever information of even the slightest communal tension was received, leaders of the Samiti along with minority representatives rushed the spot and sorted out the problem ensuring that peace and amity prevailed.

The unprecedented "Bum; Bum Bholey" agitation was massive by any standards. Women, children, and men, young and old belonging to all communities came out in an unending stream chanting Bhajans, dancing to the tune of "Bum Bum Bholey." It made history when one lakh and twenty thousand men, women of all ages including young mothers holding suckling infants offered arrest on one single day. There were neither adequate number of policemen available to arrest them nor space enough to accommodate the huge number. Jammu had woken after a long slumber. Be aware.

It was historically and authentically documented that the Yatra was going on for centuries. No one (including the fundamentalists like Ali Shah Gellani) could afford to be against the yatra. Umar Farooq and Mehbooba Mufti had taken the same position. Speaking in the Lok Sabha, Omar Abdullah went to the extent of asserting that "as long as a single Kashmiri Muslim is alive, the yatra will continue." That being so, necessary and adequate facilities had to be provided for the yatra which had in recent years come to attract lakhs of people every year. On this count also there was no disagreement. Obviously, such facilities could only be erected on the land falling on the Yatra routes. The only objection raised was regarding the agency that should provide these facilities and own the land? The first part of the objection was based on the "apprehension" that this land may be misused for settling "outsiders, thereby posing threat to the demographic profile of the valley."

Howsoever, ill conceived, misplaced and fanciful or mischievously implanted, these needed to be addressed. The directions of the Division Bench of J&K High Court dated 17/5/2005 took care of such apprehensions. The question of any one settling on the land, which was habitable only for less than four months in a year simply did not arise under arrangement which required security clearance from the state even in respect of those who wished to set up 'langars' (free kitchens for serving food to the yatris). It was a pity that a set up that would provide employment to fair number of locals, open up opportunities for small business for them and also arrange sheds for ponies, local pony wallahs, 'Pithus and Palkiwalas' should be presented as inimical to their interests. Contrary to the New Delhi's perception, the common Kashmiri was in no way "emotionally involved in the land row." In fact, there was no reason for his such involvement. The land, was already under use and he found no problem with it. His hackles were, however raised and emotions charged on the baseless and concocted projection through a well oiled propaganda machine that putting up of structures on the pretext of upgrading facilities for the yatra was, in fact the first step towards execution of India conspiracy to establish settlements of Hindu non-citizens of the state thereby changing the Muslim majority character of Kashmir. It took only a couple of days for the distortion, disinformation and falsehood to be exposed. The Kashmir civil society and the local stake holders including travel agents and tourist agencies fully understand the realty but were cowed down by the noisy and violent minority that straddled the Kashmir scene.

It was indeed a pity that while the common man in Kashmir had seen through the subversive designs of the secessionists, the truth should have continued to elude the mighty Government of India resulting in the policy fiasco and disoriented initiatives. In any case, the economic interests of the local stake holders were inextricably woven into any up gradation of yatra facilities. After prolonged dithering, mostly at the political level the good sense prevailed. The Negotiating Team headed by Governor's Advisor, Dr S.S. Bloeria engaged the Amar Nath Yatra Shangarsh

Samiti spearheading the agitation with realism and sensitivity. A mutually acceptable resolution was hammered out and the deal between the Dr. SS Bloeria, Advisor to the Governor and Advocate Lila Karan Sharma, Convenor Shri Amar Nath Yatra Shangarsh Samiti signed and sealed on the mid night of 31st August, 2008. This helped restore peace and normalcy in Jammu.

(2) The Bogey of Economic Blockade

Realising that the "Change in demography" gimmick had misfired, the secessionists and their Pak ISI masters coined the "Economic blockade" scare. It was shouted from the house tops that the "Hindu communalists" of Jammu were resorting to "economic blockade" with a view to starve the Muslims of Kashmir. They would continue to choke the National Highway, the economic life line, making the life of Kashmiris hell, it was vociferously propagated.

It was inconceivable that Ali Shah Geelani and Co were not conversant with the difference between the 'Road Blockade' and the Economic Blockade. Road Blocks were almost routinely resorted to by the population residing close to the Highways to protest mundane problems like electric load shedding, erratic supply of drinking water, paucity of irrigation water or even to obtain release of person allegedly illegally detained by the Police. Such obstructions of road traffic temporarily disrupted movement vehicles including those loaded with essential supplies. But these disruptions of the supply line were by nature brief and erratic productive of scarcity and inconvenience which the community could absorb. Economic Blockade, on the other hand aimed at total and prolonged stoppage of supplies to and from the target area through deployment of large number of committed and motivated cadres at various points over a sufficiently long time.

Obviously, the response of the administration in such eventuality would be stern and swift including use of force which could result in casualties, including fatalities. For embarking on such extreme course the leaders of the movement had not only to assess their own capability but also mobilise sufficient number of volunteers willing to join battle and be prepared for grave consequences. There was and is no evidence to suggest much less to establish that the Shri Amar Nath Sangharsh Samiti had ever contemplated any such move. The Samiti leading the agitation had categorically and forcefully contradicted the allegation of enforcing the Economic Blockade against Kashmir. Stray off the cuff remarks by an odd politician or two and irresponsible utterances of some non-entities on such a serious matter were to be ignored with the contempt that they deserved. The government claimed that at the most "difficult" time, the valley had food and petroleum stocks for two months. Against this in Jammu, for at least three days no petrol could be obtained due to curfew restrictions and for some days motorists had to stand in long queues as only two Petrol pumps were authorised to sell petrol. Rations disappeared from the Depots. Milkmen were unable to make deliveries. Vegetables and mutton were similarly unavailable. This was not to trivialise the inconveniences faced by the people of Kashmir on account of disruption of supplies but only to stress that people on both sides of the Pir Panchal had to face similar hardships due to obstruction of traffic. Srinagar population would, perhaps suffered in a greater measure due to its location 300kms farther away from Jammu.

Kashmir administration was slow and sluggish in responding to the brief "obstruction of traffic" on the National Highway and its predictable consequences. This kind of dereliction was unacceptable under any dispensation, not to speak of Governor's Rule which was expected to be model of what the public services could do free from the constraints traditionally placed by interested and self-seeking amongst the political masters. This lapse on their part merited notice of the Governor especially when the Secessionist leadership, already on political rampage could be relied upon to overplay the scarcity card and fully exploit peoples' anxiety on this account. Let us take the case of medicines which constituted the core concern in Kashmir. It was only on 17th August that the committee appointed by the Divisional Commissioner, Kashmir inspected various Drug sales establishments in Srinagar city and came up with the findings that "80 per cent of drugs were available while the other twenty per cent were available in substitute brands in the market." This inspection should have been conducted on the very next day of the disruption of traffic so that any deficiency could be made good even if the consignments had to be flown. The Commissioner Secretary Health was similarly late in reviewing the availability of drugs which he did on 18th August. In such like times of distress the Public Servants should have been proactive and seen to be making things move and fully harvest opportunities to earn people's good will through timely, transparent and efficient intervention. This was a case of low investment and high profit. The state administration, sadly appeared to have forgotten this basic tenant of good and responsive governance. Assuming for arguments' sake there indeed was an Economic blockade of Kashmir, whose responsibility it was to ensure supplies any way? Samiti or the government? By making the alleged Economic blockade a Jammu versus Kashmir issue, were the agitators not barking the wrong tree. Ironically, the March to Muzaffarabad was undertaken three days after the government had ensured smooth flow of traffic that ferried supplies for Kashmir.

(3) "Muzaffarabad Chalo"

The popular resentment in Kashmir on account of dwindling supply of essential commodities due to ongoing agitations on both sides of the Jawahar Tunnel and inept and inefficient handling of the situation by the bureaucracy offered a tempting opportunity to secessionist leadership to press the political demand for "opening up" the Jehlum valley road to Muzaffarabad for unrestricted movement. Such like difficulties which were "common" during winters, it was ague could be overcome if Jhelum Valley Road was opened to traffic connecting Srinagar with Muzaffarabad (POK). This would enable perishable commodities like apples and other fruits to be transported quickly and in time to Muzaffarabad and beyond for timely marketing. Similarly, the necessities of life could then be quickly and regularly obtained there from. Given the surcharged political climate and supply deficit the move prima facie appeared to be politically deft and strategically sound. To the common man, it prima facie made sense. The resumption of cross-border movement of people and goods for the limited purposes of uniting divided families and permitting trade under prescribed conditions with effect from 17th April, 2005 appeared to have further vetted the appetite.

Moreover, the Pak ISI smelled the opportunity to use the March as expression of solidarity with Pakistan at the cost to be born by the common man of Kashmir. According to usually reliable reports a Strategy Review session was held in ISI Hqs sometime in the January-February, 2008. It was decided to cast the over ground segment of the network in Kashmir in the pivotal role with the terrorists assigned the responsibility to provide back up so as to provide teeth to the street action. They were simultaneously to keep enacting terror strikes albeit of low cost variety. The 'sudden' almost maniacal outburst on the non-issue of Land use for the duration of the Yatra by the Shri Amar Nath Shrine Board followed by 'Muzaffarabad Chalo' march had to be viewed in that context. A conspiracy of circumstances gifted them some other issues but there was no doubt that one or other issue would have been found, an ordinary incident blown out of proportion or even fabricated to serve as "justification" for initiating street action.

Historically, the demand for opening "the Rawalpindi road" was as old as the Kashmir issue itself. The opening of the Jehlum Valley road was the begin with projected by the pro-Pak elements in Kashmir as the symbol of union with Pakistan. The Lion of Kashmir shot the demand down. The pro-Pak leadership was shipped over to Pakistan to enjoy the fruits of the 'Mumalkat-i-Khudadad'.

People were lured, motivated and incited into joining the self-destructive march complete with 'fruit loaded trucks'. The congregation that constituted the march was massive by any measure. Why did the administration allow the collection of such huge crowd for an avowed illegal purpose was, to say the least baffling. One did not have to be clairvoyant to foresee that a bloody confrontation between the administration and the highly charged, incited and motivated huge crowd 'determined' to cross into the POK, which obviously could not be permitted was inevitable. Nothing short of firing would dissuade and disperse the violent and huge crowd. There were bound to be casualties, some fatal. And this was exactly what happened. The huge procession was blocked at Chahlu, a place about 45 km short of the LOC, by police and CRPF. As the crowd turned violent and refused to heed warnings, the forces were compelled to resort to firing, in which a separatist, leader Sheikh Aziz and four other people were killed. About 100 policemen and CRPF personnel were also injured, four of them seriously. Two of the injured were later airlifted to Srinagar for treatment.

The organisers of the march were fully aware that they would never be allowed to reach its declared destination. The march was intended to be a show of strength, a publicity stunt for the benefit of their masters in Islamabad. It would also provide ammunition to ISI lobbyists like Ghulam Nabi Fai to fire at the US Think Tanks. The inevitable clash with Police/security forces and consequent loss of precious human lives was of no consequence to them. Thus, the organisers deliberately and wilfully gambled with the lives of innocent and gullible Kashmiris who had the misfortune of coming under their spell. The perpetrators of mischief from across had no stake whatsoever. But then, wasn't 'Jihad' all about sacrifices and martyrdom? And Pak ISI was determined to fight in Kashmir to the last Kashmiri Muslim.

To the utter dismay of organisers of the "March" the people in general and relatives of those killed in Police firing in particular were extremely angry and agitated.. They openly and squarely blamed Geelani and Co. for sending their men to what they knew was going to be "a slaughter." Predictably, his call to continue Muzaffarabad Challo" endorsed by Umar Farooq was ignored.

Governor Vohra took serious note of the "The Muzaffarabad Challo" fiasco. Some heads rolled, the policy frame was drastically re-cast and a well crafted professionally sound Standard Operating Procedure (SOP) put in place. This resulted in the administration snatching the initiative. After trying out some tentative agitation moves like "Lal Chowk Challo" which flopped, the separatist chose to back off and avoid confrontation with security forces.

It must be said to the credit of the Governor Vohras' administration that the policy fiasco was checked in time following bold, honest, objective and realistic introspection followed by specific and transparent corrective measures. The new innovative policy focussed on pro-active preventive action from a position of strength retaining initiative and handling of any challenge to state authority with firmness. A loud and clear massage that "enough was enough." produced welcome results. The entire law and order scenario in Kashmir underwent a radical change.

As the administration began to reassert its authority and got down to discharging its governance, economic and public welfare responsibilities the situation gradually moved towards normalcy. However, there was a broad consensus that restoration of complete normalcy and creation of conditions necessary for holding free, fair and credible elections enabling maximum possible peoples participation would take time. This appeared to have prompted the Governor to constitute Jammu and Kashmir State Advisory Council to make his government participatory in nature. The thirty four member council comprised of representative of political parties, educationalists, eminent Civil Society opinion makers, social activists, religious leaders and representatives of trade and commerce organisations. I was also take on board as a member. The Election Commission, however had their own perception and plans.

PART—4

National Conference-Congress Coalition at the Helm

Verdict-2008

The suspense regarding holding of elections was broken in somewhat dramatic manner. The State Advisory Council was in session in Raj Bhavan, Srinagar with Governor Vohra in the Chair. As expected political leaders were at their best delivering lengthy sermons pushing their party agenda. There was somewhat disproportionate emphasis on long-term measures as if like the State assembly, the council had also a life of six years. In between the proceedings a senior Raj Bhavan functionary entered the conference hall, went straight up to the Governor and whispered in his ears. The Governor promptly excused himself and departed. He returned after few minutes, took the chair and speech making continued. Soon, it was lunch break during which it became known that the Election Commission had decided to conduct elections to the State assembly. The formal announcement to hold elections to Jammu and Kashmir assembly in seven phases between November. 17 and December 24 (both dates included) was made by the chief election commissioneri. N. Gopalaswami in New Delhi on October 19, 2008.

For the Election Commission it was veritably a toss up. The arguments for and against holding of Elections 2008 at that point of time were evenly balanced. Only when the National Conference veered around to support the commencement of the electoral process without delay that the Election Commission of India decided to take the plunge.

The sceptics were scandalised. The prophets of doom forecast a disaster—the lowest voter turn out ever. The security and political environment, it was argued was completely hostile to any such 'misadventure." Some so called Kashmir experts recklessly cited the secessionists contrived June 2008 demonstrations in Srinagar against the allocation of land for Amarnath Yatra as the "Kashmir version of Intfada" and rubbished the very idea of elections as suicidal. Some equated the secessionist acrobats "with the Azadi upsurge of early nineties." Others went to the extent of making an absurd and sacrilegious comparison with the agitation against the theft of "Moai-Muqadas" from the Hazratbal Shrine in 1964 forgetting that the sea of humanity that spontaneously burst out into the streets of the entire valley of Kashmir was powered by faith and driven by religious fervour. The million dollar question was, will people of the Kashmir valley participate in elections under the given circumstances? No way, the doubting toms asserted. Not to be left behind, the self serving intellectuals and media dons imprisoned in their cocoons of make believe who had earlier successfully pressurised the establishment into taking a U-turn on the Amar Nath Yatra Land Use order were also up in arms making all kinds of dark predictions. But the Election Commission was not impressed. It did make bold to go ahead with the declared election schedule. Not only the people of Jammu and Kashmir but that of the country indeed the world awaited with baited breath the effect of this crucial determination–the level of response from the masses. Will they or will they not? This was the billion dollar question.

The subsequent developments proved the commission right. The parties quickly slipped into the election mode, frantically worked out their vision documents/manifestoes and quickly set their electoral machine in motion in top gear. The season of rallies followed confounding the anti-election lobby unable to figure out what hit them. The voters in this sensitive and most vulnerable state of the Union of India had come of age.

The voters were, as usual bombarded with pleas in the name of religion, caste, sub-caste, tribe and creed. Money and muscle power were mobilised without due regard for the prescribed norms **"Kayunkay is hamam mein sab hi nangay hain"**, no one was making an issue of it. In the ensuing noise, hustle and pressures, the voters were called upon to decide not only the fate of the candidates and the contesting political parties but also their own fate for the next six years. Obviously, the capability and reputation of a candidate, judgement of competence and credibility of the party to fulfil their electoral pledges and serve their common interests of the people hugely influenced the voter response.

Come polling day, the people of J&K in general and those of the Kashmir valley in particular delivered a land mark judgement in favour of democracy and good governance. Through massive participation in the election and an open and unambiguous affirmation of their faith in the democratic process they proved all doubting toms and prophets of doom wrong. 1,354 candidates stood for election including 517 independents and nominees from 43 political parties for just 87 seats in the Legislative Assembly. The voting percentage rose from by 43.70 per cent in 2002 to 60.5 per cent in 2008 recording a whopping 17 per cent increase. This indeed was "*a triumph of Indian democracy.*" The people of Jammu and Kashmir rubbished all predictions and calculations, bravely defying the terrorist threats and the much trotted boycott call by the secessionists leaving their Pakistan masters red faced. A peoples' agenda for peace and economic development aimed at securing for masses a better quality of life was loudly and categorically proclaimed by voter after voter, men and women alike across the vast and varied landscape of the state. After more than six decades of freedom democracy had finally arrived in the state unmindful of two decades of terrorist blood bath.

The people of the state in general and those from the valley and the terrorist infested areas of Jammu in particular were the real heroes of this revolution. The credit for creating a favourable security environment facilitating free exercise of franchise by the voters was also richly deserved by the Governor's administration, the J&K Police and other security forces. The master strategy of securing the constituencies going to polls from meddling and pressurising by outsiders ensured that no individual or party could resort to intimidation, cajoling or coercion of those wanting to participate in the electoral process. Thus a clear and rational distinction was made between voters' right to exercise or not to exercise his franchise and the licence to force a particular point of view on voters inclined otherwise.

The voters in their wisdom returned a fractured verdict favouring different parties as shown below.

Sl. No.	*Party*	*Seats*	*Seats*
	won	*Changed*	
1.	Jammu and Kashmir National Conference	28	1
2.	Indian National Congress	17	- 3
3.	Peoples Democratic Party	21	+ 5
4.	Bharatiya Janata Party	11	+ 10
5.	Independents	4	- 9
6.	J & K National Panthers Party	3	- 1

(*Contd....*)

7.	CPI (Marxist)	1	- 1
8.	J & K Democratic Party Nationalist	1	+ 1
9.	People's Democratic Front	1	+ 1
	Total	**87**	

The gains of seats by the PDP was attributed to the "backing" by Separatists. The credit for increase in number of seats gained by BJP was given to its candidates enjoying sizeable public support to which their dedicated participation in "Bum Bum Bholey" upsurge further enhanced their chances. However, the argument that BJP improved performance because of "polarisation arising from the Amarnath land transfer controversy" was way off the mark. In fact, BJP candidates were humbled in constituencies like Kathua, Samba, Gandhinagar, (Jammu), Udhampur, Nowshera, Ramnagar which witnessed tremendous impact of the "Bum Bum Bholey" agitation. In fact, the faction ridden Congress party facilitated the BJP electoral gains through fielding weak and unpopular candidates in most constituencies, selection being influenced by extraneous considerations.

The party position thrown up by Election-2008 made a coalition arrangement inevitable. And the circumstances in which the Congress and PDP had parted ways in 2008 completely ruled out any possibility of a coalition between the two. The Abdullah and the Gandhi families, on the other hand had come to revive their traditional cosy relationship fortified by friendship between the gen next- Omar and Rahul. A NC-Congress coalition government therefore emerged as the natural choice.

National Conference went to polls under the leadership of Dr Farooq Abdullah who was projected as the Chief Ministerial candidate. In fact two days before the Congress-NC coalition under the chief ministership of Omar Abdullah was announced, Farooq had reiterated that he would head the NC-Congress coalition. It was widely believed that 10 Janpath had strongly batted for Omar Abdullah. Dr Farooq was accommodated in the Union cabinet. A NC-Congress government was sworn in by Governor N.N.Vohra on 9th January, 2009.

Congress President, Sonia Gandhi sensibly blessed the classical model of parliamentary democracy by deciding that the chief minister of the majority party will lead the coalition for the full term of six years. The stipulation, however was that there would be an "annual review" of the performance of the coalition. A Coordination Committee under the chairmanship of Jammu and Kashmir Pradesh Congress President Saif-ud-din Soz was constituted to sort out any problem or issues on which there was divergence of opinion between the partners. Of course 10 Janpath would be watching all the time and intervene where necessary. No need was felt for having a formal Common Minimum Programme.

(1) Expectations

(2)

With Young Omar Abdullah taking over the reins of government in the troubled border state the expectations ran high. Voters who staked their lives, defied terrorist Diktat of boycott of elections and massively exercised their franchise watched keenly for speedy and substantive initiatives to take care of their basic need of PANNI, SARAK, BIJLI *et al.* They wished to see some definite and visible initiatives by the coalition government towards accelerated development and improvement of the quality of their lives. The government had to be focused on the vital and fundamental issue of good, responsible, responsive and transparent governance without wasting any time on symbolism and frivolities.

The first and the foremost duty of the democratically elected government was to get down to the serious business of governance. The new political executive was expected to pursue a definite chartered course discarding the 'chaotic' management it inherited. The transition had to be deliberate, sincere, principled, determined and totally transparent.

The chief minister, it should be recognised was personally accountable for the performance–good, bad or indifferent—of his government. The dedication and seriousness that informed his motivation and conduct of affairs of the state-political and administrative must therefore permeate the thinking and functioning of all members of the council of ministers, the top leadership of the coalition and the bureaucracy. People were not going to be satisfied by symbolic showmanship. They demanded that the serious business of governance be conducted through norms rooted in fair play efficiency, integrity and impartiality promoting people's participation and producing visible positive results.

For the public servants to give their best it was imperative that they were trusted and treated with decency and consideration, the deviants being taken to task under due process of law and rules. Speedy and stern punishment following quick and fair regular departmental inquiries on specific charges would obviously be a better option. More over you cannot get the best out of an official/officer through arms twisting and harassment. Only the conviction that excellence and free expression of opinion and tendering of advice shall receive recognition and reward while failure to deliver shall earn reprimand and punishment would motivate public servants to contribute their best. A strict adherence to this policy was imperative to revive the positive work culture and ethos of efficiency, integrity and professionalism in the services which had evaporated over the decades. At the same time there should be absolute clarity about the criteria according to which administrative decisions and actions would be judged. In this context the views of John A Veig, an international authority on administration may bear repetition. "It (the administration) was", he wrote " the systematic ordering of affairs and the calculated use of resources aimed at making those things happen which we want to happen and simultaneously preventing developments that fail to square with our intentions. It is the marshalling of resources in order to gain that what is desired at the lowest cost in energy, time and money." The plans, actions and priorities of the NC-Congress government had to square with these criteria.

NC-Congress government was on test. At the least it was expected to:

1. Have learnt lessons from the disastrous functioning of the predecessor coalition and strictly conform to the letter and spirit of Cabinet system based on the principle of joint responsibility.
2. To function as a harmonious team focused on ushering in an era of peace, justice and development without regional discrimination?
3. To strive diligently, persistently and determinedly to rein in the "galloping corruption."
4. Above all to deliver on the promises of good, responsive, responsible and transparent governance.

The people of the state nay the entire nation keenly watched the performance of the coalition in this sensitive border state.

(3) Handicaps

Celebrations and felicitations on the stitching together of the coalition government, however could not mask the unease within an influential segment of the National Conference at the sudden unexpected turn of events that placed young Omar in the driving seat. The senior leaders of the party found it difficult to come to terms with the reality and make the required adjustments. The decision of Dr Farroq Abdullah, the party president and a Union Minister to set up office with a Political Advisor in the toe signalled his desire to keep track of "mundane developments" in the state far beyond contacts with Omar Abdullah, the chief minister and the Acting President of the National Conference at one to one level. Reports also suggested that senior ministers in Omar Abdullah cabinet consulted and took direction from Dr Farooq over the head of the chief minister and that the activities of National Conference Presidents' Political Advisor did indeed encroach into the administrative domain. The situation, to put it mildly was confusing and far from conducive to harmonious and efficient functioning of the state government. Wasn't Confusion universally recognised as the mother of mis-governance, administrative waywardness and breeding ground for corruption?

The chief minister had the option of reaching out to his cabinet colleagues, treat them with due deference, take them into confidence without compromising the pre-eminent position of the institution of the chief minister. Of course, some hassles were possible in the initial stage but tact, firmness and persistence would have ultimately settled equations, improved personnel rapport, established spirit of confidence and mutual understanding–which was good for the health of cabinet system.

Chief minister Omar Abdullah, however decided upon a course of non-interference and let individual cabinet ministers conduct their business according to their own lights. The impression given was that the CM had no problem with non-consultation even in important matters pertaining to their departments. He also did not insist upon being kept in the loop. Consequently the NC-Congress coalition became a cluster of fiefdoms at the best loosely and tenuously connected. This placed the permanent civil services particularly the higher bureaucracy in a dicey and somewhat embarrassing position. Senior bureaucrats who found certain decisions taken by individual ministers contrary to the declared policy and cabinet decisions or not in conformity with rules and regulation did not dare to inform the chief minister or even the chief secretary for fear of annoying the powerful minister concerned.

The chief minister decided to "strengthen" his office by inducting two Advisors with the rank and status of Ministers of State. Both belonged to his generation, were close friends and confidants. They were efficient go –getters and totally loyal to the person of chief minister Omar Abdullah. A third one was added some time later. Opinions were strongly divided as to advantages and efficacy of this arrangement. It was argued that Advisors acted as eyes and ears of the chief minister, provided the much needed linkage with the bureaucracy and extended his reach to the common man and ground realities. The others saw the set up as a barrier that barred direct access to the chief minister thereby furthering his isolation. He was also denied the advantage of one to one interaction with political workers, public servants and eminent members of the civil society which adversely impacting his capability to make fair, appropriate and well informed decisions. In any case the set up was recalled, two of the Advisors, Devinder Rana and Nissar Ahmed Wani were appointed Presidents of Provincial National Conference committees of Jammu and Kashmir. The third Advisor Mubarak Gul landed the prestigious job of Speaker of the Legislative Assembly.

The Congress party, on the other hand was riddled with factionalism endemic to the grand old party and the main cause of its undoing. The faction patrons -Ghulam Nabi Azad, the then Union Health Minister and Saif-ud-din Soz, the PCC president were located in Delhi. As the source of the "mischief", its direction and control were in the national capital, any corrective at local level was out of question.

The Congress intra-party confrontation, which the party national leadership omitted to address resulted in total lack of mutual consultation/ coordination. Individual ministers ran their "empires" independently. There were occasions when driven by their personal agendas or ego hassles they worked at cross purposes and clashed both inside and outside the cabinet.

The in-fighting amongst the Congress ministers caused grievous neglect of the multifarious problems and hardships faced by people of Jammu region and indeed promoted perpetuation of regional discrimination in the main constituency of the party. The failure of Jammu Congress ministers to stand united for the interests of people of Jammu region and espouse their cause forcefully and convincingly did violence to the regional interests. The adverse impact on this kind of political naivety and resultant administrative waywardness of the overall governance of the state needed no elucidation.

The coalition partners, however managed to avoid any major public controversy. Even those unhappy at the National Conference senior ministers abrogating to themselves the right to speak for the government in their own vein chose to mind their own business. The chief minister made "off the cuff" political statements and articulated state policies on "Twitter." It appeared to be free for all.

(4) Journey Towards Normalcy

The huge Voter turnout in Election-2008 evidenced peoples rejection of violence and confrontation and intense desire and thirst for peace, development and good governance. By rejecting the terrorist/separatist call for boycott of election they signalled their preference for an early and orderly transition to normalcy. The decimation of terrorist command structure and blocking of cross-border infiltration by the Security forces immensely helped in this significant change in the public mindset. The people had unambiguously proclaimed their abhorrence for violence and conflict. It was now up to the state and central governments to create conditions favourable for the promotion and sustenance of the environment of normalcy.

Assumption of its mandated functions of maintenance of law and order by the Jammu and Kashmir Police relieving the central security forces of this responsibility and making Police stations completely, efficiently and effectively functional was fundamental to herald the return of normalcy. It may, however be empathised that the central Paramilitary forces would still be required in backup role and be strategically positioned for that purpose.

The question of reallocating the central security forces and remanding the responsibility of maintainance of law and order back to Jammu and Kashmir Police was hotly debated in the context of perceived return to normalcy in the valley. The secessionists and other opposition formulations were using the issue as a political weapon to accomplish their own unhidden agenda. For the central and the state governments, on the other hand it was a matter of politico-strategic determination.

The terrorist groups like Lashkar-e-Tyeba, Jaish-e-Mohammad, Hizabul Mujahiden, though decimated were still active and retained the capability to strike at will. The spate of encounters and the broad day light point blank shooting of a police constable and his CRPF equivalent illustrated the point tellingly. The terrorist training infrastructure across the borders in POK and Pakistan was functional training and equipping terrorists to be infiltrated into Jammu and Kashmir. In fact, hundreds of trained and armed terrorists were holed up in 'Launching Pads' across LOC waiting to infiltrate. The over ground faces of terror were visible and active.

The claim of HM chief Mohd Yusuf alias Syed Sallah-ud-din' in a tele conversation with a local paper (summer of 2009) that the wide spacing of attacks by his outfit was "tactical" represented only partial truth. Actually peoples' support for the so called 'Jihad' had drastically declined and local recruitment sources dried up. The tight vigil on the borders had made reinforcement from across the LOC very difficult and costly. Moreover, the world public opinion was unanimous in condemning terrorism anywhere and in any form. There were no takers for the claim that the ongoing terrorism in Jammu and Kashmir was 'a struggle for freedom'.

Finding the position becoming untenable, the strategists in Islamabad had taken the crucial decision sometime in the first quarter of 2008 to integrate the terrorist operations with the "over ground segment" and mount a huge push for street action. Even a casual glance at the happenings since then would establish the desperation and determination with which the valley had been kept on the boil on one pretext or the other. All the hysterical outpourings and breast beating on the issues of "demilitarisation" and revocation of the AFSPA needed to be viewed in this context.

A mixture of JEI cades, mercenaries and lumeons was marshalled and charged to rush to the streets to incite emotions on false, fabricated and exaggerated allegations. A sensation hungry section of the media was ever ready to do the honours. So were the so-called liberal bleeding hearts.

The main objectives of all these exertions may be listed as follows:

(a) To provide breathing space for the terrorists so that they may, regroup, reinforce, consolidate and enhance strike capability.

(b) To put pressure on the government of India through over ground collaborators and vulnerable political parties/ groups to thin out if not withdraw, or at the least relocate troops away from the urban and sub-urban strategic locations.

(c) To mount and enhance political pressure and escalate street action for de-militarisation, revocation of the AFSP or at least making it toothless.

(d) To brow beat the peace loving majority into silence.

Given the security environment and the nature of the proxy war, the central security forces and the State police had to supplement each other in the war against the common enemy. The military prowess had to be reinforced by an efficiently operating police network positively connected with the people and capable of providing critical strategic and intelligence inputs. Only such a combination would pave the way for ultimate victory.

It was indeed tragic that the glorious record of loyalty and steadfast devotion to duty of Jammu and Kashmir Police should be sullied by a panicked Governor and an imported chief of the state police in early days of militancy. Their atrocious and irrational decision to equate the entire police with a tiny lunatic fringe of Srinagar Police which for reasons not far to see want only and recklessly openly displayed indiscipline was a unmitigated disaster. Even worst was to practically confine the entire Force operating in Kashmir on that account in their barracks branding them as "untrustworthy." The Paramilitary forces thus wily nily came to assume the total responsibility of maintenance of law and order injecting predictable but avoidable complications in an inherently complex situation. It was an answer to the prayers of the promoters of the proxy war especially the "Dirty tricks" department of the Pak ISI who merrily conducted the psychological warfare targeting a highly vulnerable population almost unhindered. The ISI indeed did pretty well on this sensitive front.

The process of retrieval of J&K Police began after a J&K cadre officer took over as the chief of state Police during Gen. Krishna Rao's tenure as the Governor. It was a welcome and somewhat overdue step. Not unexpectedly, the hurt and humiliation of suspect loyalty led to somewhat disproportionate focus on anti-terrorist operations to the neglect of the equally important basic police work which would have earned public confidence and acclaim and proved more remunerative. The STF/SOG became the star performers. The J&K Police, however did regain its stature as a anti-terrorist fighting force though at a heavy cost.

A consensus on the identification of district or districts considered acceptably free from secessionist terrorism and manageable by local authorities was a pre-requisite to any movement on the resumption of responsibilities by local authorities especially the Jammu and Kashmir Police. This done, measures necessary for drafting, training, motivating and equipping the police force to successfully handle an unprecedented and unfamiliar situation generated by nearly two decades of bloodshed shall have to be carefully and proficiently crafted. The obvious objective should be to deploy only selected, professionally competent, result-oriented and people friendly officers and men for the pilot project.

The new era in policing in the state on resuming the total responsibility for maintenance of law and order must most importantly take cognizance of the element of "brutalisation" that was bound to have crept in after prolonged battling with terrorist gangs who recognised no rules or convention of war.

The current enemy strategy of employing the armed terrorist gangs and their over ground supporters and collaborators in an integrated and coordinated game plan should inform the counter-measures. The armed forces should continue to engage major terrorist gangs with the assistance of police while crowd control and other unlawful activity by unarmed agitators became exclusive responsibility of the police. The police shall have to be trained and motivated to handle with extreme care and caution the stage managed situations in which terrorists used unsuspecting civilians as human shield.

The conflict situation also spawned some measure of permissiveness during operations. Appropriate correctives were required to be put in place most urgently, highest priority be accorded to the change of the mindset of the officers and men. The insistence on compliance with the rules, standing orders and prescribed procedure for use of firearms and 'Tear Gas' on unarmed though violent mobs must be absolute and deviants taken to task. Obviously, well designed refresher training courses in use of tear smoke, a "Squad weapon" required to be used only under orders and prescribed condition was a pre-requisite.

Some of the other critical areas demanding attention and revamping may be identified as fallows:

Manpower Reorientation

The quality of human resource, level of professionalism, standard of training/equipment and the conviction that they were defending a righteousness cause were fundamental to win the war against terrorism. Unfortunately, the most important amongst these–the conviction about the righteousness of the cause—either received nil or little attention. Many Police officers with outdated ideas and jaundiced view of dividing line between political practices end national duty still cling to the colonial perception that the less the policeman knows about the issues involved and their implication the better.

This reduced the man in uniform to the demeaning status of a mercenary robbing him of his dignity and the energising and motivating power of national duty to which he was sworn in. This must change and change quickly. There was an urgent need to put the entire district police force under the scanner so the only the very best of the officers and men were selected for duty for the first district to become the complete responsibility of Jammu and Kashmir Police. It was, therefore, imperative for the police Hqrs to constituted a high powered committee for the purpose armed with standard profile of various ranks. The J&K Police must put its best foot forward.

Revival and Toning up of the System

The policing network rooted in the Beat system provided the most comprehensive and intimate point of contact and source of information and influence. This had by and large fallen into disuse and should be revived on top most priority. The network of Police stations and Posts must become efficiently and responsively functional to provide maximum citizen satisfaction. The groundswell of goodwill so secured would decidedly prove an invaluable asset in dealing with law and order situations and investigation of crimes.

The records of the police stations, if properly maintained were the treasure of information and knowledge about the population, crimes/criminals and social assets. These should be reviewed and updated. Similarly, history sheets should be brought up-to-date by including local recruits to terrorism, their supporters and sympathisers in the category of history sheeters. This would enable surveillance of what in police parlance were called "Bad characters" and take preventive and other action in fit cases.

To ensure that Police Station records were indeed properly maintained a committee comprising of an Gazetted officer, two NGOs and two lower subordinates experienced and well versed in the maintaining Police records may be appointed to visit every police station and post in the district to certify that all records as prescribed by the Police Rules/Standing orders were maintained correctly and brought update. All deficiencies and inaccuracies should be corrected on the spot and the PS staff counselled appropriately.

Arms and Equipment

The weapons issued to the Police Station should match those of the terrorists. The protective equipment and Night Vision gear should be of the best available quality. This would inculcate the feel of power and boost confidence. The stock of Tear Gas Shells etc should be examined and outdated material discarded. Communications setup should be dedicated, multi-channel and secure.

The citizens must be guaranteed unrestricted round the clock access to the Police Stations and posts. Complains/ problems should receive immediate, effective and sympathetic response. Experience has shown that such positive interventions produced immense confidence and good- will.

Training

Pre-deployment Reorientation Capsule courses should be organised for all ranks posted in the district. Apart from professional elements, the curriculum must lay great and enlightened stress on the service content, sympathetic and decent behaviour with citizen especially women. The citizens must find police persons not only willing but keen to help and come to their rescue where necessary. Both the language and the body language must conform to the best standards of decency. The course should be supplemented by interactive workshops on specific subjects in which all ranks at the cutting edge level should be involved.

Rule of Law

It is axiomatic that to enforce law with any degree of efficacy the police must themselves meticulously observe law in both letter and spirit. Legal authority unless backed by moral authority not only proved ineffective but degenerated to the extent of being hated and perceived as oppressive. This comprehension must underscore the thinking and practices in police working if the organisation was to outlive the century plus stigma of an instrument of oppression and exploitation of the despotic rulers and their minions.

There must be conviction that the laws, 'ordinary laws' if diligently, honesty, and impartially enforced with professional competence would earn the confidence and goodwill of the citizenry and help create a socio-cultural environment that negated inroads by negative forces including terrorism. The use of special powers even in a terrorist situation must be an exception rather than the rule and justified by strict standards.

Legal action, stringent or otherwise must precede, accompany and follow any disturbance of law and order. It should always be remembered that while merged in the collective personality of a crowd each individual felt invincible. As individuals, each one was extremely vulnerable. Preventive arrests, arrests during disturbances and follow up legal action even for mere violation of Sec. 144 of the CRPC, if speedily pursued in the court had tremendous deterrent effect. The mere knowledge that the riot scenes were being video-graphed thereby establishing the identity of the participants put individuals on the defensive even under those surcharged conditions. In this context I recall the incident of day long ding dong battle in Lal Chowk Anantnag on 26th January 1964. I was determined not to use fire arms to disperse the crowd and the mob reformed after every Lathi charge. The sun was about to set and the men were showing signs of fatigue and frustration which was bad. Suddenly an idea struck me. We had a constable nick named 'Toofani'. I called him and asked if he recognised any one amongst the crowd. On his replying in affirmative I whispered in his ears. Instantly he took up the microphone and shouted in Kashmiri "Hey Gulla, I have recognised you and by God I am going to fix you wait and see." Saying this, he along with the police party rushed in his direction. Gulla ran and so did the crowd not to reassemble.

Most often than not advantages like social stigma, bothersome and costly consequences of prosecutions requiring engagement of lawyers, finding witnesses and ensuring their presence in the court date after date were not recognised. Then, there was the stigma of 'conviction', the consequential denial of job opportunity under the government and access to government contracts etc to content with. In short, judicious and intelligent use of legal provisions, backed by credible, timely and actionable intelligence can and will turn tables on the terrorist who would find it hard to recruit youngsters and find over ground collaborators. Obviously, these suggestions were illustrative and not exhaustive.

It may sound somewhat strange, particularly to the uninitiated that the most efficacious remedy for the plague of terrorism lay in good policing. There was indeed consensus amongst the scholars and practitioners of counter-terrorism on the issue. "Counter-terrorism" already high in the list of priority of subjects taught in the Armed forces Staff colleges all over the world received greater emphasis after 9/11 especially in the United States and Europe. The philosophy, history, practices and experiences of Pan Islamic Fundamentalist terrorism were since intensely and exhaustively discussed in seminars, workshops and numerous interactions of military and police top brass with "Think Tanks" and eminent scholars and experts. "The best way to counter-terrorism is by police work" intelligence gathering and defensive security measures" emerged as the gist of all these exercise and endeavours. This was also corroborated by the strategies determined by the leading practitioners of guerrilla warfare and international terrorism and numerous memoirs, manuals and manifestos.

The J&K Police was poised to tread the historically certified 'best way' to win the war against terrorism. It must stay the chartered course with faith, determination and conviction that it was destined to be victorious.

The above analysis and a specific recommendations were placed in public domain through Print media and also communicated to the powers that be prior to 2010 Stone pelting era. The Rip Von Winkles were apparently not interested nor impressed. The real and fatal problem with the establishment mindset was their unwillingness to remain professionally, politically and administratively updated and inability for "out of the box thinking." The consequences were there for all to see.

(5) Armed Forces Special Powers Act

As the success achieved by our security forces in the war against terror and peoples urge for peace and development gained momentum danger bells rang in Islamabad. Consequently, the demand for demilitarisation grew louder and louder. AFSPA was in the centre of the thrust. This was one dimension. On the other hand lobbies in Kashmir argued that with situation turning normal the presence of army in what they called "peace zones" was an unnecessary "irritant for the public" and that there was no more justification for the Special Powers conferred on them to deal with situation that existed no more. Some called it a "draconian legislation" that must be repealed. Such demands had been raised in North Eastern states also from time to time.

Chief Minister' Omar Abdullah raised the issue in Chief Ministers Conference held in Delhi on August, 2009. He made a "good case" for reviewing the continuation of AFSPA particularly in areas wherein a distinct improvement in the security environment in Jammu and Kashmir was discernable. "Even though this is a highly emotive issue which has provoked extreme positions, a pragmatic view about the continuation of the AFSPA should be taken with a view to remove its applicability from areas where such activities were marginal or insignificant," he pleaded. This appeared to be a rational and reasonable position which merited consideration.

The controversy over AFPSA like the secessionist terrorism it sought to help quell had both external and internal dimensions. At the external level, Pakistan missed no opportunity to drum beat the "draconian nature" of the Act in each and every international forum and recklessly hurled wild allegations of "human rights violation by the Indian security forces in Jammu and Kashmir under the cover of powers conferred by the enactment. Such allegations were also used to buttress their primary demand for demilitarisation of Jammu and Kashmir forgetting their own perfectly illegitimate military presence in Galgit Baltistan and POK. Unfortunately, the horrendous Tehrik-Taliban Pakistan assault on the Army Public School, Peshawaer had to happen in which more than 150 school children and teachers were massacred to bring home to the Pakistan establishment of the indispensability of a strong special law to deal with terrorism. Confronted with the TTP challenge it went to the extreme by setting up Military courts to try the terrorists. Similarly, the abrogation of the Armed Forces (Jammu And Kashmir) Special Powers Act, 1990 (AFSPA) was high on the list of priorities of the secessionists. The Kashmir centric mainstream parties also found it politically expedient to join the chorus for repeal of the Act. In fact, the twists and turns of Kashmir politics promoted a mad race between the main stream parties to run an extra mile in support of the separatists demand in their questionable quest for separatist space. Consequently, sizeable support for the demand built up amongst a section of people in Kashmir. Whether the motivation was prompted by the Pak ISI machination, unpleasant experiences of some people, perceived or occasional misuse of powers by security forces under the Act was immaterial. Protest demonstrations, media criticism and presentations in seminars and conferences testified to this reality. It would be unrealistic and unwise to completely ignore such sentiments and demand based hereupon.

Was AFSPA a draconian legislation deserving immediate repeal or was it indispensible for combating the proxy war launched by Pakistan and patronised by Pan Islamic fundamentalist machine of terror? Only a well informed debate could help resolve the issue in a sensible manner. Interestingly, most of those taking to streets or indulging in acrimonious denunciation were not even conversant with the provisions of the Act.

Section 3 of the Act specified the activities for the prevention of which the provisions of the Act may be made applicable in "the whole or any part of the State"…"in such a disturbed a dangerous condition" necessitating "the use of armed forces in aid of the civil power."

(a) activities involving terrorist acts directed towards overawing the government as by law established or striking terror in the people or any section of the people or alienating any section of the people or adversely affecting the harmony amongst different sections of the people;

(b) activities directed towards disclaiming, questioning or disrupting the sovereignty and territorial integrity of India or bringing about cession of a part of the territory of India or secession of a part of the territory of India from the Union or causing insult to the Indian National Flag, the Indian National Anthem and the Constitution of India.

That such activities were still being carried on by the terrorists and their over-ground collaborators in the territory of the state of Jammu and Kashmir was a reality sufficient to negate the demand for abrogation of the Act at this pint of time.

Powers under the Act were not absolute. These were required to be exercised with due care and caution. An element of accountability was in-built.

In each and every case the determination had to be made by the concerned officer. The act provided that such action will be taken "If in his (Officers') opinion it is necessary to do so."

While assessing the justification for grant of such "sweeping and excessive powers" to the armed forces in disturbed areas it should be remembered that the men and women in uniform were arrayed against well trained, brainwashed fanatical terrorists fully equipped with most modern sophisticated weapons in a fight to the finish. This proxy war launched by Pakistan had already claimed thousands of innocent lives of non-combatants including women and children. Thousands of our brave officers and soldiers were also martyred. It was a war, call it proxy war if you will in which in most cases only the one who fired first survived. These facts were well known, documented and incontrovertible.

It should also be remembered that AFPSA was enacted by the parliament to deal with the extra ordinarily disturbed situation prevailing in Jammu and Kashmir. It was not intended to be permanently on the statue book. As it is, the provisions were enabling not mandatory. Moreover, the very purpose of arming the forces with special powers was to speedily bring down the level of violence and finally quell it to the extent that the normalcy prevailed and the Act could be abrogated.

The moot question today was when, how and in what manner should the applicability of the act be dispensed with as the situation improved? Should the withdrawal of powers under the Act be piecemeal or made contingent upon the return of normalcy to the whole area declared as disturbed ?

In this connection lessons from the experience of Manipur may be rewarding. The Manipur government, withdrew the applicability of the Act from some of the constituencies in August 2004. The experiment created more problem than it solved. The areas exempted from the AFSPA became safe haven for the terrorist who after conducting operations elsewhere quickly moved therein for safety and shelter. The exempted area also turned into centre of extortion rackets. There was no reprieve for the civil population from terror either.

It may be recalled that the death of Thangjam Manorama in Assam Rifles' custody aroused severe public anger which spilled into massive and persistent street protests demanding the repeal of the Act. In the wake of the furore the Government of India set up a five-member panel headed by Justice B.P. Jeevan Reddy, a retired judge of the Supreme Court. According to Justice Reddy, "We have three opinions on the Act. First, the Act should be repealed and the Army should return to the barracks; second, the Army should stay but the Act be replaced with a more humane legislation, and third, the Army should stay and the Act modified."

As may be seen none of these options catered for the necessary balance between the needs of National Security and "respect for human rights" of the citizens in view of the ongoing militancy in the North East and certainly not in Jammu and Kashmir where a full-fledged proxy war was being waged by Pakistan backed by Global fundamentalist and militarised Islamic zealot for two and a half decades. In my opinion there is an option beyond Reddy panel recommendations meriting serious consideration.

No law was bad by definition. It's irresponsible use or misuse made it so. Extreme situations dictated grant of extreme powers to organs of the state to be exercised only in relevant circumstances in accordance with the letter and spirit of the law. Once this principle was conceded window opened up for resolution of problems germane to the ground realities.

In Jammu and Kashmir a Unified Command headed by the State Chief Minister determined strategies and oversaw anti-terrorist and other related operations. As the complaints and problems related to the alleged misuse of special powers under the Act the debate needed to be de-politicised and the issue remanded to the Unified Command for hammering a solution around which consensus could be built.

To begin with, the Unified Command may by consensus identify areas where in the words of Chief Minister Omar Abdullah "militant activities are minimal or insignificant," and direct that in such areas ordinarily the force should act only under normal law and follow laid down procedures. As almost all anti-terrorist operations these days were jointly conducted with the State Police, there should be no problem in shifting to this mode of action. And in cases where the Security Forces felt compelled to take recourse to the use of powers under AFSPA, or were requisitioned by the local authorities of "peace zones" the commissioned officer/ Gazetted officer of CRPF or other para military force ordering action be required to submit a report detailing circumstances under which he was compelled to invoke special powers and provide justification for going so.

In more and more such areas responsibilities for maintenance of law and order and operation against the remnants of terror machine should become the responsibility of the J&K Police after the force underwent reorientation, restructuring and was adequately provisioned. A small committee constituted by the Unfired Command should regularly monitor the situation on the ground to ensure compliance of the policy directives.

This option had the merit of denying ground for usual accusations that the men and women in uniform were being sent into action with their hands tied behind their backs. The special powers would still be available but to be used under controlled conditions. At the same time the civil society will be assured that an element of specific accountability had been built into the system to ensure against misuse of powers under AFSPA, and forbidding routine invocation in the areas designated as reasonably free from terrorist activities. The increased involvement of local police would add to the feel of environment of normalcy. The hope and scope of more and more areas being included in this category was bound to promote and enhance the peoples' participation in ushering in peace and strengthen the urge for normalcy for which people of the state yearn.

(6) The Saga of Stone Pelting

By the end of 2007, there were no takers in the world community for "the struggle for freedom" cover for ongoing terrorism in Jammu and Kashmir. The 9/11 episode had rendered terrorism a dirty word. Locally, the people were fed up with senseless killing. Terrorism had begun to yield diminishing returns and provoking public apathy bordering on hostility. The unprecedented voter participation in Jammu and Kashmir assembly elctions-2008 and the enfeeblement of terrorist machine in Kashmir due to loss of cadres and decimation of terrorist command structure was giving nightmares to ISI bosses. The desperate situation called for desperate remedies.

In an emergency review of the politico-strategic ground realities conducted in Islamabad sometime in January-February 2008 it was reportedly decided to cast the over ground segment of the network in Kashmir in the pivotal role. "Calibrated Youth mobilisation supported by targeted terror strikes albeit of low cost variety" was the prescription arrived at. Innocent, gullible and excitable Kashmiri teenagers were accordingly sucked in as pawns in the diabolical chess game of secessionist terrorism. This translated into a combination of over ground violent mass street action with youth in the vanguard and spaced terrorist strikes on specific targets to provide teeth to the street action. The violent street action with stones as the weapon of offence would, invite the use of force by the security forces resulting in civilian casualities exposing the Indian state to charges of Human Rights violation *et al.* to which the world community was highly sensitive. The resulting situation would facilitate repairing the weakened strike capability of the terrorists and act as force multiplier. The Pak determination tactically intensified the ongoing debate in Kashmir on whether Islam sanctioned the practice of stone as a weapon in Jihad with a view to obtain favourable verdict.

Afhad-ul-Mujtaba, who headed operations in Srinagar as senior superintendent of police for more than three years joined issue by quoting a tradition (Hadith) of Prophet Muhammad declaring the practice of stone - pelting as un-Islamic and sought the support of religious leaders to put an end to the "regular feature in Srinagar." He questioned the propriety of the practice in the name of religion. Kashmir's Grand Mufti, Mufti Bashiruddin shared the view and issued a fatwa (decree) against stone-throwing, saying: "It is against the spirit of the teachings of our Prophet. He has prohibited the practice." The debate further intensified when Jamiat-e-Ahle Hadees chief Molvi Showkat Ahmad supported the fatwa. "It is an un-Islamic practice and no individual or group should indulge in it," Showkat declared. Molvi Showkat was later assassinated.

While the state did nothing to cash this windfall, the Pak proxies joined issue in defending the practice. A seminar on the issue organised by Islamic Students League (ISL) brought together writers, scholars and separatist politicians to justify stone-pelting. Those opposed to stone-pelting asserted that the practice fuelled a cycle of violence inviting use of force by "trigger happy" security forces. They alleged that those promoting Stone Pelting ask the neighbourhood boys to indulge in the practice but send their own children for higher studies to India. The voice of salinity was expectedly drowned by the fear of gun and those arguing against the pernicious practice considering discretion as the better part of valour retreated to safety of their homes. The anti-stone pelting tilt had lost the punch. Stone pelting procedures and practices thereafter became extensive, better synchronises and fine tuned.

The 2008 phase of Stone pelting had almost petered off when the Ghulam Nabi Azad government surrendered on the issue of allocation of land for Amarnath ji Yatra arrangements. The pot was kept boiling through exploitation of the Shopian rape cum murder case, in which two women – Nelofar Jan (23), and her sister-in-law Asiya Jan (18) – were alleged to have been raped and then murdered on May 29, 2009. The finger of suspicion was pointed towards Police personnel. But the entire focus of the agitation was the Army and the Central Paramilitary Forces (CPMFs). The incident was also used to reinforce demand for demilitarisation.

The criminal case as well as the agitation were badly handled. After initial show of bravado the state authorities went into confused and vacillating mode. In an uncalled for intervention much before the investigation had made any worthwhile progress and just a day after the bodies of the two women were recovered a State Cabinet Minister addressed a Press Conference almost concluding the investigation. The Chief Minister was similarly ill advised to speak to the press catapulting the incident onto the national centre stage.

In a bizarre turn of events the state government decided not to hoist the National Flag at Lal Chowk in Srinagar on the Republic Day, over a case that was evidently fraudulent. The investigation by the Central Bureau of Investigation had established that "the vaginal swabs" of the two women taken to support the allegation of rape in the Shopian case were actually substituted by the woman doctor by her own vaginal swabs. The indefensible decision was the first of its kind since the birth of the Republic in 1951.

Contrary to the outpourings of breast beating bleeding hearts in the Indian capitol, the 2010 protests were neither "spontaneous" nor peaceful. Premeditated attacks by violent mobs on security forces locations indulging in stone pelting, arson and rioting telecast alive on numerous TV channels exposed the true picture. In fact, the cycle of violence was fed on a chain of violent protests and pre-planned attacks on security force bunker/locations provoking firings that resulted in injury and death of killing. In fact, the programme of action was routinely declared and widely publicised.

This was particularly true of the calls given by Ali Shah Geelani who had ironically appropriated the "Quit Kashmir" call given by the late Sher-I-Kashmir Sheikh Mohd Abdullah in ninety forties against the Maharajah. Yes, the teenagers set up for "martyrdom" were certainly of age of innocence but the role of rioters in which they were cast by the merchants of death could by no definition be described as innocent. The stones were transported and strategically located. That many of the stone pelters were hired was public knowledge. "The stone-pelters are being financed by businessmen and people from across the border. The stone throwers want CRPF to open fire so that an issue is created out of that," said Mr Reddy, IGP CRPF. A PTI dispatch from Srinagar dated February 05, 2010 reported arrest of Irshad Ahmed of Bemina colony on outskirts of the Srinagar city, alleged to be the kingpin of stone pelters in Kashmir valley. During investigation Police claimed to have seized documents, which suggested that Stone Pelting had turned into a lucrative 'business' for unemployed youths offering their 'service' for a price. Official sources also mentioned recovery of several documents suggesting his involvement in stone pelting business for nearly last two years. Dozens of SIM cards, threat letters, fake press identity cards, cheque books and well maintained account registers which listed the expenditure for stone pelting incidents in various parts of the valley were also seized. "The first register contained 294 names along with their photographs and mentions the details of money paid to them for their stone pelting activities in the last one year in downtown city", the sources said.

Inspector General of Police (IGP), Crime Investigation Department, Kashmir, A.G. Mir, revealed another disturbing dimension of the 2010 campaign–the intimate nexus between the drugs and the public protests. "There is a co-relation between addiction and stone throwing, and those addicted to prescription drugs, cannabis, or opium, find stone pelting a lucrative way to support their habit. They show bravado under the influence of drugs, they feel they are invincible. That's why they indulge in risk taking behaviour. We have found that there are people who organise these events and mobilise people for political gains. The conflict environment is conducive to addiction, with unrelenting tension and uncertainty, and soaring unemployment rates. The young seek escapism, Mir reasoned, and wanted to prove its worth through deeds on the street.

Further a survey revealed that 72 per cent of Stone Pelters were drug addicts.

During police interrogation many arrested youths confessed to addiction to drugs which they claimed was provided to them by a local supplier in return for their participation in stone pelting and violent protests. On the strength of information provided one Shezad resident of Khanyar in the downtown area of Srinagar was picked up and interrogated. Shezad disclosed that he was getting heroin from a resident of Natipora, in the outskirts of the city, which he used to distribute among groups of youths in downtown areas. Some other steroids and drugs used to be also given to the youth besides cigarettes loaded with charas. In one of the raids, police seized hundreds of disposable syringes and vials of heroin, steroids and analgesic injections. A well knit network also provided drugs free of cost to young addicts and in return they were asked to indulge in stone pelting on security forces, the sources said.

"The stone-pelting" wrote Dr Wasim Ahmad in his perceptive piece titled "The Politics of Stone Pelting" "has become an everyday phenomenon. It seems organised on an ambitious scale and aspires to become an all-encompassing Valley-wide reality. There is a high degree of synchronisation in the way assaults are launched at various places in the city and some major towns. What is more, the juggernaut at times gets rolling without any apparent cause. A death in the process has a metastasising effect with protests soon swirling the entire Valley right from Islamabad to Varmul."

Regarding the motivation for this phenomenon he said "The second theory is that these are organised events by people seeking political mileage by cashing on our blood. No matter where the incident occurs the locality, the groups involved and the stereotyped methodology used by the stone-pelters is always predictable. If this is the reality behind these "protests" to instigate a trigger happy police force for more killings and perpetual violence, then only God can save us from the hidden schemers. No matter what their intentions are, but by getting innocent people killed they can only be described as demonic. In this context the civil society should identify these groups and make sure they never succeed in their motives." These sentiments penned and published on 14 February, 2010 mirrored the feelings of vast majority of members of the Kashmir civil society. The tragedy, however was that not many had the requisite courage of conviction and intellectual integrity to speak out openly and help avert the disaster that stared them in the face. Dr Wasim Ahmad rounded up his article in the following words:

"Lastly what one can say is that the killings we are witnessing are gruesome but "stone pelting" by no way is the right form of protest as it does no good to the souls of slain people, destroys our society, encourages more killings while allowing certain sections gain political mileage from our blood that has been rendered so cheap."

The game plan of "gaining of political mileage from the blood of the youth of Kashmir" was exposed by the intercepts of tele conversation between two functionaries of Geelani led Tehrik_-I-Hurriyat Jammu and Kashmir "wanting at least 10 to 15 martyrs" during a particular demonstration.

Two deaths which occurred as a consequence of stone pelting shocked the people most and caused tremendous anger against the Stone Pelters and their leaders. First death occurred on February 22, when the vehicle carrying 11-day-old Irfan to hospital was waylaid by stone throwers who were imposing a shutdown. The passengers were harshly ordered to disembark and in the melee, the infant fell from the lap of his mother, blood oozed from his nose and he died before reaching the hospital. In second such incident, a government employee from Natipora was hit by a stone while travelling in a passenger bus which was subjected to stoning by the rioters. Syed Ali Shah Geelani was personally blamed for the death as he had given the call for a "peaceful protest" on that day.

The 2010 Stone pelting spree brought about a significant and qualitative change in the personality and mindset of gen-next terrorist leadership' which embarked upon harnessing the huge potential of social media in their "war against Indian occupation." The credit for this transformation was given to Masarat Alam, Geelanis' right hand man, and Director of Operations. He was also given credit for converting 'Kashmiris anger', against Indian state, the cornerstone of the 2010 war of nerves into "raging hatred" what with nine-year-olds, teenagers and the youth combining forces with the womenfolk in the daily street combats with the police and other security.

Masarat Alam Bhat (38), the lynchpin of the 2010 agitation utilised the Internet as a force multiplier. The tech-savvy separatist went underground right after authority's cracked following the killing of a 17-year-old and an alleged staged encounter. "Please upload videos; they're real testimony. Use whatever you have: Cell phones, cameras whatever," read a post on one community on Facebook. Many like Koshur Mazloom (oppressed Kashmiri) regularly posted pictures of funerals, corpses, wailing women and limbless teenagers, writhing in pain on their profiles.

Masarat Alam Bhat, used the web to publicise "quit J&K movement." In one of the many videos on Youtube, he asked soldiers to defy orders. Bhat, who remained on the run despite 100 raids across the Valley, issued periodical protest calendars on social networking sites. "Two pictures of a nine-year-old boy killed near Baramulla and a father being beaten up while trying to shield his dead son's body in Batamaloo became defining images of the 2010 summer agitation. They provoked outrage like never before," said a local journalist, adding that it was at a time when authorities had cracked down on the local press and newspapers were unable to hit stands for days. "The no-holds-barred Internet campaign has skirted all attempts to silence dissent," he said. Masarat Alam released two video statement urging people "to take the ongoing movement to its logical conclusion.". The accompanying manoeuvres by the Pak ISI in successful management of Public Perception confounding the civil society, unhinged the political class gained immense public sympathy for the "movement" and squarely placed, security forces and J&K Police in the dock.

Masarat Alam Bhat was arrested by Police on Monday (2nd week of October, 2010) from Srinagar city outskirts. The question as to why and under whose authority Alam released on bail after 21 months on June 08, 2010, was allowed to go Scot free knowing his huge potential for mischief remained a mystery. Even though the 2010 agitation fizzled out, internet and social networking have come to stay as potent avenues of spreading the ideology of militarised Islam and spewing communal venom.

The Pakistan establishment-Pan Islamist Jihadi Lashkars combine were no doubt guilty of committing the grave sin of offering unsuspecting Kashmiri youth as sacrificial goats at the altar of their sinister agenda. At the same time it had to be conceded that security forces also did not exactly cover themselves with glory in their response to the highly emotive and sensitive situation. Watching the clashes on television one got the impression that two violent mobs, one wearing uniform and other in assorted civilian dresses were engaged in street fight. The CRPF/J&K Police men were totally at sea and appeared unsure of what was expected of them.. The manner in which Tear Smoke guns, shells and grenades were used defied fundamentals of police training.

Tear smoke equipment was a "Squad weapon" to be used only under order of the Squad commander or his senior under controlled conditions. For instance, firing of Tear Gas shells was dictated by the wind direction, the distance between the Squad and the crowd and the calculated trajectory of the shells fired at a predetermined angle. In no circumstances were the guns to be aimed or fired at the crowd direct. To cut the long story short officers were most of time missing from the scene, the men could be seen running helter shelter, individuals firing Tear Smoke Shells at crowd haphazardly on their own. It will, however be unfair to fault the men. Over a long period they had operated in an environment which spawned what may for a better word be called "the encounter mind set." They appeared to have forgotten that this time around the objective was to disperse the mob and arrest the leaders and Not repeat Not to kill "the enemy." If the mandatory requirement of firing toward lower extremities of mob were complied with, large number of deaths of demonstrators could have been avoided. I had foreseen these problems as these were inherent in the situation and made pointed recommendation as detailed above under head "Challenges of normalcy." But those in power were too busy with more rewarding matters. The advise was ignored at a prohibitive cost.

Chief Minister Umar Abdullah had spoken of the "denting" of his personnel as well as his government's image by the turmoil which "needs to be built brick by brick." To be productive any exercise in introspection shall have to be in depth, clinically objective, brutally frank and totally honest. He sure had to rebuild the image of his government but for heavens' sake let him not use the same bricks and material. In fact, the architecture of the structure needed to be changed. As it is, the structure had rotted to the core and was domed to collapse. The recent upheaval only hastened the inevitable and saddled him with the blame because he was not only new to the job but also relied on individuals who were bereft of the requisite vision and were not adequately equipped with the administrative and political acumen and robust will power. In their wisdom or lack of it they chose to treat alike Stone pelting youth -hardliners, drug addicts, mercenaries, bystanders and those who participated just for kick. The government tied itself into knots even after January 2011 police recruitment rally in downtown city which got a huge response. Hundreds of youth turned up for recruitment in the police. They queued up for hours in the bitter cold for their physical *measurements. Even those who didn't meet the criteria didn't leave but stayed on until the end* of the rally in the late afternoon, many of them pleading with the police officers to reconsider their candidature. Number of former stone pelters got selected which was good. But, for obvious reasons they had to be put through rigorous reorientation. This aspect did not appear to have received due attention.

The latest proposal of general amnesty was equally flawed and legally impracticable. Making promises or raising hopes which cannot be fulfilled was a sure recipe to invite public scorn.

My analysis of the happenings during the 2008-2010 turmoil and interaction with Kashmiri friends including the youth forcefully brought to fore two very critical and troubling questions. Firstly, How come the establishments in Delhi and other state capitals have come to equate the fundamentalist fringe with the entire Kashmiri Muslim society and create the impression that all of them were suspect? What would it take to decisively dispel this root cause of alienation? Secondly, what made the Kashmiri Muslim youth so vulnerable to and such easy prey for manipulation by Pak ISI and their local collaborators despite unprecedented financial allocations by the centre, special economic packages, huge inputs in infrastructural development, sanction of central universities and other institutions of higher education and government claims of massive employment generation? The crucial Tourist industry including Pilgrim tourism never had it so good. Was it frustration, desperation, hopelessness or total loss of faith in the system and conduct of governance? The governments at the centre and the state, the political class, the intelligentsia and the civil society would do well to urgently and seriously mull over these questions that spawn serious issues and persistent alienation. Correctives must be devised and applied without further loss of time.

(7) Panchayat Elections

In a determined assertion of their democratic right of self-governance voters and candidates in strife torn Kashmir defied the Terrorist Diktat to make 2011 Panchayat polls a resounding success. Panchayat constituencies in Kashmir region recorded a huge voter turnout of 80 per cent making the world community to sit up and take notice. The people of Kashmir also reiterated their secular credentials by electing 25 Sikhs and two Kashmir Hindus as Panches in areas overwhelmingly inhabited by Muslims. This was easily the first real election to Panchayats in Jammu and Kashmir after thirty two years. The 2001 Panchayat elections proved a miserable non-starter. In almost every district of Kashmir, the number of candidates was less than the total number of constituencies necessitating, declaration of a large number of constituencies vacant. No voting could take place in Badgam district. As many as 63 per cent of the total Panch constituencies in Srinagar district and 60 per cent in Baramula district were declared vacant. The

Congress-PDP coalition government during Mufti Sayeed stewardship sensibly, promptly summarily scrapped the farce through legislation the very next year. The earlier elections were held in 1978.

A word about the history of Panchayat Raj in Jammu and Kashmir. The Jammu and Kashmir Village Panchayat Regulation No.1 was promulgated by by Maharaja Hari Singh in 1935. The Department of Panchayats and Rural Development was created in 1936 to administer the regulation. By virtue of 1941 amendment a fixed amount was earmarked for the Rural Development activities. The Panchayats were also vested with power to levy taxes and toll for mobilising the resources for performing their designed functions. The Maharajah was apparently way ahead of our democratically elected rules who till the other day were quibbling about setting of the Finance commission. After independence, the 1951 Act Panchayati raj listed institutions and defined various features of their activities and allied objectives. This Act further provided for adult franchise for the election of Panchayat. This Act was replaced by Village Panchayat Act in 1958. Jammu and Kashmir Panchayat Act (1989) was thereafter enacted three years before the 73rd amendment of the constitution. The Panchayat rules were framed in 1996.

The electioneering was hectic. Buoyed by good public response candidates indulged in reckless competitive promise creating great expectations all around. The commitment by the ruling coalition as well as the opposition to empower the Panchayati Raj institutions further strengthened the feel good factor. Results declared and celebrations over, the Panchas and Sarpanchas were eager to get on with their jobs. Large number of people thronged residences of Panchayat functionaries demanding redress of grievances and solution to their problems.

As the victory euphoria evaporated, the reality hit the newly elected Panchayat functionaries. They had little power and even lesser recognition by the establishment. That the bureaucracy should behave in this manner despite public exhortations to the administration by chief minister was indeed shocking. The chief minister was on record having exhorted public servants "to be responsive to the grievances of people." He pointed out that "Panchayat elections after a period of over 33 years have opened a new window in the development process, and public representatives at grass roots would be actively involved in launch, implementation and monitoring of schemes at Panchayat level." "The public representatives and the administration" he said, "have to work in coordination and cohesion on the development front and complement each other in realising the goal of equitable and holistic development of the state." This was music to the ears of the Panchas, Sarpanchas and more importantly to the people in rural areas.

Its violation provoked frustration and angry protests. The mood for agitation took hold. People were unable to understand or appreciate why chief minister Omar Abdullah and his party National Conference were dragging feet on the issue of empowerment of Panchayats to which they were committed. And then Omar Abdullah spilled the beans. He revealed that not only "MLAs' cutting across party lines were opposed to the delegation of more powers" of Panchayats, even two Congress ministers had opposed the move for empowerment of the institution in a cabinet meeting. The accusation against Congress ministers was contested by PPC president Saif-ud-din Soz. To put it bluntly, the resistance by MLAs was rooted in feudal mind set of those who treated constituencies as their pocket boroughs but in reality lacked popular acceptability. Otherwise, a really popular MLA would have his own supporters elected to the Panchayat Raj institutions and be in control. At any rate the Panchas became fully cognizant of the source of mischief, were scandalised and determined to teach the "Dushman", a lesson, "he would never forget."

Predictably the issue got politicised, the ruling Coalition partners, Congress and National Conference taking opposing positions on extending 73rd Amendment of the Indian Constitution to the State. The 73rd Amendment, it may be mentioned provided for appointment of a Finance Commission by the State Governments to make recommendations for, (a) determination of the taxes, duties, tolls and fees which may be assigned to panchayats, (b) distribution between the State and panchayats of the net proceeds of taxes, duties, etc; (c) grant-in-aid to the panchayats by the States. The J&K law had no such provisions. It did not envisage any autonomous machinery for objective allocation of funds. In short, under Panchayat Raj institutions were neither financially viable nor autonomous.

The environment of confusion, agitation and confrontation proved to be the God sent opportunity for terrorists licking their wounds after the humiliating rejection of their call for boycott of elections to strike. Posters demanding that Panchas and Sarpanchas resign or face consequences appeared on the walls. Threats were backed by action. Killing of a Sarpanch in Baramulla's Palhalan area in the beginning of September 2012 yielded resignations by 15 Panches and Sarpanches. Pressing the advantage further, terrorists shot dead Dy. Sarpanch Mohammad Shafi

Teli, two weeks later. This triggered panic among the grass root level representatives prompting 40 of them to resign. The number of killing of Panchayat office holders would be negligible in the context of on-going terrorism in Kashmir, if the targeted persons were not elected panchayat representatives who were perceived and projected as the harbingers of peace in the Valley and enabled the percolation of mainstream politics to the grassroots.

The initial response of the state government to the legitimate demand for security cover, was a flat "No'. "We just do not have resources for providing each and every Panchayat functionary personal security" was the strain. To put it mildly, this was perhaps the most tactless positioning considering the situation, the stakes and the fact of terrorist involvement. Softening the blow, the chief minister promised to "discuss providing security to these grassroots representatives in the next united headquarters meeting." Of course there were ways and means to infuse confidence, bring them under the security blanket and deny the terrorist time and opportunity to harass and eliminate the elected peoples representatives. I sent a note to Chief Minister Omar Abdullah detailing practical, doable and efficacious steps based on my experience to inculcate a sense of security amongst the Panchayat functioneries. But to no avail.

By the end of November, 2012 *about 900 panchayat leaders had resigned following threats from militants and selective execution of those found defiant. The local papers were full of paid advertisements by Panchas and Sarpanchas proclaiming 'IZHAR-E-LA TALIQI" (declaration of disassociation). The state government's persevered in reluctance to devolve powers for self-governance. The three-tier Panchayati Raj system was not put in place more than a year after the village panchayat polls. Powerless, panchayat leaders increasingly faced the anger of their constituents. Caught between militants threats and restless voters, quitting seems to offer the best way out.*

Continuing targeted killings persistent terrorist threats and delaying tactics adopted by the National conference leadership further widened the rift between the Coalition partners meriting intervention by Congress General Secretary Rahul Gandhi. On 27 September, a delegation of Sarpanches met Rahul at his 10, Janpath residence in Delhi and requested him to visit the state and intervene on their behalf. Rahul, accordingly visited Srinagar on 5th October, 2012 and interacted with a gathering of over 3,000 Panchayat members who converged from different parts of Kashmir at the Sher-e-Kashmir International Convention Centre (SKICC).

During the Interaction Rahul Gandhi stressed on the need to empower Panchayats. He referred to the 73rd Amendment saying that if this was not possible to be implemented in Jammu and Kashmir, its provisions could be incorporated in the state law for empowerment of the Panchayats. The issue of safety of Panchayat members also came under discussion during interaction. Rahul advised restraint all round and promised to have the needful done. Rahuls' intervention led to kind of ceasefire.

Elections to four seats reserved for its representatives in 36-member Legislative Council was the next step in the Panchayati institutions' electoral process in which 33,540 Panchs and Parpanchs were to exercise their voting rights on 19 November, 2012 in 155 Polling booths across the state. These vacancies were being filled up after a lapse of thirty two years. The opposition, including the Peoples Democratic Party and the Panthers Party, fielded candidates for all four seats. The Bharatiya Janata Party contested three seats–two in Jammu region and one in the Kashmir valley. There were 44 candidates in the fray for the four seats–28 in Jammu and 16 in the Valley. Despite their persisting differences the Coalition partners entered into pre-poll alliance and put up consensus candidates. A record number of 90 per cent exercised right of franchise electing the NC-Congress candidates to all the four seats. This was a big shot in the arms of the coalition government and perhaps significantly influenced the decision to contest 2014 Lok Sabha elections. The Lok Sabha election turned out to be an entirely different ball game.

(8) The Report Card

The six year constitutionally mandated tenure of National Conference - Congress coalition would come to end on 19 January, 2015. The partners had already decided to contest the forthcoming Assembly election separately but agreed that the coalition government would complete its full term. "After extensive talks with Congress leaders and workers, the party has come to the conclusion that we are going to fight the election on our own strength," said general secretary in charge of the State, Ambika Soni on 19 July, 2014 in Jammu. Chief Minister Omar Abdullah claimed to have informed the Congress President Sonia Gandhi of his party's similar decision earlier. Hopes of civilised parting of ways were, however dashed to the ground when Congress leaders accused National Conference ministers of corruption and their own government of governance deficit. Be it as it may, it was time that the performance of the Coalition government came under the scanner.

Chief Minister Omar Abdullah led National Conference-Congress coalition government was set to complete its tenure with a mixed bag of achievements and failures. For starters the state government was conferred the "Best State Award" in 2013 for improvement in infrastructure development by "India Today", country's premier news magazine. In fact, Governor N.N. Vohra in his address to the joint session of Jammu and Kashmir Legislature made a laudatory reference to this achievement. The coalition government also bagged the "Best State Award" for improvements in the health sector where by Jammu and Kashmir moved to the top in 2013 from 2nd position in 2009. The award was received by Chief Minister Omar Abdullah personally.

"India Today" conducted the annual study of state governments performance to "rank the 20 major states in India in order of their performance." An overall composite ranking of the states' performance was determined on eight major indicators in relation to each other.

As detailed elsewhere, the overall ranking of J&K, under the current coalition government had, according to the survey dropped from number 7th position in 2009 to 10th ranked state in 2013. Considering the inevitable margin of error the ranking in 2009 and 2013 in respect of Macro economy may safely be taken at par.

For the last five years Omar Abdullah government operated upon a budget of approximately 1,18,000 Crores, out of which about 38,000 Crores was the capital expenditure spent on development. Two major variables were recognised as critical in a state budget: capital expenditure, which laid down the foundation of growth and the non-plan deficit which indicated the financing pattern. Both were interlinked in the sense that a lower non-plan deficit enabled the government to fund its investment programme without creating financial liabilities in the form of borrowings. The Congress-NC government, according to experts fared badly on both counts. Its capital expenditure declined from 32 per cent in 2008-09 to just 20 per cent in 2012-13. To add to fiscal waywardness, the government allowed the non-plan deficit to increase from Rs 2,900 crore in 2008-9 to Rs 9,500 crores in 2014-15: a more than three-fold increase. This deficit was said to have arisen because of a more than doubling of the non-plan revenue expenditure from Rs 11,735 crore to Rs 29,553 crores!

In his Republic day speech which was televised and broadcast on the radio, chief minister Omar Abdullah, highlighted following achievements of his government:

1. Empowered the people and institutions through Panchayat polls.
2. Reviving State Accountability Commission.
3. Right to Information.
4. Public Services Guarantee Act.
5. Empowering youth through Sher-I-Kashmir Employment and Welfare Programme (SKEWPY), Himayat, Udaan and Umeed, besides providing 'Sadak', 'Bijlee' and 'Pani'.

Chief Minister's Political Secretary, or is he the Advisor now, Tanvir Sadiq echoed his leaders' claims with greater gusto. "In the State sector", he boasted, "the total energy generated during the year 2007-08 was nearly 879.34 MUs, which has grown to 2670 MU in 2012-13, which is a threefold increase." This touched a raw nerve adding insult to injury. I was working on my computer late night with electric supply shut as happened more frequently than one could keep the count. The over loaded 'Inverter' had conked off. The battery of the computer dying by the minute, I was feeling miserable. The experience of others I spoke to was no better. Mind you, I live in an area serviced by digital meters and pay my hefty bill every month in time. The government had assured uninterrupted electricity supply in these area. The shutdowns some notified but mostly sudden and unannounced were becoming more and more frequent. Earlier one could contact a PDD officer and at least have the satisfaction of remanding the problem to someone who could do something about it. But since about last three years the PDD officials and stations just ignore the calls whether on land line or cell phones. This was neither the time nor the place to discuss the disastrous mismanagement of our power sector. But where was Tanvir hiding the bonanza of additional power generated?

You can not fault the chief minister on the achievement he had listed on a day which also happened to coincide with the completion of five years of his coalition government. His government did deserve the credit for holding landmark Panchayat elections, gains whereof were frittered away by the suicidal policy pursued thereafter. The sad state of affairs of the Accountability Commission was public knowledge and a subject of regular public criticism in public and the media. The legislations and schemes mentioned had either yet to take off or were perceived to have flopped.

The truth was that Omar Abdullah scored high in the realm of macro conceptions but touched low mark in micro management. This created a tragic paradox. If the announcement of public welfare and youth capacity building schemes generated public enthusiasm and soaring hopes their failure, dismal performance or snails' pace implementation only bred disillusionment and anger. Apparently, the chief minister expected his colleagues in the council of ministers and the bureaucracy to take care of the speedy and purposeful implementation. These expectations were perhaps based on his working experience in the Ministry of External Affairs in Government of India serviced by a well oiled, highly motivated and accountable administrative machinery tuned to instant response and zero tolerance for any laxity or delay. Moreover the ministry had no public dealings. The work culture in the state administration on the other hand was infected with inefficiency, sycophancy and absence of accountability. Regular monitoring, constant prodding and frequent pushing were the needs of the hour. Neither the chief minister nor his aids appeared to have taken care of these 'essentials'. Of course there were honourable exceptions-public servants of integrity, probity and efficiency and professional commitment. It was on their strength the flabby, lazy and routine oriented administration was able to deliver what it did.

As elections drew near the CM appeared to be becoming conscious of the highly unsatisfactory state of affairs in the field of implementation of projects. Stung by allegations of tardy and slow progress in project implementation, he took stock of no less than sixteen "on-going" projects during his visit to Jammu on 10-11 August, 2014. These projects included crucial upgradation of the Jammu airport, Mubarak Mandi Heritage complex, 200 bed Maternity Hospital and the mega Water Supply based on the natural resource of the nearby flowing mighty Chenab which would quench the endemic thirst of water starved Jammu city and its many suburbs. People were eagerly waiting for the critically deficient water supply to be augmented. Every time the issue was raised, pat came the assurance for early commissioning of the project. The truth, the shocking truth got blurted out in the review meeting. According to press release the Chief minister was told that "financial aid is being sought from the Japan Bank of International Commerce." The chief minister was told that 51 crore rupees had been spent on the controversial Tawi Lake project. One does not really see much evidence of such huge expenditure. One would have expected the chief minister to demand breakup of the expenditure and take the trouble to at least visit one site for on-the-spot verification. The government also needed to come clean on whether this amount was spent on training/plugging numerous gutters that discharge hundreds of tonnes of filth in the venerated Tawi-the Suriya Putri. You do not need an expert to certify that unless the gutters were treated or otherwise diverted in the very initial phase, the proposed lake runs a very real risk of turning into a gigantic reservoir of filth, an obvious health hazard and an insult to the people of Jammu.

(a) Employment

Ghulam Nabi Azad heading the Congress-PDO coalition had undertaken to fast rack filling up one lakh vacancies in the government services. Omar Abdullah who succeeded him had to acknowledge after being in the driving seat for four years that the recruitment was proceeding at snails' pace and promised "fast track recruitment of 80,000 educated youth in government service through service selection agencies within next some months." An assessment one year down the line revealed the noteworthy "progress." Only his Fast track consultant Mushtaq Peer had landed in jail. The much publicised coalition government's employment schemes for youth, the Sher-e-Kashmir Employment and Welfare Programme, centrally sponsored schemes viz Himayat, Udaan and Umeed were generally perceived to have 'flopped.' His opponents and some social scientists also laid the blame for the Kashmiri youth turning to drug abuse on account of stress and strain of living, with uncertainty about their future as also other ills that flowed from the "all pervading depression amongst the Kashmiri youth at the doors of the coalition government."

(b) Trust Deficit

The credibility rating of the political class in Kashmir has never been lower. This fall from popular grace was the fate of the mainstream as well as the separatist camps. The leaders were perceived as lying, double speaking and riding in two boats. The mainstream parties were labelled as opportunist vying with each other to grab some separatist space. Similarly, the Hurriyat led by Mirwaiz Farooq and JKLF were accused of doing the bidding of Pakistan simultaneously maintaining "Good working relations" with Government of India.

During the last one decade or so the political scene in the Kashmir valley has been muddied beyond recognition. The once neat delineation between those committed to reality of the state's accession with India and others opposed to it had been rendered vague or oblitered. "Those" confided an old political activist of South Kashmir, the cradle of Kashmir politics "were days of integrity of political commitment. Everybody knew where the other stood. Congressmen and National Conference workers openly and proudly claimed credit for forging the accession of Jammu and Kashmir with secular India under the leadership of Sher-I-Kashmir. The Bakra party, under whatever garb they may have operated were with Pakistan so were the Jamaatees — (adherents of Jamaat-i-Islam) then there was a smattering of those Azadi Wallahs." He took a deep breath and added somewhat ruefully "Gone are the days when hundreds of Congress workers defied the mighty Sheikh and came out in the streets of Bejbehara shouting Azad Hindustan Zindabad on the call of Mufti Mohd Syed, the then Congress President. One young man, the son of a very close aid of his and a dedicated Congress worker was killed in police firing. Now we do not know where Mufti himself stands and what is his agenda?" "There are no real Hindustanis in Kashmir today", chipped in his companion. "Even people in power or those who were running the government till the other day chose to be vague on the basic issue of accession." And what about the horde of ex-MLAs including Geelani (Ali Shah Geelani) who line up before treasuries every month to collect pensions for having sworn loyalty to India? he quarried. And said "SAB JHOOTHEY HAIN, PAR AWAM SUCH JANTEH HAIN." No objective political analyst could have summed up the position more accurately.

The position of mainstream politician was pitiable. In an attempt "to stay in tune with popular mood they spoke in separatist idiom and generally sought to convey the impression that they had an open mind on the fact and extent of accession with India. In the current political parlance they practiced "soft separatism." As a consequence their cadres became confused and apathetic. There was a near total disconnect between the people and the traditional leadership.

When Omar Abdullah propounded his new thesis of separation of elections from the resolution of "MASLA-I-KASHMIR" for the first time many analysts considered it a clever tactical move to persuade the fence- sitters to participate in electoral process. After all, they pleaded the election were indeed about installing an elected government to at the least provide "ROTI, KAPDA AUR MAKAN." But soon it became the scared MANTRA. Even his Republic day speech began with its recitation. And now after the parting of ways of Congress and National Conference a new stridency had been introduced in the formulation. The position taken by him on the latest repeated Pak violations of ceasefire agreement and targeting of civilian population further queered the pitch.

In a constitutional democracy people elected their representatives to run the affairs of the state in the best interests of the electorate for a specified period where after they must again seek their mandate. "Rooti, Biji, Pani, Kapda" were indeed the basic needs of under developed and developing countries and figured prominently in the manifestos of contesting political parties. Up to this point there could be no quarrel with Omar Abdullahas' thesis. All elected bodies be it a Panchayat, state assembly or parliament were the creation of the constitution which referred to a geographical entity called a country whose physical boundaries were delineated and held sacred. All elected representatives were required to and indeed did take oath of allegiance and swear in the name of God to uphold the constitution and preserve the integrity of India. Therefore for them and all those who chose to live in the union of India, register as voters and contest elections, the finality of accession of Jammu and Kashmir with India in an incontrovertible reality and act of faith.

For them there was no scope for ambivalence on this score and hence no MASLA-I-KASHMIR as far as our side of the LOC was concerned. Yes, "MASLA" does exist in respect of area under the illegal occupation of Pakistan where in Lakhs of our fellow citizen were held hostage subjected to untold hardship, ethnic cleansing and torture. That is why the 1994 parliament resolution directed the Government of India to have the occupied area vacated. As such we do need to engage with Pakistan to resolve this MASLA in accordance with the Shimla agreement "peacefully and bi-laterally."

Any other view particularly which dangerously approximated even remotely to the so-called Kashmir separatists pro-Pak ranting, under whatever pretext would neither behave Omar Abdullah and the National Conference which spearheaded the accession with secular India in preference to theocratic Pakistan nor would it be countenanced by anyone in this country. In fact such convoluted political formulations confused the cadres and bred disillusionment and uncertainty. No grass root level NC political worker worth his salt would like to be perceived as singing tune borrowed from his opponents reducing him the statue of "B team" of the Hurriyat or for that matter that of the PDP. The National Conference leadership will do well to assess whether this kind of confusion and wavering political commitments had something to do with the 2014 Lok Sabha disaster.

(c) Achievements

Let us now turn to some of the major achievements of the Omar Abdullah led NC-Congress coalition.

1. The controversy about the abrogation of the Armed Forces Special Powers Act (AFSPA) was not allowed to impact the excellent equation and co-operation between the central security forces and the Jammu and Kashmir Police in counter-terrorist operations. As a result the state recorded significant reduction in terrorist incidents (80 per cent according to Omar Abdullah) during last five years. The resultant improvement in peace and security environment proved congenial for boost in the economic and development activities.
2. The Yatras to the holy shrine of Shri Amar Nath were well managed despite ever increasing rush and adverse climatic conditions. The enormous economic benefits accruing there from enriched the economy. After many years people smiled as they greet each other.
3. The tourist boom year after year saw Hotels full to capacity, Shikaras crowded the Dal lake while the illuminated Houseboats cast magical shadows on the placid waters creating fantasy of bewitching images. The overall environment was relaxed and comfortable.

   Economic benefits apart, the return of normalcy and enhanced business activity had deeper meaning for the people of Kashmir. It more than justified their conscious decision to opt for peace and development rejecting senseless violence and fortified their resolve to tread the chosen path. Economic security enhancement of quality of life and securing bright future for their children now topped their agenda.
4. Attention was focused on preservation of heritage sites in Saher-I-Khas (Srinagar) which yielding rich dividend. This would be an ever-lasting contribution of the Coalition government more specially of chief minister Omar Abdullah, minister Ali Mohd Sagar and INTACH chief Salem Beg but for whose dedicated efforts so much quality progress could not have been made.

(d) Conclusion

The Congress-PDP (2002-2008) and Congress-NC (2008-2014) coalition governments, as may be seen largely failed to satisfy the hopes and expectations of the people of Jammu and Kashmir. Both coalitions, jointly and severally, reneged on their solemn commitments as contained in the PDP-Congress government Common Minimum Programme and strings of solemn promises of accelerated non-discriminatory development, Infra-structural constructs and upgradations and honest, people friendly and efficient governance regularly reeled out by Chief Minister Omar Abdullah. Neither of the coalition governments passed muster on even the most relaxed criteria of good, responsible, responsible and competent governance. While the PDP-Congress coalition was plagued by intra coalition dissentions, mutual suspicions and conflict of political interests, the Congress-NC brand found itself gravely stricken by lack of cohesion, absence of unity of purpose and administrative and political waywardness.

The state of Jammu and Kashmir comprising of three distinct regions of Kashmir, Jammu and Ladakh had a unique political character. In the post- accession era Kashmir region dominated the political landscape and its regional interests were always held paramount whether National Conference, the premier Kashmir-based political party was in power or All India Congress ruled the state. With National Conference back to power following 1975 Indira-Abdullah accord, the Congress constituency primarily shrunk to Jammu and Ladakh. But still the Congress policies remained Kashmir centric. Actually, the electoral arithmetic was so "contrived" that the Kashmiri dominance would be a permanent feature. A delimitation of constituencies in accordance with the nationally adhered to criteria would have resolved the issue in an equitable and fair manner. In fact setting up of a Delimitation commission was part of the Common Minimum Programme of PDP-Congress coalition. However, the Delimitation commission was not constituted nor there appeared to be any hope of this happening under current constitutional formulation. The mounting frustration in Jammu region largely driven by this unjust treatment was fuelling the demand for division of Jammu and formation of a separate state of Jammu region.

Elections 2014 were round the corner. Parties including a somewhat unrealistically over-ambitious BJP were busy working out strategies and the game of AIYA RAMS AND GAYA RAMS were being unashamedly played. The geographical, demographic and political configurations indicate a fractured verdict once again.

Whatever judgement the history may pass on the two coalition governments, the seasoned Mufti Mohd Sayed would have the distinction of having presided over a cabinet perennially at war with itself, whose ministers clashed in the state legislature and vehemently criticised in media and public decisions to which they were party merely because at the given point of time Mufti or Azad happened to be in the driving seat. As for Ghulam Nabi Azad, he was on record, as having described his cabinet as a body "half of whose ministers (the PDP component) would not work and the other half (the Congress WALAS) were incapable of working." In respect of Omar Abdullah, it may be rewarding to quote Dr Sheikh Showkat Hussain, who teaches law at the Central University of Kashmir who opined "Omar Abdullah came with the promise of jobs. The vacancies could not be fulfilled because the administration is beyond his grips as he remains preoccupied with his Twitter handle." Whatever judgement historian pass on the performance of Omar Abdullah, the label of "Twitter CM" will stick to him.

(e) Epilogue

As decreed by the Election Commission, **Jammu and Kashmir Legislative Assembly election, 2014** was held in five phases from November 25 to December 20, 2014. The six-year term of the outgoing assembly was to expire on January 19, 2015. The result was declared on December 23, 2014. Peoples Democratic Party bagged 28 seats. Bharatiya Janta Party secured 25 while Jammu Kashmir National Conference and Indian National Congress to content with 15 and 12 seats respectively. The position in respect of the rest was; Jammu Kashmir Peoples' Conference (2), Communist Party (Marxist) (1), Peoples' Democratic Front (1) and Independents (3), Modi's Mission 44+, the bid to form a BJP government.

Jammu and Kashmir on its own thus collapsed. As may be seen, Jammu region massively voted for Modi/BJP, in response to an aggressive campaign led by Prime Minister Modi. The Indian National Congress drew a blank in the Hindu dominated belt of Jammu region. Kashmir region, on the other hand consciously, determinedly and solidly voted against Modi and his party. Ladakh rejected all the three major parties, PDP, NC, and BJP and embraced the Congress party...Jammu and Kashmir Assembly elections-2014 thus returned a somewhat uniquely fractured verdict— the kind of which was never witnessed before…An unprecedented stalemate prevailed in the process of government formation. However, after protracted red and torturous negotiations through 49 days of Governors' Rule, BJP-PDP hammered out a Common Minimum Programme. The PDP-BJP coalition government was accordingly sworn in on March 01, 2015 in Jammu.

The Coalition government was mired in somewhat unsavoury controversy from day one. It all commenced with a press conference by Chief Minister Mufti Mohd Sayeed who chose to give credit to Pakistan, the Hurriyat as well as the militants for facilitating peaceful conduct of polls. This was followed by a group of PDP legislatures criticising the hanging of Parliament attack convict Afzal Guru and demanding transfer his mortal remains to Kashmir.

The release of Muarat Alam, the chief of Pro-Pak Muslim League, a constituent of Hurriyat (G) led by Ali Shah Geelani, operational commander of the 2010 Stone Pelting upsurge which claimed 112 lives and a notorious Pakistan agent involved in over twenty criminal cases created a storm of protest in the country, the media and the parliament. The BJP and Government of India distanced themselves from Mufti's decision, utterances and the demand relating to remains of Guru. An acutely embarrassed and provoked Prime Minister Modi unequivocally and strongly disapproved of all that had been said or done by Mufti and his men since assumption of office which impinged on the security and integrity of the country. While the controversies rage, the nation awaits the outcome of efforts to sort out the mess. The fate of PDP-BJP coalition appeared to be hanging in the balance.

How the PDP-BJP coalition government (if in survived) dealt with the developmental demands and political aspirations of people of Jammu and Ladakh regions could determine the future of Jammu and Kashmir state as a single political and administrative entity. The kind of political acrobats the Kashmir based parties/groups were indulging in and regional (some call it religious) sentiment becoming blatantly assertive should be a cause for serious concern to all those who were committed to maintain the integrity of Jammu and Kashmir and unity of its people as a proud and prosperous integral part of the Union of India.

Appendices

Appendix– A

Common Minimum Programme for Congress-PDP Coalition Government (2002)

Objectives

1. The Goal of the Coalition Government is to heal the physical, psychological and emotional wounds inflicted by fourteen years of militancy, to restore the rule of law in Jammu and Kashmir State, to complete the revival of the political process which was begun by the recently concluded elections, and to request the Government of India to initiate and hold, sincerely and seriously wide ranging consultations and dialogue, without conditions, with the members of the legislature and other segments of public opinion in all the three regions of the State, to evolve a broad-based consensus on restoration of peace with honour in the State.

2. Ensuring safety of lives and properties, restoring dignity and honour of all persons in the State will be the foremost concern of the government. The Coalition Government will take all possible measures, within its power, to protect all the people in the State of Jammu and Kashmir from violence and militancy, whether originating from within or outside the State, and to encourage those young men from the State who have resorted to militancy to return to their families and the mainstream, with the belief that they will receive security and justice according to law. At the same time, the State Government will fully cooperate with the Government of India in combating cross-border militancy originating from Pakistan.

3. *Restoring Peace and Normalcy and Curbing Corruption*: The Government shall review all cases of detainees being held without trial for long periods. It shall release all detainees held on non-specific charges, those not charged with serious crimes and those who have been held on charges that are such that the period they have spent in exceeds their possible sentence.

4. The Government shall review the operation of all such laws that have been used in the past decade to deprive people of their basic rights to life and liberty for long periods of time, without due legal process. Where the government deems that some special powers need to be retained, it will ensure, by instituting careful and transparent pre-screening and monitoring procedures, that such powers are used sparingly and those entrusted with them are held accountable for any misuse.

5. All cases of custodial killings and violations of Human Rights shall be investigated and persons responsible for them will be identified and punished appropriately.

6. The Government shall strengthen the State Human Rights Commission to make it an effective instrument for addressing the grievances of the people of the State.

7. The Government shall formulate a comprehensive relief and rehabilitation package for those families affected by militant violence over the past decade. The ex-gratia relief at Rupees one lakh per deceased person in militant violence will be raised to Rs 2 lakhs. In recruitment to Government posts, preference will be given to one member of each family where an innocent member has been killed in the militancy related violence.

8. The Government shall implement special schemes to rehabilitate former militants who have forsworn violence and rejoined the mainstream.

9. The Government will reach out to the children, widows and parents of the deceased militants and make endeavours to provide free education to the militancy affected orphans.

10. The Government reaffirms that the return of Kashmiri Pandits to their mother land is an essential ingredient of Kashmiriat. The government will seek the cooperation of all elements in the society to create an atmosphere conducive to their safe return, will take all necessary steps to ensure their safety and devise effective measures for their rehabilitation and employment.

11. Persons living close to the line of control and the international border face special difficulties due to recurrent tension and cross-border violence. Permanent shelters will be constructed in all vulnerable areas to prevent loss of life. The government will also devise a scheme to provide, wherever feasible, alternative land to such families in safe zones.

12. The Government shall give top priority to ridding the State administration of corruption and nepotism, especially in the award of government jobs and contracts and places in institutions of higher learning. It will endeavour to make the selection process to all those positions and institutions fully transparent.

13. The Government shall establish an institution or "Ehtisab" for enquiring into complaints received against Chief Minister/Ministers and legislators. The appointment to this post shall be made by the Chief Minister in consultation with the Chief Justice of the State High Court and the Leader of Opposition in the Legislative Assembly.

14. A Commission will be set up to make recommendations for reform of the Police Administration to make it a more effective and humane instrument for investigation of crimes and for the enforcement of law and order. The government will ensure that the personnel in Special Operation Group (SOG) are assimilated /relocated within the regular police establishment.

15. The Congress-PDP coalition government considers that there are enough laws in existence to deal with militancy. Therefore, it will revoke/ not implement POTA in the State. Employment Oriented Development Strategy.

16. Our Government shall make sincere efforts to ensure that all the three regions of the State—Jammu, Kashmir and Ladakh receive an equitable share of resources available for development. It shall set up a State Finance Commission with a statutory status for this purpose and the effort will be to ensure that the backlog of development and employment at the regional and district levels is made good within a specified time frame.

17. The Government shall press for the inclusion of Dogri in the 8th Schedule of the Indian Constitution.

18. The Government shall grant full powers to the Autonomous Hill Council for Leh which has hitherto been deprived of its legitimate powers. Efforts will be made to persuade the people of Kargil to accept a similar Autonomous Hill Council for Kargil.

19. Our Government will give top priority to the preparation of an employment oriented medium term development plan laying particular emphasis on the development of agriculture, horticulture, handicrafts, tourism, information technology, food processing and environment friendly industrial activities. Efforts will be made to evolve a development strategy which provides at least one productive job per family.

20. The Government shall accord due consideration to the recommendations of the Wazir Commission.

21. Employment and welfare of the youth will receive special attention. Measures will be taken to help those youth who have fallen victim to drug abuse and narcotics due to frustration and unemployment.

22. The Government shall constitute Delimitation Commission for delimiting the Legislative Assembly constituencies, as required by law.

23. High priority will be given to the development of power resources of the State and to extend the benefit of electricity to all villages of the State. The State Government will ask the Central Government to ensure that the power generation in the State should be available to the maximum extent possible for meeting the needs of the State.

24. Special emphasis will be laid on provision of basic minimum needs such as provision of safe drinking water, sanitation, rural roads, primary health-care and elementary education and school buildings.

25. A new scheme will be prepared to universalise access to elementary education for all children. Services of unemployed graduates will be utilised for this purpose.

26. A comprehensive plan for the development of environment friendly tourism in all the three regions of the State will be prepared bringing the hinterland districts on the tourist map of the State. Special measures will be taken to facilitate and protect pilgrim related tourism.

27. Panchayati Raj institutions will be given both functional autonomy and adequate financial support for making them an effective instrument for decentralised development. Early elections will be held wherever they are due.

28. Keeping in view that women have borne the brunt of violence in more ways than one over the past decade, special welfare programme will be designed for women such as widow pensions, subsistence allowance for women headed households and self employment schemes for young women.

29. Special emphasis will be laid on promotion of welfare of backward communities including Gujjars and Bakerwals, scheduled castes and tribes. The government will strive for the extension of scheduled tribes status to the Pahari speaking population of the State.

30. Effective measures will be taken to check unplanned and unauthorised growth of towns and cities. Jammu and Srinagar municipalities will be given the status of corporations to ensure orderly development of all civic facilities. Effective measures will be taken for orderly growth of towns and cities and for provision of basic civic amenities thereof.

31. All the three regions of the State have got religious minorities which face special problems. The government shall give full protection to the minorities and safeguard their rights. A Minority Commission will be constituted to look after the interests of minority communities.

Appendix-B

A Background Note on the Diversion of Forest Land to Shri Amarnathji Shrine Board circulated by Jammu and Kashmir Government (June 25-2008).

The pilgrimage to Amarnathji has been going on for centuries. Local population had always taken an active role helping the pilgrims in performing the pilgrimage. State Government also had been involved in making arrangements for the pilgrimage. Indeed the Deputy Commissioner of the erstwhile Anantnag District used to be designated as the Yatra Officer and was made responsible by the government for the smooth conduct of Yatra.

With the passage of time, it was felt necessary to build sufficiently strong structures en route the Shrine which could withstand the fury of the elements during the winters and also provide shelter to the pilgrims in case the weather turned hostile during the course of Yatra. The need for such structures was reinforced in 1996 when a very large number of pilgrims died during blizzard lasting four days. Thereafter, some structures in form of toilets and Sarais were put up at vulnerable points en route the Shrine.

In order to institutionalise the arrangements for smooth conduct and management of the pilgrimage to Holy Shrine of Shri Amaranthji, the State Legislature passed the Jammu and Kashmir Shri Amaranthji Shrine Act 2000. The Bill had been piloted by the Tourism Department pursuant to the Cabinet decision No.182/16 dated 1o/10/2000. Shri Amarnathji Shrine Act received the assent of the Governor on 14th November, 2000 and the Act was enforced vide notification SRO 54 dated 12/2/2001 with effect from 21.2.2001.

A Project Report was received by the State Government in the Forest Department dated 15.10 2004 from the CEO Shri Amarnathji Shrine Board requesting for the transfer of 3642 kanals of Land for 7 halting places on the Baltal -Amamathji Shrine and Chandanwari- Amarnathji Shrine routes. The matter was examined in the Forest Department at various levels and the case was finally submitted to the Hon'ble Minister by the Principal Secretary of the Forest Department recommending that the proposal be approved.

The Hon'ble Minister of Forests and Environment recorded his decision 28/3 /2005 as under;—

"If there is no violation of the J&K forest (Conservation) Act, 1997 and the Cabinet decision regarding, diversion of Forest Land the proposal at Para 13 and 14 of the departmental note file is approved with the conditions laid down in para 9 ante of the file."

The Forest Department then issued a Government Order No. 148—FST of 2005 dated 29.3.2005 granting permission to Shri Amarnathji Shrine Board for using Forest Land for constructing prefabricated structures for Yatris in compartment no. 21/AC. 8/AC. 6/AC of Lidder Forest Division and compartment No. 62 of Sindh Forest Division. –

In the meanwhile, it was learnt that some people had already agitated the matter before the Hon'ble High Court of J&K vide OWP No. 732/2004- in Rampal Bathoria Vs State. The High Court on 15/4/2005 ordered as under;

"Since the Board intends to upgrade the infrastructure across the tracks and at different places, the state shall immediately permit the use of Forest Land by the Board if not already allowed to enable it to carry out the developmental activities for the benefit of the Yatris. I am informed that the Forest department had already granted permission to the Board for the purpose."

The State Government went in appeal to the Division Bench of the High Court. The Division Bench vide its interim directions on 17.5.2005 ordered as under:-

"The land to be allotted by the Board would be only for the purposes of user and would remain limited for the duration of Yatra. The Board shall also identify the sites to be allotted for the purpose of Langar erection of detachable/prefabricated Huts and toilets etc. which would not be permanent in nature and are liable to be removed after the period of Yatra is over. The Board shall identify the person/agency to whom the Site would be allotted so as to enable the State Government to screen the antecedents of the said person or agency. In case the State Government may have "any valid objections in regard to any of the person or agency then permission shall not be granted to the person/agency and in that eventuality the board shall make alternate arrangement."

Earlier on 5/5/2005, the Chief Conservator of Forests Kashmir had sought a clarification from the Principal Chief Conservator Forests J&K whether the Land was to be allowed to be used by the Amarnath Shrine Board free of cost or on royalty basis. The Principal Chief Conservator of Forests J&K referred the matter to the government for Orders.

On receipt of the letter dated 20 /5/2005 from the Principal chief conservator of Forests J&K, the matter was re-examined. After re- examination, the following observations were made by Commissioner/ Secretary, Forests and the case was submitted to the Hon'ble Minister for Forest on 20/5 /2005.

"It is apparent that the Government Order issued is not fully in the same spirit as the order passed at para 15. Same shall be withdrawn as proposed. The PCCF shall be asked to process the case-on overriding priority basis under the relevant provisions of the Forest Conservation Act and Cabinet decisions on the subject. A fresh order shall be issued after the required procedure is followed (expeditiously) and all aspects including the applicable Court directives are taken into account."

The Forest Minister then approved that the Government Order No. l48 FST of 2005 dated 29/03 /2005 should be withdrawn. Accordingly Government Order No. 21 0-FST of 2005 dated 20/5/2005 read with corrigendum dated 20/5/ 2005 was issued withdrawing the earlier Order.

In the meanwhile the Chief Secretary had received some complaints' against Government Order No.148FST of 2005 dated 29/3/2005. The Chief secretary on 21/5/2005 advised the GAD to call for the file of the Forest Department and examine the matter. The GAD called for the file of the Forest Department and re-examined it.

The re-examination of the case revealed the following:

"The provisions of the Forest (Conservation) Act had been violated as the proposal was not considered or placed before the Forest Advisory Committee/Cabinet for orders. Unnecessary haste was shown to allow

SASB to utilise the said land. The Hon'ble Minister of Forests was not advised properly and his observations were not considered before issuing the Government Order no. 148-FSTof2005 dated 29/3/2005 granting permission to the SASB for using the Forest Land for non-forestry purposes. There were no compelling reasons for the Forest Department to issue the impugned Order."

In the meanwhile, H.E., the Governor sent a message to the Council of Ministers on 25/5/2005 under section 44C of the Constitution J&K urging it to reconsider the decision to withdraw Government Order 148FST of 2005 dated 29/3/2005.

The cabinet considered the message from H.E. in its meeting held on 7/6/2005 and vide its decision No. 109/8 decided as under:

"Cabinet desired that the copy of the reference from HE the Governor and the memorandum of the Hon'ble Chief Minister be circulated among all the Cabinet Ministers and the matter be discussed in the next Cabinet Meeting. Memorandum of the Hon'ble Chief Minister and the message from HE the Governor annexed herewith."

There is no record to indicate whether the matter came up before the cabinet for discussion as desired by it.

The case then remained under correspondence between the office of the PCCF and the Amarnathji Shrine Board. The Land was jointly surveyed to assess requirement of the Amarnathji Shrine Board on the Baltal Amarnath Shrine Axis in the first instance. As a result of the Joint survey an area of 39.88 hectares was recommended for being diverted for non- forestry purposes for use of the Amarnath Ji Shrine Board in 2007.

The forest Land measuring 39.88 hectares fell under compartment No. 63a Sindh in Block Kullan, Range Sindh, Sindh Forest Division. The land was recommended for being used for raising prefabricated structures only for camping purposes of pilgrims without going in for permanent structures in Baltal and Domel.

The matter was placed before the Forest Advisory Committee which is headed by the Chief Secretary and has among others, the Principal Secretary of the Forest department, Principal Secretary Planning and department Commissioner/Secretary Finance department, Principal Chief Conservator.Forests, Wild Life Warden. Financial commissioner revenue. Director Soil conservation department, Director Environment and Remote Sensing department, Shri Sadiq Ali Ex-MLA, Dr S.P.S Datta. ex-HOD Department of Environment Jammu University as members. Conservator

Working Plan and Research Circle is the Member Secretary. Commissioner/ secretary Law had been invited as a special invitee for the meeting.

The Committee was initially supposed to meet on 28/6/ 2007 but the meeting had to be postponed due to the visit of the Parliamentary Committee on Environment. The meeting was finally held on 12/07/2007. Since the proposed area was adjacent to the Thajwas Sanctuary the Advisory Committee sought the opinion of Chief Wild Life Warden. The Chief Wild Life Warden informed the Committee that he had already submitted his report under no. WLP/Tech / 1971/07 dated 11.06.2007 after spot inspection on 27.5.2007. The relevant portion is reproduced as under;

"It was noticed that the proposed site for construction of Shri Amarnathji Shrine Board Complex falling in the compartment 63(s)/ Sindh/Kullan is located on the right side of the Sindh rivulet. The proposed complex does not seem to have any significant impact on the ecology of Thajwas Wild Life Sanctuary. The apprehensions of DFO Sindh and the Wild Life Warden, Central, that the said complex may have adverse impact on the Wild Life Sanctuary appeared to be "Over Cautious" and environmentally conservative approach." It is also given to understand that the Amarnathji Shrine Board is using prefabricated structures as such likely pollution due to discharge of muck and garbage etc. shall not be significant. It is presumed that Shrj Amarnath ji Shrine Board will take necessary environmental safeguards as applicable for such development Projects.

In view of the above report of the Chief Wild Life Warden, the Forest Advisory Committee cleared the diversion of the requisitioned Forest Land to the Amarnathji Shrine Board on the standard terms and conditions of the government.

Earlier on 27.4.2007 in the case titled T.N. Godavaraman Vs. Union of India and Others the Supreme Court had directed that "all cases where clearance was given by the Forest Advisory Committee should be placed before the-Supreme Court for approval. A copy of the clearance should also be given to the Central Empowered Committee (CEC) so that CEC would give its response to the clearance expeditiously. The Supreme Court had stated that it would thereafter, examine each Clearance and decide whether to grant or not to grant the approval, thereto."

The Forest Department requested the Law Department on 4.6.2007 to give its opinion on whether this order of the Supreme Court dated 27.4.2007 was applicable to the State of Jammu and Kashmir. The law department opined on 16.7.2007 as under:

"The order of the Hon'ble Supreme Court dated 27.4.27 is with regard to the Forest Conservation (Central) Act and rules framed thereunder. The said Act is not applicable to the State as forest continues to be in the State List. Earlier similar case was examined and vide DO. No. LD (Opn) 2006/77-FST dated 6.3.2007 the Department was advised to move application before the Honb'le Court to the effect that Forest Conservation Act, 1990 (Central Act) is not applicable to the State. The State has its own Forest Act as well as Forest Conservation Act, 1997 and seek clarification from the Hon'ble Court. The department is advised to pursue the said matter vigorously with the Hon'ble Supreme Court and await clarification in the matter.

The Forest Department incorporated the view of the Law department on the subject and prepared a memorandum for submission to the Cabinet. After obtaining the approval of the Hon'ble Minister for Forests on 17 /7/2007, the Forest department referred the memorandum to the GAD for placing the matter before the Cabinet.

The GAD returned the file to the Forest Department on 1.8. 2007 requesting them to intimate whether the Hon'ble Supreme Court has passed any Order in the case titled T.N. Godavarman Vs. Union of India and others on 20.7.2007 i.e., the date when the case was listed for hearing.

Meanwhile, the Principal Chief Conservator Forests (PCCF) vide his letter No. PCCF/FC/GEN/5/106 dated 21. 7.2007 had approached the Central Empowered Committee constituted by the Hon'ble Supreme Court regarding clarification about the aforesaid order of the Apex Court. The Central Empowered Committee vide their letter No. 1/26/CEC/SC/2007-Pt-XXIII dated 2.7.2007 opined as under;

"The non forest use of the Forest Land falling within the State of Jammu and Kashmir is governed by the provisions of the Jammu and Kashmir Forest (Conservation) Act, 1990 and not by the Forest-(Conservation) Act, 1980. In view of the above the CEC is of the view that the Hon'ble Supreme Court order dated 27.4.2007 regarding the functioning of the Forest Advisory Committee constituted under Section 3 of the Forest Conservation Act, 1990 is not applicable in respect of the proposal examined by the State Level Advisory Committee constituted under the Jammu and Kashmir Forest (Conservation) Act 1990 as amended from time to time.

The Forest Department again sought the advice of Law Department on the opinion of the CEC on 4.8.207. The law department advised on 24.9.2007 as under:

"The views of the Central Empowered Committee regarding the applicability of the order of the Hon'ble Supreme Court is their opinion. The said opinion confirms the views of this Department. However, it would be safe, as advised earlier to bring the legal position in the notice of the Hon'ble Supreme Court and seek their clarification as the State has its own Forest (Conservation) A ct of 1990." The Forest department thereafter considered it appropriate to seek the opinion of the learned Advocate General in the matter. Accordingly, the matter was referred to the learned Advocate General for advice on 5/10/2007. The learned Advocate- General opined as under on 8/11/2007.

"I have gone through the order dated 27.4.2007 passed by the Hon'ble Supreme Court. Since neither the Forest Conservation Act of 1980 nor Forest Conservation Rules made there under are applicable to the State of J&K. J&K State is governed by the J&K Forest (Conservation) Act 1997 and Forest Conservation Rules 2000. The Forest advisory committee has been constituted under aforesaid Forest Conservation Rules."

Therefore the order dated 27.4.2007 does not have any applicability with respect to the State of Jammu and Kashmir in as much as since the Forest (Conservation) Act of 1980 and the Rules made there under are not applicable to the State of J&K. More so as the communication issued by the CEC on 27.7.2007 which is on the file had clarified that the order of the Hon'ble Supreme Court-dated 27/4/2007 regarding the functioning of the Forest Advisory Committee under Section 3 of the Forest (Conservation) Act is not applicable in respect of the proposals examined by the State Level Advisory Committee constituted under Section 3 of the J&K Forest (Conservation) Act 1997. It is as, such advised that order dated 27.4.2007 does not pertain to J&K State and proposals in J&K have to be examined by the Forest Advisory Committee constituted under the J&K Forest (Conservation) Act of 1997 and Rules made there under."

Thereafter, the recommendations of Advisory committee along with the views of the Law, Department and learned Advocate General were placed before the Hon'ble Minister for Forest and Environment on 1/11/ 2007. The Hob'le Minister of Forest and Environment approved the submission of the proposal to the Cabinet on 3/1/2008.

The matter was then examined in the General Administration Department (GAD). The GAD again returned the file on 4/2/2008 to the Forest Department with the remarks that it should be placed before the Hon'ble Deputy Chief Minister in view of two different opinions given by the learned Advocate General and the Law Department.

"There is no material difference between the opinion to the learned Advocate General and that of the Law department. Law Department by way of abundant caution seeks to obtain clarification of the Supreme Court. I concur with the view of the Central Empowered Committee and the learned Advocate General. The Dy. Chief Minister (in charge of Law) and the Forest Minister submitted the case to the Cabinet.

The matter was brought before the cabinet on 6/2/2008. The Cabinet deferred the case along with another proposal for diversion of Forest Lands for non-forestry purpose. Subsequently, the Forest Department constituted a committee under the Chairmanship of the Chief Wild Life Warden vide Govt. Order No. 108-FST of 2008 dated 7/03/2008 to examine the feasibility of diversion of land viz-a-viz Wildlife perspective for various activities including Construction of Roads in Baltal Range, Domail area of Ganderbal District as requested by Amarnathji Shrine Board.

The committee submitted its report vide letter dated 7/5/2008 which is reproduced as under:

"The proposed camping sites of Shri Amarnathji Shrine Board (SASB), complex comprising 39.88 hectares of Forest-Land (30.88 hectares at Baltal and 9 hectares at Domail fall in the Forest Compartment No. 63/ Sindh of Sindh Forest Division, Forest Department. These proposed camping sites are located on the right side of the Sindh River. The camping sites do not involve any area of Thajwas Wild Life Sanctuary, which is located on the left side of River Sindh. The forest Compartment No. 63/ Sindh and Thajwas Wild Life Sanctuary are divided by the Sindh River. The representative of SASB informed that SASB will be using prefabricated structures, for the camping purpose of the pilgrims and will not go for construction of permanent structures."

"The Committee also recommends that Shri Amarnathji Shrine Board should take all possible environmental safeguards in consultation with the State Pollution Control Board to ensure that no damage is caused to the ecology of the area."

In view of the recommendation of the Advisory Committee, the opinion of the Law Department, the opinion of the learned Advocate General, the opinion of the Hon'ble Deputy Chief Minister in charge of Law and the report of the Committee constituted vide Govt. Order No. 108/ FST of 2008 dated 17.03.2008 the Forest Department felt that diversion of 39.88 hectares of Forest Land to Shri Amarnath ji Shrine Board at Baltal/

Domail be agreed only for raising prefabricated structures for camping, purposes of pilgrims without going in for construction of permanent structures, after taking all possible environmental safeguards in consultation with the State Pollution Control Board prior to them being put to use by the pilgrims to ensure that no damage is caused to the ecology of the area.

The matter was then submitted to the Hon'ble Minister for Forest and Environment. In view of the recommendation of the Advisory Committee, the opinion of the Law Department, the opinion of the learned Advocate General, the opinion of the Hon'ble Deputy Chief Minister (Minister in charge of Law) and the report of the Committee constituted vide Govt. order No. 108/FST of 2008 dated 17.03.2008, the Hon'ble Forest Minister cleared the proposal of diversion of 39.88 hectares of Land to Shri Amarnathji Shrine Board and approved its placement before the Cabinet for consideration on 17.05.2008.

The Cabinet, on 20.052008, vide its decision no. 94/7 approved the proposal of the Forest Department for diversion of 39.88 hectares of Forest Land to Shri Amarnathji Shrine Board at Baltal and Domail and Government Order No 184 FST of 2008 dated 26.5.2008 was issued containing the terms and conditions for the use of the Forest Land by Shri Amarnath ji Shrine Board.

Appendix—C

Joint Statement Signed By Governor's Adviser and Convener SAYSS dated 31 August 2008

The deal between Governors' administration and SAYSS.

The text of the joint statement issued by Governor's Advisor Dr SS Bloeria and SAYSS convener Shri Leela Karan Sharma at a joint press conference in Jammu.

1. The Shri Amarnathji Yatra, which has been going on for many centuries is a shining symbol of communal harmony and brotherhood in Jammu and Kashmir and reflects the State's composite heritage. The Yatris have been welcomed with open arms by the people of the Jammu and Kashmir Divisions and all required facilities have been made available for them. Sadly, certain decisions of the State government relating the Yatra created misunderstandings which led to controversy and agitation and loss of many precious lives. Apart from damage to property there has been a colossal loss to the states' economy in different sectors like transport, trade, industry, horticulture and tourism.

2. The Yatra to Shri Amarnathji Shrine has traditionally benefitted a large number of local residents many of whom have crucial dependence in the annual pilgrimage for their livelihood.

3. There has been no occasion in the past in which the State government has failed to provide the required support for the conduct of the Amarnath Ji Yatra. On the contrary, the extent and nature of governmental support to the Yatra has been progressively, enhancing, from year to year.

4. In view of the need to seek a peaceful resolution of the fundamental issues, to settle all existing doubts and clarify the continuing responsibility of the Shri Amarnathji Shrine Board (SASB), the Governor of Jammu and Kashmir had constituted, on 6 August, 2008, a four-member Committee comprising: Dr S.S. Bloeria, Advisor to Governor Justice (Retd) Shri G.D. Sharma, Professor Amitabh Mattoo, Vice Chancellor, University of Jammu, Shri B.B. Vyas, Principal Secretary to Governor and Chief Executive Officer, Shri Amarnathji Shrine Board.

5. The Committee held three rounds of discussions with the four member Committee nominated by the Shri Amarnathji Yatra Sangharsh Samiti (SAYSS) which comprised: Shri Tilak Raj Sharma Brig (Retd), Suchet Singh, Professor Narinder Singh and Shri Pawan Kohli.

6. The Governor has also held discussions with the leaders of political, social, religious, academic and other organisations in the Kashmir valley. The predominant view, emerging out of the consultations, is that the Amarnathji Yatra, which is a centuries old tradition of J&K's rich composite heritage, will continue to be welcomed and supported by the people of Kashmir, in every possible way. It was also felt that while the Shrine Board could continue to use the land, as in the past, for Yatra purposes, nothing should be done to alienate or transfer the land. While an assuring convergence of views has emerged, the Governor is committed to continuing the consultative process to ensure against any remaining misunderstanding whatsoever on an issue which has earlier led to serious misperceptions and great human and economic loss. Based on detailed discussions and deliberations held in the recent weeks, the following framework of action for resolving the issue relating to the use of land for the period of yatra by the Shri Amarnathji Shrine Board at Baltal and Domail has been agreed to:

(A) The State Government shall set aside for the use by Shri Amarnathji Shrine Board, exclusively, the land in Baltal and Domail

(Compartment No. 63/S, Sindh Forest Division) comprising an area of 800 Canals traditionally under use for the annual Yatra purpose.

(B) The proprietary of status/title /ownership shall not undergo any change.

(C) The Board shall use the aforesaid land for the duration of the Yatra including the period of making required arrangements and winding up the same for the purpose of use by various service providers according to its needs and priorities.

The aforesaid land shall be used according to the Boards' requirements from time to time including for the following:

1. Raising of temporary pre-fabricated accommodation and toilet facilities by the Board.

(i) Establishment of tented accommodation by private camping agencies (local permanent residents of the State),

(ii) Setting up of shops by shopkeepers (Local permanent residents of the state),

(iii) Facilities for Ponywallahs and Pithuwallahs,

(iv) Provision of the healthcare and medical facilities,

(v) Setting up of free Langars by private persons and groups which are licensed by the Board,

(vi) Provision of the healthcare and medical facilities,

(vii) Setting up of free Langars by private persons and groups which are licensed by the Board,

(viii) Facilities for helicopter operations! parking of vehicles,

(ix) Arrangements of security by local police/para-military forces and other security agencies as per the arrangements in place heretofore, and

(x) Undertaking measures relating to soil of conservation, land protection and preservation of ecology.

2. It has further been agreed that the Board shall continue to remain responsible for the overall arrangements on both the routes during the Yatra period, including all arrangements as mandated under the provisions of the Shri Amarnathji Shrine Act, 2000 A.D.

3. Apart from the above, the Committee set up by the Samiti had, during the course of discussions, presented a fourteen- point "Charter of Demands" for consideration by the State Government. The main demands relate to withdrawal of criminal cases against various persons during the

period of agitation, provision of compensation to the families of the deceased and to the injured and working out of appropriate packages of financial assistance to compensate losses of the transport sector, trade and industry, horticulture sector, hoteliers and tourist operators. The State Government has agreed to examine all these demands in an appropriate manner on time-bound basis.

4. In particular, as regards the registration of criminal cases against various persons during the period of agitation, it is agreed that all cases of non-serious nature which mean bailable and compoundable will be withdrawn. The remaining cases will be reviewed, on the merits of each case, by a Committee headed by Shri Anil Goswami, Principal Secretary (Home) within 60 days. Till the completion of this process, no action will be taken in such cases. Also, specific allegations of atrocities on agitators, based on prima-facie evidence, could also be looked into by this Committee.

5. Ex-gratia relief will be extended in favour of the next of the kin of the deceased and in favour of permanently disabled and the injured in all cases covered under the existing rules of the State Government.

6. Further, a Working Group, under the Chairmanship of Chief Secretary will address all compensation issues relating to both Jammu and Kashmir Divisions and the Central Government will be approached for extending enabling financial support to the State Government for this purpose within a period of two months. To make the exercise meaningful, one representative from each of the affected sectors will be associated with the deliberations of the Working Group.

7. Shri Amarnathji Shrine Board will be reconstituted keeping in view the provisions of the Act and the past precedents.

8. It is agreed that the Law Department of the State Government will examine the issue of disposal of LPA in terms of the understanding made hereinabove within one month. Sd. Dr. S.S. Bloeria Lila Karan Sharma Advisor to Governor of J&K Convenor Shri Amarnath Yatra Sangharsh Samiti Jammu dated 31-Aug-2008.

Appendix—D

Prime Ministers' Package for return and rehabilitation of Kashmiri migrants (June 2008)

The Hon'ble Prime Minister during his visit to the State on April 25-26, 2008, announced, inter-alia, a package for return and rehabilitation of

Kashmiri migrants who wish to return back. Following are the main components of the package involves an amount of 1618.40 crores.

Housing: Assistance @ Rs 7.5 lakhs for fully or partially damaged house. Rs 2.00 lakh for dilapidated/unused houses.

Rs 7.5 lakh for purchase/construction of a house in Group Housing Societies for those who have sold their properties during the period after 1989 and before the enactment of "The J&K Migrant Immovable Property (Preservation, Protection and Restraint of Distress Sale) Act, 1997" on 30-5-1997.

Transit Accommodation: Construction of transit accommodation at three sites @ Rs 20.00 crore each for a total of Rs 60.00 cr. Alternatively, Rs 1.00 lac per family towards rental and incidental expenses to those families who may not be accommodated in transit accommodation.

Continuation of Cash Relief to Migrants: Migrant families at Jammu and Delhi who are recipients of cash, relief and free ration would continue to receive the same @ Rs 5000 per family per month (including rations) for a period of two years after their return to the Valley.

Students Scholarships: The children of migrants will be provided scholarships @ 750/- per student per month.

Employment: It has been decided to provide employment opportunities to 15,000 unemployed migrant youth. Out of which, 6000 youth will be accommodated in State Government jobs. To assist the State Government in providing such employment opportunities, the Central Government will bear the cost towards salary for 3000 youth till they are absorbed against regular posts in the State Government, within the specified time-frame. Remaining 9000 unemployed youth would be facilitated to get financial assistance to come up with self-employment/business ventures. For this purpose one-time assistance of Rs 5.00 lack in each case will be provided out of which 50 per cent will be grant and 50 per cent as loan.

Assistance to Agriculturists/Horticulturists: One time financial assistance of Rs 1.00 lac would be provided to those having agriculture holdings. Rs 5000 per kanal, subject to maximum of Rs 1.5 lakh would be provided for restoration of orchards. Waiver of interest on loans: It has been decided to waive off the interest component of the loans taken by Kashmiri Pandits before migration from the Valley.

Appendix-E

The Jammu and Kashmir state Lands (Vesting of Ownership to the Occupants) Act, 2001

Act No. XII of 2001

[Received the assent of the Governor on 9th November, 2001 and published in Government Gazette dated 13th November, 2001].

An Act to provide for vesting of ownership rights to occupants of State Land for purposes of generating funds to finance Power Projects in the State.

Be it enacted by the Jammu and Kashmir State Legislature in the Fifty-second Year of the Republic of India as follows :–

1. Short title, extent and commencement. – (1) This Act may be called the Jammu and Kashmir State Lands (Vesting of Ownership to Occupants) Act, 2001.

(2) It extends to the whole of the State of Jammu and Kashmir.

1[(3) It shall come into force on such date as the Government may, by notification in the Government Gazette, appoint and different dates may be appointed for different areas].

2. Definitions. – In this Act, unless the context otherwise requires, -

2[(a) "authorised occupant" means a person who on the date of the commencement of the Jammu and Kashmir State Lands (Vesting of Ownership to the Occupants).

(Amendment) Act, 2004 is in actual physical possession of the State land, personally or through an authorised agent, by virtue of an existing valid lease or grant made by the competent authority;

(b) "authorised overstayed occupant" means a person who on the date of the commencement of the Jammu and Kashmir State Lands (Vesting of Ownership to the Occupants) (Amendment) Act, 2004 is in actual physical possession of State land, personally or through an authorised agent, but whose lease or grant has expired and respect of whom no notice for eviction or assumption of lease has been issued by the competent authority;

(c) "3[available State land]" means any State land, which is not in possession of any person 4[x x x];

1. The Act has been enforced in the State w.e.f. 01-03-2002 vide SRO-94 dated 01-03- 2002 except in Ladakh and Kargil Districts.

2. Existing clauses (a) and (b) substituted by clauses (a), (b), (c), (d), (e) and (f) vide Act No. XVI of 2004 w.e.f. 21-05-2004, s.2.

3. Substituted for the words "available land" by Act No. III of 2007, s.2, w.e.f. 20th November, 2006.

The words "or which has been encroached upon by any person" omitted ibid. 2.

(d) "Committee" means the Committee constituted under sub-section (1) of section 12;

(e) "Occupant" means a person who is in actual physical possession of any State land on the commencement of the Jammu and Kashmir State Lands (Vesting of Ownership to the Occupants) (Amendment) Act, 2004, personally or through an authorised agent;

(f) "Price" means the value determined for any State land in accordance with the provisions of this Act and the rules made thereunder;]

1[(g) "prescribed" means prescribed by rules made under this Act;

(h) "State land" means the land recorded as such in the—

2[Revenue Records] and includes any land which has escheated to the Government under the provisions of any law for the time being in force in the State but does not include any Government or State land mentioned in section 3 of this Act:]

3[Provided that for purposes of section 3-A of this Act, the State land shall include Kahcharai and Forest land;]

4[(i) "unauthorised expectant occupant" means a person who on the date of the commencement of the Jammu and Kashmir State Lands (Vesting of Ownership to the Occupants) (Amendment) Act, 2004 is in actual physical possession of the State land, personally or through an authorised agent, and in respect of which lease has expired but no notice for resumption of lease has been issued by the competent authority or who pursuant to this Act has applied in terms of section 5 thereof; and (j) "vacant land" means any State land which is not occupied by any person and in respect of which there is no existing lease or grant made by any competent authority.]

3. Act not to apply to certain lands. – The provisions of this Act shall not apply to such State land as is:–

(a) recorded or used as pathway, grazing ground, graveyard, cremation ground, camping ground or Kohl (irrigation channel);

1. The existing clauses (d) and (e) renumbered as clauses (g) and (h) respectively by Act No. XVI of 2004 w.e.f. 21-05-2004, s. 2.

2. Substituted for the words "Record of Rights" by Act III of 2007, s. 2. w.e.f. 20.11.2006.

3. Proviso added by Act XVI of 2004 w.e.f. 21-05-2004, s. 2. 4 Clauses (i) and (j) added *ibid.*

(b) held by any Government Department or institution under the control of the Government;

1[(c) earmarked for a specific purpose in any 2[x x x] Master Plan;

(d) covered by fields floating over water;

(e) forest land or wooden waste];

3[(f) held by a person in terms of Government Order No. LB 6/C of 1958 dated 5-6-1958 read with Government Order No.S/432 of 1966 dated 3-6-1966 irrespective of the fact whether mutation in his favour has been attested or not;

(g) held by a person by virtue of Government Order No. LB 7/C of 1958 dated 5-6-1958;

(h) held by a displaced person of 1947, 1965 or 1971 by virtue of Cabinet Order No. 578/C of 1954 dated 7-5-1954 read with Cabinet Order No. 254/C of 1965 dated 7-7-1965 and Cabinet Order No. LB – 40 of 1969 dated 1-1-1969;

(i) held by a person in a Residential Colony which stands regularised by the Housing and Urban Development Department up to 18-3-2005;

(j) held by a person in pursuance of permission granted or allotment made by the Government under the provisions of Jammu and Kashmir Big Landed Estates Abolition Act, Samvat 2007 (1950 A.D) or Jammu and Kashmir Agrarian Reforms Act, 1976; in respect of land which has escheated to the Government under the provisions of any of the said Acts; or (k) held by a person which is barred by the Limitation Act, Samvat 1995 (1938 A.D)].

4[*3-A. Mapping of State land.* – The mapping of the State land shall be carried out by such authority, in such manner and within such time, as may be prescribed.]

5[*4. State land.*– *6*[(1) Without prejudice to the powers of the Government to lease out State land under the Jammu and Kashmir Land Grants Act, 1960 or any other law for the time being in force on the subject, the State may, in such manner as may be prescribed, auction the State land in favour of the permanent residents of the State in the following order and subject to the conditions specified hereinafter:-

1. Existing clause (c) omitted and clauses (d), (e) and (f) renumbered as clauses (c), (d) and (e) respectively by Act No. XVI of 2004, s.3.

2. The word "District" omitted *ibid.*

3. Clauses (f) to (k) inserted by Act III of 2007, s. 3 w.e.f. 20-11-2006.

4. Section 3-A inserted by Act XVI of 2004, s.4.

5. Section 4 substituted *ibid*, s.5.

6. Sub-section (1) substituted by Act III of 2007, s.4, w.e.f. 20-11-2006.

Vacant land for commercial use:

(i) State land for commercial use in the cities of Srinagar and Jammu and tourist resorts;

(ii) State land for commercial use in such other cities and towns in the State as may be notified by the Government from time to time;

(iii) State land for commercial use in such rural areas as may be notified by the Government from time to time:

Provided that nothing herein shall take away the power of the Government to lease out land on bid or negotiated basis for development of tourist resorts in such tourist areas as may be notified by the Government, from time to time, under this Act;

(iv) subject to the directions of the Government, the competent authority to auction such vacant land shall be the Committee;

(v) the reserve price for such land in any specific area shall not be less than the registered sale price of the migrant property in such area or the market value of land determined for purpose of stamp duty under the Stamps Act, Samvat 1977 and the rules made thereunder or the highest sale deed registered in the area, whichever is higher;

(vi) the Committee may fix higher reserve price, in respect of any vacant State land, wherever it is of the opinion that the reserve price fixed under sub-clause (v) is lower than the potential value of such land as determined in accordance with sub-section (2) of section 12; (1-A) State land in possession of:—

(i) an authorised occupant may be converted into freehold rights by the Committee in favour of the occupant unless he opts for exercising his lease hold rights;

(ii) an occupant at the commencement of the Jammu and Kashmir State Lands (Vesting of Ownership to the Occupants) (Amendment) Act, 2004 may be considered for conversion into freehold rights by the Committee in such manner as may be prescribed: Provided that the State land falling within 50 feet and 75 feet from the centre on either side of any interior road and highway, respectively, shall be considered by the Government only for grant of leasehold rights initially for a period of forty years subject to conversion in the term of lease or resumption of such State land in the public interest on expiry of the initial term of lease.]

(2) The price at which the freehold rights shall be granted under sub clause (vi) of clause (a) and sub-clauses (i) and (ii) of clause (b) shall be determined by the Committee in the manner prescribed under Section 12 1[xxx].

(3) Notwithstanding anything to the contrary contained in any other provision of the Act,—

(i) the vacant State land falling within the territorial limits of Srinagar Development Authority and Jammu Development Authority shall stand transferred to the respective authority; and

(ii) the Ladakh Autonomous Hill Development Council and the Kargil Autonomous Hill Development Council shall be the competent authority for disposal of the State lands falling within the limits of a Council and the proceeds thereof shall be utilised for development purposes by the concerned Council.]

5. Application for vesting or transfer of State land. – (1) Any occupant of the State land may within the period specified in 2[clause (b) of sub-section (1) of section 8] apply in the prescribed form to the territorial Tehsildar for having such land vested in or transferred to him under the provisions of this Act.

(2) The application under sub-section (1) shall be accompanied by–

3[(a) documentary proof to the effect that he is an occupant of a particular category of the State land in question];

(b) extract of 4[Girdhawari];

(c) Shajra Kat (Tatma Shajra) of such land;

(d) a certificate by an officer not below the rank of Naib Tehsildar that he has verified the Tatma-Shajra with reference to the position obtaining at the spot; and

(e) an affidavit to the effect,

5[(i) that he is an occupant of a particular category of the State land in question]; and

1. The words "which shall be subject to the approval of the Government" omitted by Act III of 2007, s. 4, w.e.f. 20-11-2006.

2. Substituted for "clause (ii) of sub-section (1) of section 4" by Act III of 2007, s. 5, w.e.f. 20-11-2006.

3. Clause (a) substituted by Act No. XVI of 2004, s. 6.

4. Substituted for "Girdhawari Kharief, 1990" *ibid.*

5. Substituted, *ibid.* 6

(ii) that he shall neither be entitled to such land nor to refund of the cost paid in case any averment made in is found incorrect or false.

6. Preliminary action on application. – (1) On receipt of an application under section 5, the Tehsildar shall make an entry in a register duly numbered and also attest each such entry date-wise.

(2) The Tehsildar shall, after holding such enquiry, as he thinks fit, and after verifying the contents of the application, make a report to the District Collector of the area recommending that the application may be allowed for the whole or any part of the area of land to which it relates or that it may be rejected.

(3) The District Collector shall on receipt of a report under subsection.

(2) and after such further enquiry as he may deem fit 1 [forward the application along with his report to the Committee] within two months from the date of its receipt in his office.

2[(4) The Committee shall pass appropriate orders for disposal of such land within two months from the date of receipt of application under sub-section (3) and also determine the price 3[x x x], to be deposited by the applicant for vesting of such State land]:

4[Provided that the Government may grant such rewards and incentives, and in such manner, as may be prescribed to the officers/ officials showing excellent performance in administering the scheme under this Act.]

5[*7. Appeal.* – Any person aggrieved of an order passed by the—

6[Committee] relating to the price for vesting of free hold rights in favour of an occupant may file an appeal before the 6[Government] who shall, as far as practicable, decide the same within 30 days of its filing. The decision of the 6[Government] shall be final and binding.]

7[*8. Vesting of rights.* – (1) Notwithstanding anything contained in any law for the time being in force but subject to the provisions of this Act, all rights, title and interest in any State land shall vest in the occupant or head of the family in case of two or more occupants belong to a family subject to the following conditions, namely:-

(a) that he is a permanent resident of the State:

1. Substituted for the words "pass appropriate orders on such application" by Act XVI of 2004, s. 7.

2. Sub-section (4) of section 6 substituted *ibid.*

3. The words "subject to the approval of the Government" omitted by Act III of 2007, s. 6, w.e.f. 20-11-2006.

4. Proviso to sub-section (4) inserted *ibid.*

5. Section 7 substituted *ibid*, s. 8.

6. The words "Committee" and "Government" substituted for "Administrative Department of the Government" and "Chief Minister" respectively by Act III of 2007, s. 6, w.e.f. 20-11-2006.

7. Section 8 substituted by Act XVI of 2004, s. 9.

1[(b) that he has applied or applies in the prescribed manner for transfer of vesting of such land within such period as the Government may, from time to time, specify;]

(c) that he pays the price as is determined in the prescribed manner for such land to the Government; 2[x x x]

3[(cc) that the land shall be used in conformity with the provisions of the Master Plan, wherever existing, and if there is no Master Plan for any area, it shall be put to prescribed land use, if any; and]

(d) that the land is not required for any public purpose.

(2) The total land in possession of any person or a family including the land vested in such person or a family under sub-section (1) shall not exceed the limits of 4[hundred kanals].

Explanation: - The expression "family" and "head of the family" in this section shall have the same meaning as are assigned to these in the Jammu and Kashmir Agrarian Reforms Act, 1976.

5[(3) The occupant shall, within such period as may be prescribed, deposit the price as determined and notified, with the District Collector concerned against proper receipt who shall thereupon issue a formal order conferring ownership rights upon the said occupant.]

(4) The Tehsildar shall attest mutation in favour of such occupant, on payment of a mutation fee of rupees twenty per kanal in rural areas and rupees fifty in urban areas, conferring upon him the ownership rights in respect of such land within one month from the date the occupant produces receipt of the money deposited with the District Collector.

(5) Any occupant who fails to deposit the price of land under subsection.

(3) shall be evicted from such land by the Assistant Commissioner (Revenue/Nazool) within two months from the date the period for its payment expires and report to the District Collector forthwith.

(6) On receipt of a report under sub-section (5), the District Collector shall cause such land to be put to auction by the Committee].

6[***8-A. Restriction on land use.*** – (1) The land use in respect of agricultural land which vests in an occupant under this Act shall not be—

1. Clause (b) to sub-section (1) of section 8 substituted by Act III of 2007, s. 8.

2. The word "and" at the end of clause (b) omitted *ibid.*

3. Clause (cc) inserted *ibid.*

4. Substituted *ibid* for "121/2 standard acres as provided under the Jammu and Kashmir Agrarian Reforms Act, 1976."

5. Sub-section (3) substituted *ibid.*

6. Section 8-A inserted *ibid*, s. 9. changed after such vesting without permission of the Committee or such other authority as may be prescribed.

(2) Any occupant who desires to use agricultural land for any other purpose after vesting in due process of law may be accorded such permission by the Committee or such other authority as the case may be, on payment of price as per the rates prescribed for vesting of State land for commercial use.]

9. Power to evict. – 1[(1) The 2[Assistant Commissioner (Revenue/Nazool)] for the purpose of eviction under 3[sub-section (5)] of section 8 shall be the Estates Officer within his jurisdiction and he shall have all the powers of Estates Officer for the said purpose as are exercised by an Estates Officer appointed under the Jammu and Kashmir Public Premises (Eviction of Unauthorised Occupants) Act, 1988.

3[(2) Notwithstanding anything contained in sub-section (1) the concerned Assistant Commissioner (Revenue/Nazool) shall give only five days notice for eviction to the occupant and shall complete eviction proceedings under this Act within fifteen days.

(3) On the eviction of such an occupant from the land in question, the District Collector shall cause such land to be put to auction].

4[**10. *Creation of Fund.*** – Finance Department shall create a separate Fund under a proper account number in the Jammu and Kashmir Bank in each District or allot an account head in which cost of the land realised under this Act shall be deposited.]

5[*11.*Omitted].

6[**12. *Determination of price.*** – 7[(1) The application for vesting of freehold rights on the State land shall be determined by such Committee as may be prescribed: Provided that different Committees may be prescribed for different areas.]

(2) The Committee shall, for determination of the price for the land in any area, take the following factors into consideration, namely:–

(a) potential value of the land;

(b) nearness to the road or urban areas;

(c) irrigation and transport facilities available; and

1. Existing section renumbered as sub-section (1) by Act No. XVI of 2004, s.10.

2. Substituted *ibid.*

3. Sub-sections (2) and (3) inserted by Act No. XVI of 2004, s. 10.

4. Section 10 substituted by Act III of 2007, s. 10.

5. Section 11 omitted by Act XVI of 2004, s.11.

6. Section 12 substituted *ibid*, s.12.

7. Sub-section (1) of section 12 substituted by Act III of 2007, s. 11. 9

1[(d) the market value of land determined for purpose of stamp duty under the Stamps Act, Samvat 1977 and the rules made thereunder.

(3) The Committee shall give the reasons for determining the rate in a particular area or locality:

2[xxx].

3[(4) Notwithstanding anything contained in any other provision of this Act, an occupant other than an authorised occupant, authorised overstayed occupant or unauthorised expectant occupant, shall be entitled to vesting of freehold rights on the State land up to 10 kanals, on payment of price determined by the Committee in the prescribed manner: Provided that the ceiling of 10 kanals shall not apply in respect of –

(a) Agriculture land; and

(b) land under institutional use subject to such ceiling as may be prescribed].

13. Disposal of land. – Any occupant who fails to apply for vesting of any land in his favour or does not deposit the cost of such land 4[as determined under the Act and the rules made thereunder] shall be dispossessed of such land by the Tehsildar having jurisdiction in the area and the provisions of section 9 shall apply for such dispossession, *mutatis mutandis*.

5[***13 – A. Transitory provisions.*** – The pending cases, if any, on the commencement of the Jammu and Kashmir State Lands (Vesting of ownership to the occupants) (Amendment) Act, 2007 shall be decided in accordance with the provisions of this Act.]

14. Bar of jurisdiction of Civil Court. – Notwithstanding anything contained in any law for the time being in force,–

(a) no civil court shall have jurisdiction to settle/decide or deal with any question or to determination any matter arising under this Act or the rules made thereunder; and

(b) no order of any officer or authority passed under this Act or the rules made thereunder shall be called in question in any civil court.

15. Indemnity. – No suit, presentation, other legal proceedings shall lie against an officer or authority in respect of anything done or to:

1. Clause (d) substituted by Act III of 2007, s. 11.

2. Proviso to sub-section (3) omitted *ibid.*

3. Sub-section (4) inserted *ibid.*

4. Substituted *ibid* for "at its market value under this Act", s. 12.

5. Section 13-A inserted *ibid*, s.13. be done in good faith purported under this Act or the rules made thereunder.

16. Powers of Revenue Officers. – Any officer exercising powers under this Act shall have the powers of a civil court to enforce the attendance of a witness, to call for any documents, to take evidence on oath and to issue commissions.

17. Penalty. – (1) Any person in any proceedings under this Act who,—

(a) intentionally makes a false statement during the course of such proceedings; or

(b) intentionally produces a false document; or

(c) files a statement which is false or incorrect to his knowledge, shall be punished by the Tehsildar having jurisdiction in the area with a fine which may extend to twenty thousand rupees but shall not be less than five thousand rupees.

(2) A Revenue Officer or official making any wrong entry or issuing a false or incorrect report or certificate in respect of any State land, shall be liable to punishment which may extend up to five years of imprisonment and fine which may extend up to fifty thousand rupees by the Chief Judicial Magistrate having jurisdiction.

18. Power to make rules. – (1) The Government may make rules for carrying into effect the purposes of this Act. (2) In particular and without prejudice to the generality of the foregoing power, such rules may prescribe the manner and form in which application shall be made and disposed of.

Appendix-F

The Jammu and Kashmir State Lands (Vesting of Ownership to the Occupants) Rules, 2007

[Revenue Department Notification SRO 64, dated 5th May, 2007]

In exercise of the powers conferred by section 18 of the Jammu and Kashmir State Lands (Vesting of Ownership to the Occupants) Act 2001, the Government hereby makes the following rules, namely:-

1. Short title and commencement. – (1) These rules may be called the Jammu and Kashmir State Lands (Vesting of Ownership to the Occupants) Rules, 1[(2) They shall come into force on their publication in the Government Gazette.]

2. Definitions. – In these rules, unless the context otherwise requires—

(a) "Act" means the Jammu and Kashmir State Lands (Vesting of Ownership to the Occupants) Act, 2001;

(b) "Assistant Commissioner" means Assistant Commissioner, Nazool, Assistant Commissioner, Revenue, Sub-Divisional Magistrate concerned or any other officer authorised by the Government to discharge the duties and perform the functions assigned to the Assistant Commissioner, Revenue under the Act;

(c) "Defaulter" means a person liable for payment of arrears of premium or ground rent and includes a surety;

(d) "District Collector" means the Deputy Commissioner of the district in which property claimed for ownership rights is situated;

(e) "Form" means a form appended to these rules;

(f) "section" means a section of the Act;

(g) "Tehsildar" means Tehsildar Territorial/Tehsildar Nazool or any other officer authorised by the Government to discharge the duties and functions assigned to the Tehsildar Territorial under the Act; and

(h) words and expressions used in these rules but not defined shall have the same meaning as assigned to them in the Act.

1. These rules have been published in Government Gazette dated 5th March, 2007.

3. Mapping of State land. - (1) The mapping of State land shall be carried out by the Tehsildar in such manner and within such period as may be directed by the Government from time to time:

Provided that the Divisional Forest Officer concerned shall be associated in the mapping of Forest land.

(2) Any officer may, in the discharge of his duty under the Act enter upon and survey the State Land and demarcate the boundaries under section 3-A of the Act.

4. State land to be notified. – (1) When mapping of State land has been completed and the Tehsildar is satisfied that the particular property in his jurisdiction is State land, he shall notify the same in the Government Gazette and in local Newspaper as also on the notice board kept for that purpose in his office.

(2) The Tehsildar shall intimate the District Collector within 7 days of such notification about the completion of mapping.

5. Disposal of property left by un-authorised occupants. – A person who has been evicted from any land or property vested in the Government under the Act or the rules shall be given 21 days time including holidays for removing the article or articles remaining on such property:

Provided that if the owner fails or refuses to remove the article or articles thereof after the expiry of prescribed notice or if the article is subject to speedy and natural decay, the Tehsildar may cause it to be disposed off by public auction and the owner shall be entitled to sale proceeds, after deducting the expenses incurred on holding of such auction:

Provided further that the notice of auction shall be published in at least two local dailies having wide circulation in the locality.

6. Auction. – The procedure for auction shall be as under:—

(a) The Tehsildar shall give wide publicity to the notice for auction of the land through print and electronic media, giving full particulars in the notice, and the auction shall be conducted after 15 days from the date of publication of such notice by the committee constituted under sub-section (1) of section 12 of the Act.

(b) The intending bidder shall have to deposit with the Tehsildar, earnest money equal to 2 per cent of the minimum reserve price, fixed for such land, before the auction.

(c) The person offering the highest bid shall have to deposit 1/4th of the bid amount with the Tehsildar, on the close of auction, failing which the land in question shall be re-auctioned forthwith.

(d) The balance amount shall be paid by the person in whose favour auction has been confirmed within a period of 10 days from the date of auction.

(e) In case of default of payment of the bid amount within the prescribed period, the 1/4th amount already deposited shall stand forfeited to the Government.

7. Procedure of application. – (1) An application in terms of sub clause (b) of Sub section (1) of Section 8 of the Act shall contain full particulars of the State land as per Form No. 2. It shall be stamped with a court fee of Rs 10 and shall be verified in the manner prescribed for the verification of the pleadings in rule 15 of Order VI of the Code of Civil Procedure, Samvat 1977:

Provided that an occupant shall have to furnish the requisite information, in duplicate, with respect to his proprietary land as well as the State land under occupation as per Form No. 2: Provided further that an occupant who fails to apply for vesting of ownership rights within the prescribed period shall forfeit his claim under the Act and be evicted from such land by the Assistant Commissioner under section 9 of the Act.

(2) The person verifying the pleadings shall also furnish an affidavit in support of the said pleadings.

(3) The Tehsildar may issue notice to any person whose attendance is required in his opinion or who may be interested in the proceedings. The Tehsildar may for expeditious disposal of the case issue commission for examination of any person within his jurisdiction.

8. Procedure of eviction. – (1) Where an occupant is to be evicted under the Act, either wholly or partly, from the State Land, a notice shall be issued by the Tehsildar in Form No. 1, demanding him to surrender possession of such land, within one month of issue of notice.

(2) Where a notice has been duly served under sub rule (1) and possession is not delivered as required, a warrant of eviction shall be issued under the signatures of the Assistant Commissioner under section 9 of the Act. One copy of the warrant shall be forwarded to the Police Officer of the Police Station concerned for carrying out eviction who shall forthwith take steps to effect the eviction with use of such force as may be necessary.

9. Determination of market value. – The following Committees shall determine the market value in each case in accordance with the parameters laid down in the Act: -

'A'. For Jammu and Srinagar districts:

(a) Divisional Commissioner concerned. Chairman

(b) District Collector concerned. Member

(c) Assistant Commissioner Nazool/Revenue concerned. Member

(d) Tehsildar concerned. Member

'B'. For other districts including areas falling under the Tourism Development Authorities:

(a) District Collector concerned—Chairman

(b) Additional Deputy Commissioner concerned—Member

(c) Assistant Commissioner Revenue concerned—Member

(d) Chief Executive Officer of the Tourism Development Authority concerned.

(e) Tehsildar Territorial concerned—Member

10. Structures over State land. – Where an occupant has constructed a structure, rented it out and died leaving no legal heir, the Committee may, subject to verification of the claims submitted to it, consider occupant of such structure for vesting of ownership.

11. Terms and conditions under section 4 of the Act. – (1) For the purpose of implementation of section 4 of the Act the terms and conditions shall be as under:—

(i) The prospective owner should be permanent resident of the State.

(ii) The land, for which transfer of ownership is sought, should be free from encumbrances.

(iii) The prospective owner should not be a proclaimed offender/ antisocial element.

(iv) Price fixed shall be paid in lumpsum.

(2) Arrears, if any, on account of ground rent or any other such account shall have to be deposited by the occupant, with the Tehsildar, prior to vesting of ownership rights.

12. Death of occupant. – No action initiated under the Act shall abate by reason of the death of occupant and the same may be continued by or against the legal heir of the occupant.

13. Fixation of price. – Subject to provisions of section 4 of the Act, fixation of the price payable by different categories of occupants shall be as under:-

Category of occupant Price payable

(I) In Residential use:-

(i) Authorised occupant (where lease has not expired):

(a) upto 2 kanals 25 per cent of the value of land determined by the Committee.

(b) from 3rd kanal to 10th kanal 40 per cent of the value of land determined by the Committee.

(c) more than 10 kanals: The occupant will have the option to continue with the lease beyond 10 kanals or pay full value of land determined by the Committee.

(ii) Authorised over-stayed occupant/ un-authorised expectant occupant (where lease has expired):

(a) upto 2 kanals 35 per cent of the value of land determined by the Committee.

(b) from 3rd kanal to 10th kanal 50 per cent of the value of land determined by the Committee.

(c) more than 10 kanals: The occupant will have the option to surrender the land beyond 10 kanals or pay full value of land determined by the Committee.

(iii) Unauthorised occupant (where no lease has been granted or no allotment has been made by the Government).

(a) upto 2 kanals 40 per cent of the value of land determined by the Committee.

(b) from 3rd kanal to 10th kanal 50 per cent of the value of land determined by the Committee.

(II) In Commercial Use:-

(i) Authorised occupant (where lease has not expired). 30 per cent of the value of the land determined by the Committee.

(ii) Authorised overstayed occupant/Un-authorised expectant occupant (where lease has expired). 45 per cent of the value of the land determined by the Committee.

(iii) Un-authorised occupant (where no lease has been granted or no allotment has been made). 60 per cent of the value of the land determined by the Committee.

(III) In Institutional use viz. educational, religious, charitable, non-profitable, social institutions/trusts/societies, political parties recognised by Election Commission of India:—

(i) Authorised occupant (where lease has not expired) 15 per cent of the value of the land determined by the Committee.

(ii) Authorised overstayed occupant/Un-authorised 25 per cent of the value of the land determined by the Committee, expectant occupant (where lease has expired).

(iii) Un-authorised occupant (where no lease has been granted or no allotment has been made). 50 per cent of the value of the land determined by the Committee.

(IV) Agricultural use:—Free of cost. However, a token amount of rupees one hundred per kanal shall be charged for maintenance of proper Revenue records: Provided that where the land is in residential as well as commercial use the rates of commercial use shall apply: Provided further that if an occupant in whose favour ownership right has been vested does not commence the intended activity within three years, the Government shall have the right to resume the land: Provided also that Authorised Overstayed Occupant and Unauthorised Expectant Occupant shall be treated at par with Authorised Occupant in respect of scale of payment where such occupant has applied for renewal of lease within 30 days of expiry of lease: Provided further that the following limit shall apply for regularisation of land in favour of Occupants which is under Institutional use and the land held over and above the said limit shall be resumed by the Government: -

(a) Land in religious use upto a maximum of 50 kanals, on case to case basis, to be decided by the Committee.

(b) Land in use other than religious upto a maximum of 25 kanals, on case to case basis, to be decided by the Committee: Provided further that the conferment of ownership rights for land in agricultural use shall be subject to the following conditions:—

(a) the land use in respect of agricultural land shall not be changed after the ownership is vested. However, in case an occupant desires to use agricultural land in future for any purpose, other than agriculture if otherwise admissible in due process of law, he shall have to pay as per the scale prescribed for commercial use for getting the land regularised for that purpose;

(b) the land in question should have been in cultivation at least for three years on the date of application;

(c) no transfer of Agricultural land other than by inheritance shall be permitted for 10 years from the date of conferment of ownership rights.

14. Incentive and Penalty for payment. – The following schedule of time and scale of incentive and penalty shall be adopted in the realisation of the price of land against which ownership rights are decided to be vested with the occupant, namely:-

For payments made within 3 months A rebate of 25 per cent

For payments made within 6 months A rebate of 15 per cent

For payments made within 9 months A rebate of 5 per cent

For payments made within one year A rebate of 2 per cent

For payments made within one year and 3 months A penalty of 5 per cent for payments made within one year and 6 Months A penalty of 15 per cent.

For payments made within one year and Months. A penalty of 25 per cent. For payments made within two years A penalty of 35 per cent.

15. Review by officers. – An officer exercising powers under this Act may either of his own motion or on the application of any party interested, review, modify, reverse or confirm, any order passed by himself or any officer predecessor in office within a period of 15 days from the date of issuance of such order.

16. Rewards and incentives. – The Government may devise and notify a policy of granting rewards and incentives to such officers administering the scheme who show excellent performance in implementation of the scheme: Provided that a minimum limit of quantum of land shall be fixed in case of each individual official after considering total area and value of land under encroachment in the particular unit of administration viz. Halqa, Niabat, Tehsil, District or Division.

17. Appeals. – (1) An appeal against the order of the Committee may be filed within a period of thirty days stating the grounds on which the order appealed against is sought to be challenged and shall be accompanied by a certified copy of such order.

(2) Where an original order is confirmed no further appeal shall lie.

18. Repeal and Savings. – (1) The Jammu and Kashmir State Lands (Vesting of Ownership to the Occupants) Rules, 2005 are hereby repealed.

(2) Notwithstanding such repeal, anything done, any action taken, or any order or notification issued under the said Rules shall be deemed to have been done, taken or issued under the corresponding provisions of these Rules as if these Rules were in force on the date such thing was done, action taken or order or notification issued.

Appendix-G

'Kashmir Observer', March 09, 2014

Roshni Act Biggest Scam in J&K:

JAMMU: Massive land transfers to encroachers under Roshni Act was possibly the "biggest scam" of Jammu and Kashmir, Principal Accountant General, Subash Chandra Pandey said on Saturday and criticised the administration under the then chief minister, for making rules in contravention and violation of the law.

"Possibly, yes," he said when asked whether Roshni Act could be the biggest scam in the state. "The state government has estimated such lands for Rs 25,000 crores in 2006. Today you can yourself think of the value of this land, Panday said while addressing a press conference here today."

"We cannot go out of our brief. It does not fall in our domain. The Constitution says that CAG will present a report to the Governor. So we have presented it to Governor and now it is up to the Governor and Legislature. Governor is part of the Legislature," the CAG said responding to queries on whether he would recommend a probe into it. He further said, "The legislature's rights have been violated because law has not been followed by the state government (headed by Ghulam Nabi Azad)," he said.

Referring to amendment in rules, he said, "Yes, substantial deviations in the rules from the Act happened in 2007."

Asked whether the rules of state government were made to help land mafia, he said according to the CAG, the list "includes some businessmen, politicians, bureaucrats and journalists."

The CAG has alleged irregularities in transfer of encroached land to occupants in Jammu and Kashmir from 2007 to 2013, saying the state government realised just Rs 76 crore against a target of Rs 25,448 crore, they give us. "We have filed the detailed report with regard to Roshni land transfers in the High Court," he said, adding, "I hope that they will take action."

Manish Kumar, Accountant General; Mrs Pushpa Devi, Mr A.K. Mehra and Mr T. Kashim, Deputy Accountant Generals were also present during the press conference.

Appendix-H

Nation March 10, 2014

Rs 25,000 cr: CAG sees biggest ever J&K land scam

Written by Arun Sharma|Jammu|March 10, 2014, 9:56 am

The Comptroller and Auditor General has estimated a Rs 25,000-crore land transfer scam in Jammu and Kashmir, under the much-hyped Roshni scheme, making it the biggest ever such scandal in the state.

The scheme, under the Jammu Kashmir State Lands (Vesting of Ownership to the Occupants) Act, 2001, was meant to raise nearly Rs 25,448 crore to finance power projects by selling over 20.64 lakh kanals of state land under unauthorised occupation. In a report tabled in the Assembly, CAG has alleged irregularities in the transfer of the encroached land to occupants from 2007 to 2013, saying only Rs 76 crore had been realised, defeating the purpose of the legislation. Rs 25,000 crore was estimated to have been the cost of such land worked out by then government while enacting the Act, the present value would be much more, said Principal Accountant General (Audit) Subash Chandra Pandey on Saturday.

According to CAG, among the beneficiaries of the illegal and irregular deals under the Act were the National Conference's Nawai Subah Trust and the Congress's Khidmat Trust. While 7 kanal, 15 marlas and 84 sq ft of land were transferred to Khidmat Trust, 3 kanal and 16 marlas were given to Nawai Subah at Zero Bridge in Srinagar.

This land, that was under commercial use, was transferred to the two trusts at concessional rate applicable to land under institutional use. The statutory committee under the Act fixed market rate of the land at Rs 1.10 crore per kanal in case of the Khidmat Trust and Rs 1.20 crore per kanal in the case of the Nawai Subah Trust. Both were given 85 per cent rebate, with land valued at Rs 13.10 crore transferred for only Rs 1.97 crore. This amount too was not recovered, with only Rs 1.47 crore collected so far.

There had been substantiative deviation from provisions of the Act by successive governments who provided concessions and rebates to benefit encroachers, Pandey said. State Revenue Minister Ajaz Ahmad Khan described the CAG findings as motivated. The timing of the Accountant General's press conference, pointing fingers at the implementation of a flagship scheme of the previous government at the time of elections, raises doubts, he said. The state government will, however, study the CAG findings and initiate action wherever any provisions of the Roshni scheme or the rules were found to have been violated, Khan said.

The Jammu and Kashmir State Lands (Vesting of Ownership to the Occupants) Act, 2001, or the Roshni Act, was enacted by the Farooq Abdullah-led National Conference government and came into effect on March 1, 2002. However, it was amended by successive Mufti Sayeed and Ghulam Nabi Azad governments.

Index